The
Best of
THE SHOW

The
Best of
THE SHOW

A Classic Collection
of Wit and Wisdom

Bill Scheft

WARNER BOOKS

NEW YORK   BOSTON

Warner Books

Time Warner Book Group
1271 Avenue of the Americas, New York, NY 10020
Visit our Web site at www.twbookmark.com

Printed in the United States of America

First Edition: May 2005
10 9 8 7 6 5 4 3 2 1

Library of Congress Control Number: 200592066
ISBN: 0-446-57807-X

To Zoyd, who would have gotten every joke.

Foreword by
Bob Costas

Traditionally (and you know how I feel about tradition), this is the part of the book where someone more well-known than the author gives his blessing over what you are about to read. To achieve a kind of faux legitimacy, the guy writing the foreword usually manufactures a "relationship" between himself and the author, based on a loosely knit string of "coincidences." If done correctly, it praises the author, but more important, makes the guy writing the foreword pivotal to the author's career and responsible for the success of the work.

I like to think that I am above such artifice. I like to think that over the last two-plus decades I have built up an integrity-funded equity with the American sporting public as a broadcaster, journalist and fan that has engendered a deep and abiding trust.

That said—I invented Bill Scheft, and I have proof.

Bill Scheft was a struggling, multi-Emmy-nominated writer on the world's most influential late-night comedy-variety show when I plucked him off the scrap heap in 1994 to write some after-dinner jokes for me for a sports charity function I was emceeing in Kansas City. (I forget which charity. Something like the George Brett chapter of the National Hemorrhoid Awareness Association.)

I can't remember what made me decide to call him. Perhaps it was a remark I had overheard him make at the NBC commissary: "I'll have the Julio Gotay Chicken." That doesn't matter. What

matters is that he wrote a line for me that night about then-Chiefs head coach Marty Schottenheimer: *"Marty Schottenheimer is here tonight. This is a nice change of pace for Marty. Usually, at these dinners, John Elway shows up in the last two minutes and eats his dessert."*

Screams. Where else could you go with a joke like that and not get stares? And who else could deliver it, smile impishly and move on? Letterman? At a CART awards banquet, maybe. Not here.

There were other dinners, other events, other jokes. (*"They're having 'Jamie Quirk Day' at Royals Stadium this season. All fans 14 and under get a free cap with revolving team logo in the front . . ."*) but I believe getting the opportunity to write that Marty Schottenheimer joke was the seminal event in Bill Scheft's professional life. I believe a switch went off in his head that told him, "Why can't I write sports jokes like this all the time? And why can't I get the credit when I do?" Sure, it would be another six years before he began to write this sort of joke regularly, first at *ESPN Magazine*, now *Sports Illustrated*, and build the ever-growing audience of those among us who crave smart laughs about our sports heroes and villains, peppered with cultural references obscure enough to drive Dennis Miller into APBAA. But again, that is not my point.

My point is this. That "switch" I referred to? It was flipped by me. And, I guess, some greater unseen power. But, whoever or whatever that may have been, he, she or it wasn't even considered to emcee the dinner that fateful night in Kansas City. In fact, here was the entire list: me, Roy Firestone and, oddly enough, U.L. Washington. I got the nod and fate took Bill Scheft's hand.

Whew. I am so glad we could straighten this out. God knows we can all use a laugh or two. Or a couple thousand. So read on.

Foreword by
Rick Reilly

I am insane. I'll prove it to you.

The best definition I ever heard of insanity is doing the same thing over and over again, expecting different results.

For the last three years, I have done the same thing over and over again, every Thursday. I go to the mailbox, flip open my *Sports Illustrated* (no, employees don't get the sneakerphone), and turn to Bill Scheft's column, "The Show." On my way there, I say to myself, "O.K., this is it. This is the week he runs out of jokes. Nothing humorous happened this week. Humor Took a Holiday. Sports was duller than fat-free rice cakes. Scheft's done. Emptied out. Thanks for stopping by the booth. Show's over."

And every week, after waking the dog by laughing out loud, reaggravating the bruise on my palm from banging the Formica and drying my eyes in admiration and envy, I say to myself, "The bastard did it again."

Look, I have seen some things in my life. I have seen Al Davis walk *past* a courthouse. I have heard Charles Barkley ask a waiter if there's anything light on the dessert menu. I have seen a coatroom girl try to check Donald Trump's hair. I have seen John Elway eat a minute steak and not use any of his timeouts. I have heard Reggie Jackson refer to himself in the first person. I have heard Chris Berman say he needed some quiet time.

But I've never seen a guy who can write 20 topical, funny, edgy sports jokes a week, every week. And not this AM radio sports-talk "O.K., JoeBob, you're on 'Get Off My Jock!' with Double-Down Dave and The Coach!" gratuitous cuts with laugh track. Scheft does it without a laugh track, without a net, without a staff of minions. Twenty kills. Twenty top-shelfers. Twenty line drives back at your head. Nobody can do that. No human, at least.

I'm telling you, with God as my witness, Bill Scheft is going to run out of hilarious things to say one day. Not in these next 200-plus pages, maybe not next Thursday, but one of these days. I'm going to turn back there and his page is going to be blank. And it will read at the top, "Doodle Up Some Fun," or "This Page for Autographs."

And when that happens, I'll know I should have quit the year before.

THE SHOW
Opening Act

Before we begin, here are my goals for this first chapter. I want to avoid self-indulgence. What I mean by that, what I mean to say is, I, I, I, I . . . O.K., let's get back to that.

How about if I teach you how to write a joke? You know, get a return on that $22 you just shelled out? It's very simple. You pretend your brain has double-stick tape around it. You pick a celebrity, someone universal with a lot of baggage, and free-associate. Topics, words, phrases start to stick to the tape. Pick one you like, remove the rest and free-associate off that. More words, more phrases stick to the tape. Repeat the last step and get more specific free-associating. Keep doing that, keep boiling it down, like you're making crack. Eventually, you can see the connection between each step. Add some attitude, some nonsense logic, you've got a joke.

I'll do an easy one. President Bush. Let's see . . . Dad was President, disputed election, loves tax cuts, compassionate conservative, quit drinking, former owner of the Rangers, big baseball fan. I'll take big baseball fan. O.K. . . . big baseball fan, T-ball court at White House, against steroids, honors championship teams. I'll take honors championship teams. O.K. . . . honors championship teams. Ceremony in Rose Garden. Bush among the Red Sox. What could happen during a ceremony with Bush and the Red Sox?

Wait, I got it.

The World Champion Red Sox recently visited the White House. They presented the President with a customized jersey: BUSH 43. Come on. Am I the only one thinking? How about IDIOT 1?

Basically, that is my life. I gather items from sports—people, places, things, arraignments, pharmaceuticals—and I try to logically free-associate off them. Eventually, it congeals into something resembling a joke. And if not, I just stick the word "Tagliabue" at the end. Because, come on, who are we kidding? Tagliabue is funny. Say it. No, better yet, take two gulps of water, don't swallow, now say it. Huh? Funny? Do I know what I'm talking about? Give it to me.

Other than drooling water on myself, putting the column together is a two-part process. Three, if you count paying off cops. Every morning, Tuesday through Saturday, I get up, get down on my knees and pray to a Higher Power that Mike Tyson did or said something stupid the night before. Then I make coffee. (I like my coffee with milk and two Vicodin.)

I read six newspapers a day, back to front, and not just because I'm Jewish. Every day I read the sports sections of the *New York Times, New York Post, New York Daily News, Boston Globe, USA Today* and the *Watchtower*, which has all kinds of trouble getting results from games on the coast. I also check in regularly with SI.com, Yahoo!Sports and www.allthingslizaminelli.com, which also has trouble posting late scores.

Most newspapers and websites end up sharing pretty much the same information, although *USA Today* is great with the daily roundups from all the teams. Just once, I'd love to see next to the Brewers: "MILWAUKEE—Still cheap, still sucking. No change. Check back in six months." Or next to the football Cardinals: "ARIZONA—What are you looking at? Read a book, Roto Boy!"

Believe it or not, the best items for my column come not from newspapers or websites, but something called the *Sports Business Daily*, a scarily thorough compendium of sports-related news generated five days a week out of some guy's curing shed in North Carolina.

The *SBD*, published by Street & Smith, is an exhaustive daily synthesis of both sides of the big stories, issues and trends in the sports industry, and their corresponding dollar figures. While that is fascinating stuff for you spreadsheet geeks, there is a section near the back called "Sports Industrialists," which features boldface names galore. It's there you find items such as *"Dennis Rodman sold his house in Newport Beach for a reported $3.8 million after paying $865,000 in 1996."* You see something like that, and you think, "Well, that's the first thing he's done in the last eight years that involves the world 'appreciation.'" O.K., maybe that's just what I think. And I have to go through a lot of double-stick tape to get there. Rodman, tattoos, Pistons, Bulls, Lakers, Mavericks, wedding dress, kicks a cameraman, motorcycle, drinking, hair color, Carmen Electra, Madonna, multiple piercings. Too much. So I went with house, sold, closing, mortgage, appreciation. . . . Bingo. See, just like making crack. Which may or may not bring us back to Rodman.

I try to write at least 10 jokes a day from Tuesday to Friday. That's my foundation, and if the column was a newspaper, that would be the feature and business sections. I use Saturday to write jokes on any of the marquee games. By Saturday night, around 10:00, I have about 50 jokes, which I edit down to the 30 I really like, the polish them up nice for shipping. I e-mail the column in around midnight.

Sunday morning, my editor, the frighteningly efficient Kostya Kennedy, calls me and tells me the jokes he's looking to cut. The final column is usually around 20 jokes. If there is something going on Sunday (which, between the NFL, the golf majors and the play-offs, is 40 out of 52 weeks), I usually send another five jokes before 5:00. We make our final, final cuts Monday morning (after the legal department has called and said I can't say Tonya Harding danced topless at her husband's bachelor party unless I have three signed affidavits from guys who gave her dollar bills.) I devote Monday

afternoon to my favorite charity, In God's Love We Deliver Chinese, play with my cats, Joe and Charbonneau, and pass out just before Final Jeopardy.

Tuesday, I wake up, and the process begins anew.

I did a similar column, "The Monologue," for two and a half years at *ESPN Magazine*, and this format, 20 jokes and a band, seemed to work consistently. I moved over to *Sports Illustrated* and they said, "Don't change a thing. Except the title. And make it funnier. We don't want any Tonya Harding–type trouble."

My first day at *Sports Illustrated*, I told my editor, Kostya Kennedy, "Look, there's only one rule with this column. You can cut a joke because you don't think it's funny, you can cut a joke because you think it's offensive, you can cut a joke because you think the magazine might get sued. But you are not allowed to cut a joke because you don't get it."

I know what you're thinking: "But I don't get it." Relax, you have plenty of company. My benchmark is 50%. If you get half the jokes every week, you are a well-informed, borderline obsessive follower of sports, and I will guess not very happily married. If you get more than 75% of the references, seek immediate help from your clergyman or pharmacist. Hey, I don't get 75% of this stuff, and I wrote it. I'm just trying for a sound, man.

Rather than just do a Xerox job and reprint my first 112 *SI* columns, I thought it might be interesting to annotate each column, explain or desperately justify the process behind a couple of selected jokes, include a few of the jokes that weren't selected and do half a Casey Kasem on the bands at the end. Other than that, I think we're caught up. For what it's worth, my motto has always been: Do a volume business of cheap laughs, and pass the savings on to you, the reader. And by "always," I mean, you know, just now when I wrote it.

Enough. You look like a good crowd. Enjoy The Show.

The
Best of
THE SHOW

ELS WEATHERS BRITISH Before the four-man, four-hole playoff began, Ernie huddled with his psychologist, Jos Vanstiphout. He was very supportive. I believe his exact words were, "Who do I look like, Harvey Penick? Just don't cough it up like you did against Retief Goosen and embarrass me!"

Jos Vanstiphout. That's the sound the membership board at Augusta makes when a woman approaches the clubhouse.

The tournament was full of surprises. Are you like me? Are you wondering if Tiger is suddenly using a Nike kryptonite-shafted putter?

Woods shot an 81 on Day 3, the worst 18 holes of his pro career. He played so badly that midway through the round, the Swedish nanny ducked into the scoring tent with Soren Hansen.

Brutal weather for Round 3. On the bright side the flowers on Duffy Waldorf's shirt and hat needed the rain.

Monty shot an 84 last Saturday. By the third hole he was reprimanded by course marshals for heckling himself.

ALLEN IVERSON AWAITS THE ANSWER The NBA All-Star was arrested on four felonies and 10 misdemeanors. None of the charges count as team fouls.

If convicted on all counts, Iverson faces a maximum of 65 years in jail. And his cousin gets two shots and the ball on the side.

Actually, it's 65 years, or 12 seasons with the Grizzlies.

Sixty-five years in prison. However, his lawyers are working out a deal to get it reduced to life in Reeboks.

The latest incident began when Allen allegedly threw his wife out of the house naked. That would make her the first member of the Iverson family left uncovered.

Iverson's no dummy. He's going to show up in court with Bennett Salvatore and Bernie Fryer to protect him.

MAJOR LEAGUE BASEBALL CELEBRATES 16 STRAIGHT WEEKS WITHOUT A BOUNCED CHECK Despite reports to the contrary, Devil Rays managing general partner Vince Naimoli says his team is not desperate for cash. Of course, he said it while selling candy bars at the entrance to the Tampa Mall.

The balance of power in baseball is still lopsided. The Yankees placed Roger Clemens on the 15-day disabled list. Then, for insurance, they offered $6 million to the Blue Jays to acquire Roy Halladay's groin.

The Cardinals traded for veteran lefty Chuck Finley. Not to be outdone, the Reds acquired the only person who can hit him— Tawny Kitaen.

The Indians are going through with a July 27 promotion in which they'll give out baseball cards of former Tribe's pitcher Bartolo Colon. And there are still seats available for Aug. 4 —Albert Belle Bobble-Hip Doll Night.

By the way, midnight July 31 is the insider trading deadline for Martha Stewart.

MARTINA HINGIS DATING SERGIO GARCIA She has only one complaint: He stands over her too long.

ROLAND LATINA, RAWLINGS'S "GLOVE DOCTOR," PASSES AWAY AT AGE 78 There is no truth to the rumor he was tied up with string, soaked in a bucket of water and buried under a 14-year-old's mattress.

My time is up. You've been great. Enjoy Blood, Sweat and Tears.

THE **NOTES**

(Jos Vanstiphout...) This was the last thing I came up with for my first *SI* column. I love this formula, which Johnny Carson did for years as Carnac. My favorite: *"The answer: Constantin Chernenko. The question: What is the sound a fat man makes sliding across a linoleum floor?"*

*(**Allen Iverson Awaits the Answer...**)* Timing is everything. It was a huge break to get this story the first week. The details were odd, you had a hugely public figure and 99% of the charges were dropped. It raises the question: What phrase do you think Allen Iverson has heard more, "Nice shot," or "Do you mind if we ask you some questions?"

*(**"Glove Doctor"**...)* I learned to write obituary jokes while working for Dave Letterman. The one I remember is about the guy who invented the multiplex movie theater. His funeral was at 11:00, 1:15, 3:30 and 6:00.

THE **CUTS**

How about those course conditions at Muirfield? It rained so much Saturday, they had to dump out the Claret Jug three times. Remind me to fax this to Bob Hope if he's doing any gigs in heaven.

U.S. Post Office raises first-class stamp to 37 cents. *Thanks a lot, Lance.* Lance Armstrong was about to win his fourth straight Tour de France. He was sponsored by the U.S. Postal Service. But still and all, this is a stretch.

THE **BAND**

An explanation: I started doing this to end my columns at *ESPN Magazine*. It was kind of a salute to my years as a comic opening for bands and singers. That's how you'd get offstage: *"My time is up. You've been great. Enjoy Jay and the Americans!"* Just to be safe, for this first column, I went with a well-known group that evoked some sports-like images. That was the last time I did that. From now on, it'll mostly be residents of the "Where are they now?" file. I will include their one or two hits, just to jog your memories. If they had any more than two, you probably won't see them here.

MAJOR LEAGUE PLAYERS WEIGH STRIKE DATES They've narrowed it down to three possibilities: Aug. 16, Sept. 16 or Sept. 33.

So far, the most popular date seems to be Sept. 16. That way, the players would lose only one paycheck. Thank the Almighty. You don't want to see anyone suffer financially in all this.

The players' union is unified. Curt Schilling says he's willing to walk out on only two days' rest.

But there is hope. Last Thursday the two sides had a five-hour negotiating session. There was rhetoric, there was acrimony, there was name-calling—but they finally agreed on five selections for the bargaining-table cheese tray.

I'm starting to worry about Bud Selig. Yesterday he called a press conference to announce that if you buy the Expos before Sept. 1, he'll throw in free undercoating.

In other baseball news MLB is now sponsoring the Triumphant Glory Series, where participating teams take the field wearing jerseys from their most memorable era as voted by the fans. The Texas Rangers will appear naked.

TEDDY BALL-GATE CONTINUES Last week John Henry Williams produced a hand-written note from November 2000 signed by his father, who asked to be frozen when he died. And it must be authentic because there's absolutely nothing out there with a bogus Ted Williams signature.

You know, maybe Ted Williams did want to be frozen. Just to get the chance to one day tell Walt Disney he wasn't opening the hips enough on his swing.

FORMER NO. 2 PICK RYAN LEAF RETIRED AFTER FOUR SEASONS He plans to put football behind him and concentrate on alienating people in the business world.

And the 49ers announced they expect to consume 3,600 eggs during 26 days of camp—3,800 if Ron Stone wants an extra omelette.

LANCE ARMSTRONG WINS FOURTH STRAIGHT TOUR DE FRANCE Armstrong won by 7:17. His victory margin would have been greater if he hadn't gone off course three times to deliver newspapers.

Even after Lance retook the lead in stage 11, he was never a lock for the title. Thanks to changes in the format, stages 14 to 17 involved crepe-rolling.

Did you hear a French rider was kicked out of the Tour for holding on to a team car during a climb? What an idiot. All that training, all that dedication, and the guy doesn't think to just hide in the trunk?

ALLEN IVERSON GETS A LOOKAWAY PASS You knew this was coming a week ago Saturday, when Iverson played in his charity softball game. He had one at bat, and his attorneys worked out a walk.

Despite his problems with the law, Allen Iverson jerseys are still flying off the shelves. And they've even sold a couple.

FRENCH FIGURE SKATING JUDGE ACCEPTS THREE-YEAR SUSPENSION Terrific. She'll be back in time to screw up the next Olympics.

My time is up. You've been great. Enjoy Gino Vanelli.

THE **NOTES**

(I'm starting to worry about Bud Selig...) First tip: Anytime, I mean, anytime you get the chance to do a joke about a former used car salesman, drop everything and do it.

(Lance Armstrong wins fourth straight...) Larry Jacobson, one of the great Letterman monologue writers ever, invented the quintessential Tour de France joke. *Greg Lemond won his second straight Tour de France. Finishing second, once again, was a delivery guy from Empire Szechuan.* When I say quintessential, I mean it. I think Dave has done it every year since. So, I went with newspapers.

THE **CUTS**

New Cardinals pitcher Chuck Finley hasn't had a hit in 17 years. No, wait. I'm thinking of Michael Jackson. No, wait. I'm thinking of Gino Vanelli....

Armstrong is part of the U.S. Postal Service team. Which explains the sign on the back of his seat, "Next Window Please." O.K., I tried a different tactic here. You have to do that. You have to keep trying different pay-offs. You can't take rejection personally. Those bastards....

THE **HIT(S)**

"I Just Wanna Stop"

(*Tap, tap*) Is this thing on?

SALT LAKE MOB SCENE Forget what you've heard. At the 2006 Winter Games in Turin, Italy, Ice Fixing will not be a demonstration sport.

A reputed Russian mobster, Alimzhan Tokhtakhounov, was arrested for trying to fix the ice dancing event at the Salt Lake City Games. He would have gotten away with it if he hadn't been ratted out by his brother Fredo Tokhtakhounov.

But this mob guy is no dummy. He's already hired a very sharp lawyer, who advised him to plead "Not Gillooly."

Are you like me? Are you waiting for Sale and Pelletier to hold a press conference to announce that this is not about them?

HBO REALITY SERIES *HARD KNOCKS* LANDS IN DALLAS I feel so foolish. I thought HBO already had a show about the Cowboys: *Curb Your Enthusiasm.*

The Cowboys are ready for the cameras. For the last two months Brian Billick has been giving Dave Campo bluster lessons.

Lots of inside revelations on the show. For instance, I didn't know you had to report this, but the Cowboys placed OT Aaron Gibson on the Physically Unable to Have a Salad list.

Don't miss the second installment. Dave Campo shows up with his evil sidekick, Mini-Campo.

According to a poll, 28% of NFL fans say the Dallas Cowboys improved themselves the most during the off-season. The other 72% prefer Jerry Jones's original face.

Come on. Jerry Jones's private jet is on its second nose.

BASEBALL HEADED FOR FALL It still looks like Sept. 16 may be closing time for the union. Good move. Who wants to be play-ing the same night *The King of Queens* has its season premiere?

This would be the ninth work stoppage since 1972. Tenth if you count the Braves after Game 2 in the '96 World Series.

Bud Selig may be starting to crack. He's now threatening to contract the bratwurst from the sausage race at Miller Park.

Despite all the dire possibilities, attendance in Minnesota has jumped during the last few weeks. It's a combination of two fac-tors: 1) the Twins' commanding lead in the AL Central; 2) a local classified ad describ-ing the Metrodome as a "perfect fixer-upper for newlyweds."

Tell me if I'm wrong. With all the distract-ing talk about steroids and strikes, has there ever been a better time to cork your bat?

In other news, the Red Sox designated Jose Offerman for assignment. The assign-ment: Write 2,000 words on how to earn $26 million stranding runners and drop-ping throws.

Offerman was shocked. Never saw it com-ing. If you're scoring at home, that makes 289 signs he's missed.

Boston also released RHP Rich Garces. He had to turn sideways to clear waivers.

Unlike Offerman, Garces was a real gentle-man. He offered to eat his contract.

JIM KELLY INVITES 1,200 FRIENDS AND EX-TEAMMATES TO HALL OF FAME INDUCTION And Scott Norwood made 75 bucks park-ing cars.

LAWYERS FOR FORMER NFL WR RAE CAR-RUTH APPEAL MURDER CONVICTION Remember, if the conviction is not over-turned, Rae loses one of his timeouts in the yard.

My time is up. You've been great. Enjoy Pablo Cruise.

THE **NOTES**

(Is this thing on?) The editors wanted me to start with some sort of introduction. I had done a thing at *ESPN Magazine*, *"Good to be here. How about a hand for my spiritual adviser, Mark Pope?"* but I didn't want to repeat that. Too shticky. So, I came up with this, which I figured I could use every week. It lasted a week, although I did bring it back a couple more times.

(...plead "Not Gillooly") Jeff Gillooly was Tonya Harding's fiancé and orchestrated the 1994 attack on Nancy Kerrigan. When photos of them having sex were published years later in *Penthouse*, my friend, the get-out-of-the-business funny Larry Amoros, commented, "It's not the way you like to see our Olympians."

(According to a poll, 28% of NFL fans...)

(Come on. Jerry Jones's private jet is on its second nose...) You can never have enough plastic surgery jokes. It's completely fair game. Hell, Jimmy Johnson once referred to the Cowboys owner as "Michael Jackson, I mean, Jerry Jones."

(Boston also released RHP Rich Garces...) Sure, it's a fat joke, but it's more clever than gratuitous.

(Unlike Offerman, Garces was a real gentleman...) Now this, this is gratuitous.

THE **CUTS**

Iverson works on his outside shot. *All the serious charges were dropped. The judge must have been a big Iverson fan. His decision was delayed for two hours while the bailiff arranged his cornrows to spell "case dismissed."* The story may have been played out by then. Tip: Always have a bailiff help with your cornrows.

You've all heard of the Russian mob—the Vodka Nostra. This was a tag to the skating scandal run. I'm glad it was cut. It's a little forced. Sounds like something the girls drank on an episode of *Sex and the City*.

THE **HIT(S)**

"Love Will Find a Way"

By applause, how many of you had Aug. 15 in your strike date office pool?

GILLETTE WINS NAMING RIGHTS TO PATRIOTS' NEW DIGS Too bad. For another $75 million it could have been Yankees Suck Stadium.

Meanwhile, the Tennessee Titans still haven't decided what to do about the former Adelphia Coliseum. So far, the best they've come up with is Defraud Field.

Are you like me? Did you find John Madden's *Monday Night Football* debut disappointing? Come on. Three hours, not one reference to George Lazenby, Deke Slayton or Uriah Heep.

Big production changes this season on *MNF*. For the first time ever Hank Williams Jr. will be allowed to use the telestrator.

It's official. If Steve Spurrier adds another Gator, the Redskins will be eligible for federal Wetlands Protection funds.

MLB PLAYERS EASE UP ON STEROID RAGE
Last week the union proposed that players be subject to mandatory testing. However, it must be a written test.

Actually, the MLBPA is in favor of unannounced testing. Unannounced testing. That's when a guy in a lab coat jumps out from behind your sofa with a specimen jar and yells, "Surprise!"

According to a recent phone poll, 41% said that in the event of a strike they would stop following baseball. The other 59% said, "Hey, how'd you get this number?"

The small-market owners are desperate for money. Before the plane took off on a recent road trip, the Royals had to chip in for gas.

This is shocking. Turns out the FBI knew about Reds G.M. Jim Bowden's mouth last winter and failed to act.

Speaking of diplomats, Texas Rangers reliever John Rocker issued a written apology after making antigay remarks in front of a Dallas restaurant. Hey, who said he'd never get his 1999 form back?

You know what's really sad? This latest episode occurred just when Rocker was starting to get people out with his new pitch: the ethnic slurve.

TONY STEWART FINED $10,000 BY NASCAR FOR PUNCHING PHOTOGRAPHER
Not only that, he was ordered to take a course in Frank Sinatra Anger Management.

Stewart was also fined $50,000 and placed on probation for the rest of 2002 by The Home Depot. What does this mean? He can't come in with 500 feet of Sheetrock?

In other NASCAR news, Jeff Gordon filled in for Regis on *Live with Regis and Kelly* last week. Did you see him? Looks like they tried to do his hair and makeup in under 12 seconds.

NBC UNVEILS FALL SCHEDULE Pretty shrewd. Sunday afternoon, it's a brand-new three-hour drama, *Law and Order: Special Teams Unit*.

DIKEMBE MUTOMBO TRADED TO NETS
Strange way the trade was announced. Allen Iverson allegedly kicked in Keith Van Horn's door with a contract in his waistband.

My time is up. You've been great. Enjoy Boz Scaggs.

THE **NOTES**

(It's official. If Steve Spurrier adds another Gator, the Redskins will be eligible...) You know what makes this joke work? Back then, there still were Federal Wetlands Protection funds.

(Actually, the MLBPA is in favor of unannounced testing...) Sometimes, you have to repeat the setup to get the audience focused on the payoff. This is such a case. It is also, I believe, my first recorded use of the phrase "specimen jar." There'll be more. A lot more.

THE **CUTS**

The Tennessee Titans still haven't decided what to do about renaming the former Adelphia Coliseum. So far, the best they've come up with is "Happy First Communion, Earlene" Coliseum. Earlene was the name of the least-known Mandrell sister.

Dikembe Mutombo traded to Nets. *Don't kid yourself. This is a huge upgrade for Jayson Williams's defense.* It was too early in that case. Comedy tip: With murder, you have to wait until the charges are filed. Any other felony, go nuts.

THE **HIT(S)**

"Lido Shuffle"

"Harbor Lights"

"Lowdown"

"We're All Alone"

(Much too successful, but I waived the rule here because of his name, Boz Scaggs, and the fact he's been forgotten as if he had one hit.)

Thank you. This is great. I feel like Don Fehr on Fan Appreciation Night.

UGH-UST 30 The players are being a little cute. They say that because baseball is a monopoly, the luxury tax should be $75. And you have to pay only if you land on it.

President Bush has ordered both sides to keep working. Coming from a guy who's in the middle of a one-month vacation while the economy is in turmoil, this really means a lot.

The players and owners are still about $90 million apart. No problem. Jerry Lewis can raise that Labor Day weekend.

Are you like me? Are you wondering if they'll bring in the QuesTec umpiring machine to decide if the strike is legitimate?

Fred Wilpon is now the sole owner of the New York Mets. It was an amicable separation. Nelson Doubleday got $135 million and custody of John Franco's elbow.

The Mets announced their 40th-anniversary alltime team. The fans selected Darryl Strawberry twice: rightfield and lefthanded felon.

Meanwhile, Yankee Alfonso Soriano became the first 30-30 second baseman. My question: Does that include the five homers and 10 steals he had for the Harlem Little League team?

SAINTS TRAINING CAMP BEING SPRAYED DAILY FOR WEST NILE MOSQUITOES That's funny. I thought the league moved those mosquitoes to the NFC South Nile.

The Saints have shifted Kyle Turley from right tackle to left tackle. Big adjustment. He's spent the last three weeks working on using his left arm to throw opposing players' helmets.

Not only that, he now has to protect his blind-side tattoos.

New Packers wide receiver Terry Glenn has already suffered two injuries during training camp. And today the late Vince Lombardi called him "she."

Don't miss this week's installment of *Hard Knocks: Training Camp with the Dallas Cowboys*. Former lineman Nate Newton is arrested for possession of the Cowboys' dime package.

Republican congressman and former Oklahoma quarterback J.C. Watts pulled a hamstring running sprints at the Redskins' camp. Actually, he hurt himself trying to go to the left.

Watts was carted off the field. And he fell to No. 5 on Steve Spurrier's quarterback depth chart, behind John Reaves and Norm Snead.

BEEM-ING UP AT THE PGA Amazing story. Seven years ago Beem quit the Tour to sell cellular phones and car stereos. This happens a lot. I was just talking about that with my marriage counselor, Freddie Couples.

Fred Funk finished tied for fourth, which gives him a 10-year exemption to all George Clinton concerts.

During Saturday's third round, winds gusted up to 40 mph. On the bright side, it was a nice change to hear the term *blustery* used to describe something other than Gary McCord.

CBS COLLEGE FOOTBALL REPORTER JILL ARRINGTON POSES IN SEPTEMBER ISSUE OF *FHM* Don't get excited, she's not completely naked. Help me out here. Technically, is that a Cover 2?

SHAQUILLE O'NEAL TO COSTAR IN WEEKLY DRAMA ON CBS I hope I'm not too late with a title: *Touched by a Brick.*

My time is up. You've been great. Enjoy the Little River Band.

THE **NOTES**

(President Bush has ordered both sides…) This joke got picked up by a lot of local papers. And I heard Bush was so upset, he took another two weeks off.

(Fred Funk finished tied for fourth…) I love this joke as I love few things. George Clinton was the founder of the band Parliament-Funkadelic.

THE **CUTS**

The Harlem Little League team was cleared of allegations its players came from outside the legal district. The charges proved to be totally bogus. According to Little League rules, as long as your ex-wife and kids still live in the area, you're O.K. On the heels of the Danny Almonte age scandal, this was a strong joke. But that scandal was two years old. Big heels. Christina Aguilera big heels.

*(re: **Jill Arrington**) Pretty racy pictorial. In one shot, she's wearing nothing but Tim Brando's makeup bib.* The "cover-2" line that made it into the column is better and should stand alone, as it did, but I wanted you to see how hard I was working on this.

THE **HIT(S)**

"Lonesome Loser"

"Man on Your Mind"

THE **SHOW**

(*Taptaptap*) Is this thing on?

(*Taptaptap*) Is this season still on?

HELP ME OUT HERE What do you think the chances are we'll ever see a Rob Manfred Bobblehead Night?

I don't want to complain about the pace of the negotiations, but Steve Trachsel works faster.

Alex Rodriguez offered to give up 30% to 40% of his $252 million salary if it would help move things along. And I'm not sure about the connection, but a half hour after he said that, Anna Nicole Smith had her wedding dress let out.

And San Diego Padres owner John Moores said he was willing to shut down the Padres for the rest of this year and all of next season. Well, sure—0–0 is the closest they'll get to finishing .500.

Despite a leaguewide drop in attendance, the Yankees last week were on pace to attract 3.6 million fans. Do you realize what this would mean if there was *real* revenue sharing? Yeah, I don't care, either.

Former replacement player Shane Spencer was allowed to meet with some union players. And everyone in the union agrees: He makes a dynamite gin and tonic.

Meanwhile, the man who caught Barry Bonds's 600th home run says he won't share proceeds from the sale with his friends. He said, "You can't find a person that deserves it more than me." No, wait. I'm sorry. That's what Barry said.

COLLEGE FOOTBALL SEASON BEGINS— FINALLY! I don't know about you, but I can't wait until it all culminates in the Rose Bowl on Memorial Day.

Florida State coach Bobby Bowden has come under fire for having the Seminoles use "Let's Roll" as their rallying cry. Wait a minute. I thought "Let's Roll" was the rallying cry of Nate Newton.

SERENA WILLIAMS SEEDED FIRST AT U.S. OPEN She was seeded second, but she brought a note from her father.

On the men's side, you have to feel bad for Pete Sampras. He didn't even make Bridgette Wilson's top 16.

They're really beefing up security for this year's Open. In fact, it could take another five days before they stop patting down Anna Kournikova.

PATRIOTS OWNER ROBERT KRAFT UNDERGOES SUCCESSFUL BYPASS SURGERY Very serious. Doctors went in and found his arteries blocked by Damien Woody.

In other NFL news Drew Brees has beaten out Doug Flutie for the starting QB job in San Diego. Quick impression. Chargers coach Marty Schottenheimer talking to G.M. John Butler:
"You tell him."
"No, you tell him."
"No, you tell him."
"Hey, not me. I got a family. You tell him…."

Former Colts linebacker Jeff Herrod remains in an Indiana jail awaiting extradition to Nevada on charges he passed $75,000 in bad checks. I'm confused. I thought you weren't allowed to hold a defensive player.

TOBEY MCGUIRE TO STAR IN *SEABISCUIT* FILM This is smart. Universal will audition 30 MLB owners and 750 players for the part of the horse's ass.

My time is up. You've been great. Enjoy T. Rex.

THE **NOTES**

(Florida State coach Bobby Bowden has come under fire...) My editor, the warp-speed quick study Kostya Kennedy, came up with the "Let's Roll" joke. Six weeks into the job, he's writing top-flight comedy. And you can, too. Just send $199.99 to Six Weeks to Hilarity, c/o Bill Scheft, First National Bank, Bimini....

(In other NFL news, Drew Brees...) Anytime I can shake up the form, I like to. Unfortunately, it takes up the space we could have used for another couple of jokes.

THE **CUTS**

Earlier this month, Newton was sentenced to 30 months in prison after pleading guilty to possession of 175 pounds of marijuana. The original charge was possession with intent to sell, but that went away when the cops found half a pack of rolling papers. The key to humor is exaggeration. Half a pack of papers for 175 pounds of pot? Come on. You'd need at least six packs.

THE **HIT(S)**

"Bang a Gong (Get It On)"

Good to be here. Anybody looking to buy unused strike jokes? Priced to go, like Scott Rolen.

STRIKE? WHO SAID ANYTHING ABOUT A STRIKE? Are you like me? Don't you think Bud Selig looks better on no sleep?

Both sides emerged from the MLB offices on Park Avenue and declared it a win-win. Which makes two more wins than the Mets had in New York during the month of August.

I was worried. I didn't want to turn on *Baseball Tonight* the third week of September and see Peter Gammons and Rob Dibble doing improv.

In the event of a work stoppage, the Fox network would have received more than $500 million in rights and compensation from Major League Baseball. And they would have used the money to produce a prime-time series, *That '70s Strike*.

In other baseball news, who cares?

Seriously, I think these Little League World Series players are too influenced by television. Last week Louisville's star pitcher Aaron Alvey signed with Arliss.

U.S. OPEN CLOTHED FOR ALTERATIONS In his second round match Tommy Haas was ordered to change out of a sleeveless muscle shirt. Either that or change his name to Tommy Haasselhoff.

Did you see Serena Williams's black Lycra outfit? She calls it her catsuit. And it really is a catsuit. She puts it on, then plays with a ball for 45 minutes until she gets bored.

The men's winner gets $900,000. Wow. That's enough to buy a dozen hot dogs at the Arthur Ashe concession stand.

Food prices at the Open are insane. Last Thursday, I was forced to lease some nachos.

Bomb-sniffing dogs at the National Tennis Center had to wear photo I.D.'s. It sounds like a hassle, but how else are they going to buy beer?

NFL HOSTS KICKOFF CELEBRATION IN TIMES SQUARE ON SEPT. 5 Everybody will be there. Dick Clark's going to interview his old high school teammate Darrell Green.

Little different celebration in Times Square. At midnight, the ball will be dropped…by the Jets' Richie Anderson.

NFL teams got down to their final 53-man rosters. Before being released by the Broncos, Ola Kimrin kicked a 65-yard field goal in the team's final preseason game. Ola Kimrin—isn't he married to Ethan Hawke?

John Madden will demonstrate his *Madden 2003* once a week during *Monday Night Football*. Forget the demonstration. How about in the middle of a blowout, an icon appears on your TV: "Abort game and start over"?

By the way, I just got *Madden 2003*. There was a warning on the side of the package: "Randy Moss may decide not to be included."

TIGER WOODS IS HAVING TROUBLE CONTROLLING HIS NEW NIKE DRIVER The club has been so erratic, he's thinking of getting it regripped with Ritalin.

DOMINIK HASEK TURNS DOWN RUN FOR PRESIDENT OF CZECH REPUBLIC Too bad. Political experts believe the only way he can be beaten is top shelf stickside on a screen.

MAVERICKS OWNER MARK CUBAN PRODUCING AN UPDATED STAR SEARCH First prize: a $100,000 fine from David Stern.

My time is up. You've been great. Enjoy Vicki Sue Robinson.

THE **NOTES**

(Good to be here…) We began to settle on this form for the opener, which Letterman used to call the "Hihowareya."

(I was worried…) The key to this joke is the visual. Can you see Gammons and Dibble in a club doing improv: "Give us a situation."/ "Okay, runner on second, no outs, Aristotle is the hitter and you have an eye in the middle of your bicep.…"

(Seriously, I think the Little League players are too influenced…) My biggest regret is that I never told more *Arli$$* jokes at *SI*. Here's my favorite from *ESPN Magazine*: "*Arli$$* was renewed for its seventh season. And once they get that first laugh, look out."

(NFL hosts kickoff celebration…) Dick Clark old = comedy gold. Again, I have to defer to the great Carson/Letterman monologue writers, Mike Barrie and Jim Mulholland. Every New Year's Eve, they write a joke about how as Dick Clark gets old, they move the camera back a little more to not show the lines in his face. *So, this year, Dick will be in Times Square and the camera will be in Cleveland.* Here's what's incredibly hip. Every year, Barrie and Mulholland move the camera farther away. I think in 2004 it was in Fallujah.

THE **CUTS**

(re: a work stoppage) Keep in mind, this is a tentative agreement. Tentative, like Joel Skinner signaling for Mark Wohlers with the tying run on second. Hey, another improv for Gammons and Dibble!

John McEnroe and Boris Becker will play a challenge match before the women's final at the U.S. Open. The stakes are high. The loser has to give a sponge bath to Ilie Nastase. You know, every year, they move the camera a little father back from Ilie.…

THE **HIT(S)**

"Turn the Beat Around"

O.K., by applause, how many of you think the only Grand Slam that really matters is at Denny's?

STRIKING DISSENT So, the baseball owners approved the new labor contract by a vote of 29–1. Actually, the vote was 29 "for," one "kiss my 26-time world champion large-market ass."

According to the new pact there can be no contraction until 2007. Great. That means the infield at Tropicana Field will get a second coat of paint.

Big breakthrough for the players: Rick Reed, Brian Daubach and Damian Miller bobbleheads are now eligible for union benefits.

The Red Sox have opened a street fair on Yawkey Way serving alcoholic beverages before and after games. It's all you can drink for $19.18

Boston may be packing it in. I saw a listing in the paper under today's starters: "Wakefield (9–5) or K. Couric (0–0)."

SAMPRAS STOPS AGASSI AT OPEN Hard to believe 1995 is nearly over.

Agassi-Sampras. The only thing missing from the last time they played for the title was Brooke Shields. And hair.

Andre was stunned by the loss. After the match he climbed into the stands looking for Barbra Streisand.

UPSETS GALORE IN NFL WEEK 1 Tell me about it. I dropped $550 taking under 28—on Steve Spurrier visor tosses.

The Texans won their opener. Bob McNair paid $700 million for the new franchise. Actually, the price was $11 million, plus $689 million for shipping and handling Paul Tagliabue.

Major traffic problems around the team's new facility, Reliant Stadium. Apparently, there's still a jam created by people leaving the Astrodome from a 1996 Oilers-Steelers game.

In other NFL news, the Browns announced that beer sales will be cut off at the end of the third quarter. And you must be 21 with a photo I.D. to buy kibble.

Tennessee offensive lineman Bruce Matthews finally retired after 19 seasons. Football experts believe he'll be a first-ballot Hall of Famer in 2007, and be able to come out of a three-point stance in 2008.

USA SHOWS NO MEDAL IN WORLD HOOP CHAMPIONSHIPS On consecutive nights the Americans lost to Argentina and Yugoslavia at Conseco Fieldhouse. Luckily, there were no witnesses.

Sad. By the end of the tournament Spike Lee was heckling Reggie Miller in Croatian.

BOB KNIGHT SETTLES LAWSUIT WITH FORMER ASSISTANT Knight will pay $25,000 after admitting he shoved Ron Felling three years ago. Not only that, Felling will get another $2,500 from Brian Dennehy.

According to Felling, Knight shoved him into a TV. Go ahead and laugh, but that's how Billy Packer got his start in broadcasting.

AUGUSTA NATIONAL BOLDLY MOVES INTO 12TH CENTURY I don't think Hootie Johnson is playing with a full set of clubs. He's now thinking of changing the name of holes 11 through 13 to Amen-only Corner.

And last month he paid Callaway $25,000 to make him a Big Bert driver.

RICK SCHRODER HOSTS THE *NEW AMERICAN SPORTSMAN* Did you see the premiere episode? Fascinating. Schroder and Greg Kinnear go grouse hunting, and find Sipowicz.

SPARKS WIN SECOND STRAIGHT WNBA TITLE Of course there will now be comparisons with the Comets' dynasty. But come on, it's two completely different eras.

My time is up. You've been great. Enjoy The Vogues.

THE **NOTES**

(Sad. By the end of the tournament…) This is my brother Tom's favorite "Show" joke of all time. Yeah, I know. Sad.

(Augusta National boldly moves…) First good joke on a story that had seven months' worth of legs. It's a switch on a line I wrote for *ESPN Magazine* in 2000: *They've made so many changes at Augusta, holes 11 to 13 are now known as "Amend Corner."* Every time I write a joke about "Amen Corner," I should give a hundred bucks to my uncle, the great golf writer Herbert Warren Wind, who first coined that iconic phrase in an *SI* piece on the 1958 Masters. No, you're right, a grand.

THE **CUTS**

Reliant Stadium seats 65,000. And this is clever: The stadium has a retractable roof modeled after Granville Waiters's hairline. Raise your hand if you know who Granville Waiters is. Just as I thought. He was an NBA career backup center, mostly with the Rockets, and the one guy who should have shaved his head.

I can't believe I missed the final episode of HBO's Hard Knocks: The Dallas Cowboys. *I heard Joe Avezanno put the Cowboy Cheerleaders through the nutcracker drill.* Joe Avezanno was the Cowboys' longtime special teams coach. And the only one with better hair than the cheerleaders. Believe me, I am more proud of my reference to him than the nutcracker drill.

THE **HIT(S)**

"Five O'Clock World"

"You're the One"

(*Taptaptap*) Is this thing on?

(*Taptaptap*) Is Fernando Vargas still out?

FALCONS CORNERBACK RAY BUCHANAN SUSPENDED FOR VIOLATING NFL STEROID POLICY This is sad. Buchanan bought the steroids from an undercover cop dressed as a pharmacist.

He's out for four games. But this is strange. During that time he's allowed to play major league baseball.

This is resourceful. Browns coach Butch Davis has already developed a package of five pass plays involving Dwayne Rudd's helmet.

I guess this is a good sign. New Buccaneers coach Jon Gruden has promised the offense will be 30% cuter this season.

HBO Sports president Ross Greenburg says new HBO *Inside the NFL* analyst Cris Carter has "a Charles Barkley–like presence." It's true. Last week he stole a tray of sandwiches out of Bryant Gumbel's dressing room.

Did you hear that brand-new Ford Field in Detroit features an artificial playing surface partially made of recalled Firestone tires? Does this mean that every time the Lions score, the end zone will explode? Because if that's the case, I'm there.

Bengals offensive coordinator Bob Bratkowski must serve four days in jail before Jan. 31 after pleading no contest to DUI. The Bengals should plead no contest about 11 times before then.

NOTRE DAME IS 3–0! I haven't seen any games, I just found out from reading George O'Leary's updated résumé.

More changes in the BCS. Now 40% of the index will be based on your ranking from the judges on *American Idol*.

And all ties will be decided by Brent Musberger's urologist.

BUD SELIG UNHURT AFTER MINOR CAR ACCIDENT Luckily, thanks to the new labor agreement, his $500 deductible will be paid by George Steinbrenner.

The accident occurred after Selig stopped for lunch at his least favorite fast food joint, "Thank God It's Fehr Days."

Rangers owner Tom Hicks says the team won't raise ticket prices next year to apologize to fans for the threat of a strike. They'll also start a new tradition at The Ballpark: the seventh-inning lap dance.

Everybody's trying to make up for all the protracted labor nonsense. Last week the Yankees had a wonderful promotion: David Wells Dentist Appreciation Night.

Dave Hollins is back after missing most of the season recovering from the effects of spider bites. Be honest. How many of you are thinking of a joke that ends in the phrase "web gem"?

SHAQUILLE O'NEAL CLEARED IN INTERNAL PROBE OF EAST BATON ROUGE POLICE During Shaq's ride-along with the cops, a suspect in a routine drug sweep claimed the Lakers center had physically manhandled him and stuck his head in the toilet. Sounds like somebody said something nasty about *Kazaam*....

In other NBA news Shawn Kemp signed with Orlando. Are you like me? Are you thinking two months into the season Minnie Mouse will file a paternity suit?

TIM MONTGOMERY SETS WORLD RECORD IN 100 METERS BY .01 OF A SECOND Right after the race former record holder Maurice Greene tested positive for sour grapes.

LOU HOLTZ ADMITTED AS MEMBER TO AUGUSTA NATIONAL FOR 2003 You know, if he really had a sense of humor, he'd show up at the club in drag.

My time is up. You've been great. Enjoy Dave Mason.

THE **NOTES**

(Dave Hollins is back after...) The use of *"how many of you are thinking of a joke"* is a tremendous formula, if for no other reason than it excuses the writer for coming up with an incredibly hack line.

(In other NBA news, Shawn Kemp...) Here's another formula: NBA players having children out of wedlock—tragedy. Adding a cartoon character as the mother—brilliant social commentary.

THE **CUTS**

Jaguars linebacker T.J. Slaughter was suspended after violating the NFL policy on steroids and related substances. T.J. Slaughter. Wasn't that the cop show with William Shatner?

Speaking of which, have you seen Shatner's hair lately? You could get turf toe on that thing. No matter how hard I tried, I could not convince the editors that Shatner had anything to do with sports. Although I believe that, technically, Warren Sapp's jersey qualifies as a Klingon.

THE **HIT(S)**

"Only You Know and I Know"

"We Just Disagree"

(Note: Dave Mason is the only performer both myself and Dave Letterman opened for. The difference is, I opened for him last week.)

Thanks, you're too kind. I missed the Emmy Awards. Help me outhere: Did Tom Arnold win for Best Supporting Sycophant?

PATRICK EWING ENDS 17-YEAR CAREER The Knicks plan to retire his jersey. And the Gold Club in Atlanta will retire his pants.

Ewing will spend this season as an assistant coach for the Wizards. Patrick, memorize this line: "More ice, Michael?"

FATHER AND SON ATTACK ROYALS FIRST BASE COACH TOM GAMBOA AT COMISKEY You know what's sad? This just ruins it for all the fathers and sons who want to go to Comiskey, jump out of the stands and attack Gary Pettis.

The father claims Gamboa provoked the attack. Well, sure. Gamboa was standing there with his back to the guy, clapping his hands. He had it coming.

Let me tell you something. By the time this thing goes to trial, this numskull will be swearing Gamboa gave him and his kid the sign for run and hit.

Meanwhile, there are reports that as many as seven Mets may have problems with marijuana. Apparently, some players are so high, they still think the team has a shot at the wild card.

Are you like me? Are you waiting for Mike Piazza to call another press conference and announce he's straight?

In actual baseball news, congratulations to Braves manager Bobby Cox, who won his 1,800th game. To celebrate, Leo Mazzone sat still for two batters.

This is nice. If the Angels win the AL West, Disney promised to waive the height requirement on all rides for David Eckstein.

The Orioles' Mike Bordick set a major league record for consecutive errorless games by a shortstop. (That sound you hear is Cal Ripken getting his equipment bag out of the attic.)

PANTHERS NAME 36-YEAR-OLD RODNEY PEETE PERMANENT STARTER OVER CHRIS WEINKE Pretty simple. They wanted to go with youth.

What's going on? First, the NFL refused to let Peyton Manning wear black high-tops to honor Johnny Unitas. Now there's a $10,000 fine if any player names his child Weeb.

Before their game against the Bengals, the Falcons gave away Michael Vick bobblehead dolls. Unfortunately, a gang of eight-year-olds showed up from Chicago and tried to take out the knees.

The Cowboys released 410-pound offensive lineman Aaron Gibson. Insiders believe he may come back. You know, gravity.

NFL Films is already planning a documentary on Gibson's career: My Big Fat Freak Waiving.

TIGER WOODS WINS FIFTH WORLD GOLF CHAMPIONSHIP EVENT All right, that's enough. From now on everybody else gets to play from the white tees.

The U.S. will begin its defense of the Ryder Cup this Friday at the Belfry in Sutton Coldfield, England. Sam Torrance will captain the European squad. I believe he replaces Dr. Heimlich.

HOCKEY PRESEASON IS HERE And Bryan Trottier is the Rangers' new coach. Nice touch. It coincides with the silver anniversary of the "Potvin sucks!" chant.

HOOTIE JOHNSON UNDERGOES SUCCESSFUL BYPASS SURGERY Very serious. Doctors found 90% blockage. And that's just in his membership committee.

My time is up. You've been great. Enjoy The Knack.

THE **NOTES**

(The father claims Gamboa provoked the attack...) Pure sarcasm. Paul Reiser had a tremendous joke in his act. He would look at someone in the front row and say, "Ask me who invented sarcasm." The guy would say, "Who invented sarcasm?" And Reiser would squint his eyes and say, very sarcastically, "I did."

(Are you like me? Are you waiting...) Look, I thought it was sad and demeaning that Mike Piazza had to call a press conference to tell people he's not a homosexual. That said, if I don't write this line, I can't cohabitate with myself.

THE **CUTS**

What's going on? First, the NFL refused to let Peyton Manning wear black high-tops to honor Johnny Unitas. Now, they're saying any player who gets a flat-top must have the Reebok logo cut in. The NFL's silliness about uniformity has never been lampooned enough. In fact, they had a former player, 49ers DB Merton Hanks, patrolling the sidelines looking for infractions. Which is strange, because his neck extends more than six inches above his collar, which is illegal.

THE **HIT(S)**

"My Sharona"

"Good Girls Don't"

By applause, how many of you thought Lee Westwood is where John Wooden buys jeans?

BASEBALL'S SECOND SEASON BEGINS Of course, it's not official until George Steinbrenner switches from the lightweight all-cotton turtleneck to the 50-50 cotton-poly blend.

Attendance at Atlanta's Turner Field was down 200,000 this season. So the old adage is true: Fans will only put up with a winning team for so long.

The Angels are feeling very good. Last week the players voted half a series share to Danny Glover.

In other baseball news Pete Rose returned to Cincinnati to play in a softball game with other former major leaguers. More than 40,000 fans showed up. What a shame. Pete had under 39,500.

Pete went 1 for 2 and dived headfirst into third base. His stomach should stop jiggling by Game 2 of the NLCS.

RANDY MOSS WORKS IN AND OUT OF TRAFFIC Moss was arrested after bumping a traffic control agent with his car. I guess it occurred outside the five-yard legal chuck zone.

Randy spent a night in jail. He used his one phone call to tell Daunte Culpepper he was open.

Are you like me? Were you just happy to hear about a Vikings drive that did not end in a punt by Kyle Richardson?

In other NFL news Jimmy Johnson has rejoined *Fox NFL Sunday* after a seven-year absence. Since 1995, however, his hair had been working as a consultant to Terry Bradshaw.

RYDER CUP LANDS ON WRONG SIDE OF THE POND This is smart. Next time, to ensure camaraderie, the American players will all stay in the same dormie.

To speed up play, the captains agreed on no practice putting. And no practice choking.

Incredible sportsmanship between the two teams. On the last day Jesper Parnevik let Tiger Woods take a mulligan nanny.

There were some problems with the tape delay. At one point NBC gave the Europeans credit for a hole when Colin Montgomerie made a sand save—from the 16th at Valderrama.

L.A. SUPERIOR COURT ORDERS NEW TRIAL IN RAIDERS CONSPIRACY LAWSUIT VERSUS THE NFL You know, jury selection will be the closest thing Los Angeles has had to an NFL draft in six years.

A $1.2 billion conspiracy suit. Al Davis is clinging to his "Second Paul Tagliabue" theory.

JORDAN RETURNS FOR THIRD FINAL SEASON He feels he can play 20–25 minutes a game off the bench. Well, at least that's what his knees told Rick Reilly.

Michael will turn 40 during the season. That explains Nike's new shoe, Gasping for Air Jordans.

MICHAEL ANDRETTI'S TEAM JUMPS TO IRL On the bright side, the three drivers actually left in CART are all guaranteed podium finishes next year.

You know your racing series is in trouble when the pace car is a Yugo.

It's not all bad news though. Last week Paul Newman finally developed a salad dressing using 40-weight oil.

UPPER DECK MARKETING MANCHESTER UNITED TRADING CARDS Each pack comes with a little tear gas pellet to disperse hooligans.

MARK CUBAN GETS MARRIED The newlyweds are registered at Tiffany's, Neiman Marcus and the NBA fine office.

My time is up. You've been great. Enjoy .38 Special.

THE **NOTES**

(Pete went 1 for 2 and dived headfirst…) Here I took a break from doing jokes about his hair. It felt good.

(In other NFL news, Jimmy Johnson has rejoined…) This is probably why I took a break from doing jokes about Pete's hair.

(Incredible sportsmanship…) Elin Nordegren, who became Tiger's fiancée, was Jesper Parnevik's nanny. Thus giving new meaning to the expression "match play."

(Jordan returns for third final season…) If you can get body parts talking to reporters, by all means, do it.

THE **CUTS**

Sad. Now, the Big Red Machine is the device Pete uses to paint his hair. I said I took a break. What do you expect, abstinence?

In the end, Moss was charged with two misdemeanors. And his car goes back 15 yards from the spot of the original foul. The five-yard chuck zone was the better version of this joke. If I had included both, it would have been piling on, which is another 15 yards.

THE **HIT(S)**

"Caught Up in You"

Thank you. I know you're out there, I can hear you signaling for a beer vendor.

BASEBALL PLAYOFFS: OUT WITH THE ALDS Be honest. Which catchphrase do you like better for the Twins: Kiss my A's! or Contract this!

After the Game 5 win in Oakland, the Minnesota clubhouse received a congratulatory phone call from owner Carl Pohlad. Very emotional. Manager Ron Gardenhire could barely say, "Yes, operator. I'll accept the charges."

The Yankees and the Diamondbacks were eliminated on the same day. Although the players are calling it a work stoppage.

Are you like me? Do you think the new Basic Agreement should include drug testing for that Angels Rally Monkey?

Several of the opening-round games were carried on ABC Family Channel. I don't know what kind of cross-promotional deal they worked, but the Twins had to clear playoff roster spots for Mary-Kate and Ashley Olsen.

By the way, can these games drag on a little longer? The last thing I watched on TV that long had a dead actor montage in the middle.

CLEARANCE SALE FOR BIG LEAGUE SKIPPERS: ALMOST EVERYBODY MUST GO! Six managers have been fired since the end of the season. Seven, if you count Bobby Valentine in the mustache and glasses.

The Mets dismissed Valentine after six years. Bobby knew it was coming. The last two weeks of the season he took the lineup card to home plate with his résumé attached.

The three front-runners to replace Valentine are Buck Showalter, Chris Chambliss and Dr. Phil.

CELTICS SOLD FOR $360 MILLION Actually, it was $350 million, plus $10 million for a crew to come in and remove all evidence of M.L. Carr and Rick Pitino.

Meanwhile, NBA training camps opened. The Knicks' Latrell Sprewell will be out for six weeks with a broken hand. At first Sprewell said he had no idea how or when it happened. You know that when he heard this, his teammate Kurt Thomas thought, "Amnesia. Why didn't I think of that?"

VIKINGS HAVE BYE WEEK Help me out here. Does that mean they don't play, or that Randy Moss isn't arraigned?

In addition to his four traffic misdemeanors, Moss was also charged with possession of marijuana. Police found a small amount in his car, next to a book, *Intersections for Dummies*.

Elsewhere on the NFL docket, Raiders kicker Sebastian Janikowski was arrested for driving under the influence. Janikowski may have had one too many. He blamed the arrest on a bad hold.

Typical drunken Oakland Raider: He was blacked out locally.

Kurt Warner will miss at least five weeks with a broken pinky. Serious injury. It's on his Chunky-soup-eating hand.

And Johnnie Cochran is threatening to file a class-action suit against the NFL for its lack of progress in hiring African-American coaches. He's got the statistics, all he needs is a word that rhymes with Dungy.

NEBRASKA LOSES TWO IN A ROW IN SEPTEMBER FOR FIRST TIME IN 45 YEARS On the bright side, it turns out Eric Crouch still has three quarters of eligibility left.

WE MAY HAVE A BREAKTHROUGH AT AUGUSTA Hootie Johnson is seriously considering admitting a couple of really effeminate men.

My time is up. You've been great. Enjoy Gene Pitney.

THE **NOTES**

(Several of the opening round games…) Normally, I don't like a setup this long, but then again, I do like making fun of the Olsen twins, so it's a push.

(Celtics sold for $360 Million…) You may begin to notice there are some folks I take a shine to as material fodder. Rick Pitino is many of them. Remember his career as coach of the Celtics? He wasn't there long enough to shed a layer of skin.

(Typical drunken Oakland Raider…) I wish this column had been two paragraphs long. Anytime you can construct a complete joke in under ten words, you get a check from God. You know the great Steven Wright line: *"It's a small world, but I wouldn't want to paint it"*? Eleven words.

(We may have a breakthrough at Augusta…) Here's the other paragraph I'm proud of. This line was quoted in a gay magazine. Nice to know in between bitchiness about Rick Pitino, I can make a point.

THE **CUTS**

ABC Family is a little tamer than ABC. The Bachelor *has to choose between one woman.*

The big hit show on ABC Family is 8 Simple Rules for Having a Platonic Relationship with My Daughter. Damn. We could have had these two jokes for the price of the Olsen twins.

THE **HIT(S)**

"It Hurts to Be in Love"

"Town Without Pity"

"The Man Who Shot Liberty Valance"

"Twenty-Four Hours from Tulsa"

(Again, I break the two-hit rule, but come on, it's Gene Pitney!)

(*Taptaptap*) Is this thing on?

(*Taptaptap*) Is ABC Family still on?

THERE IS A TOMORROWLAND How about that bottom of the seventh? The only Angel who didn't score was Kate Jackson.

Fox went a little nuts with the stats. I saw one graphic in the ninth: "Angels have gone to World Series every year Bo Belinsky has died."

You think those ThunderStix are annoying now, wait till the audioanimatronic kids on the It's a Small World ride get hold of them.

The playoffs are a great national showcase. The Fox Virtual Manager just had his second interview for the Brewers' job.

Fans can pay to see batting practice during the LCS on MLB.com. And for an extra $4.95 Kenny Lofton will threaten the BP pitcher.

The decibel level in the Metrodome hit 107. But it hit only 105 against lefthanders with runners in scoring position.

Elsewhere, Tampa Bay infielder Russ Johnson, a born-again Christian, is still trying to get the team to take *Devil* out of its nickname. Not only that, he'd like the Rays to replace Hal McRae with Barabbas.

SERGIO GARCÍA SIGNS WITH TAYLOR-MADE CLUBS FOR $7 MILLION A YEAR It sounds like a lot, but that works out to eight cents a waggle.

And Phil Mickelson signed a multimillion deal with Ford. Is that what he meant when he said he had to work on his drive?

And I guess this isn't a surprise. Martha Burk filed another lawsuit. She won't rest until there's a female member in Hootie and the Blowfish.

KNICKS HAND SPREWELL LARGEST FINE IN NBA HISTORY Great. Now Mark Cuban's jealous.

According to a recent CBS *SportsLine* e-mail survey, Michael Jordan is the most influential person in the NBA. Where's the SpamGuard when you really need it?

Jordan finished with 62 points, edging out Shaquille O'Neal's podiatrist.

A MISS AND ANDY In an interview with Boomer Esiason, Rooney said female reporters have no business being on the sidelines. The next day he received 200 angry e-mails—and a dozen roses from Zeke Mowatt.

Last week Marshall Faulk walked off in the middle of an interview with Bob Costas. He found out Mike Martz had scripted only five of the first 20 questions for him.

Jaguars linebacker T.J. Slaughter is back after a four-game ban for steroid use. During the ban he lost 10 pounds and three biceps.

NHL MAKES RULES CHANGES TO TRY TO SPEED UP PLAY What does that mean? They've added express checking?

Many people are saying this could be the year for the Sharks. And even more people are saying, "Wait a minute. The NHL has a team in San Jose?"

Toronto coach Pat Quinn dropped 55 pounds over the summer. He put in a neutral zone trap in front of his refrigerator.

INDIANA PRESIDENT MYLES BRAND NAMED PRESIDENT OF NCAA His first order of business: transfer the Texas Tech campus to Baghdad.

NEW YORK CITY HOLDS FAKE TICKER TAPE PARADE TO ATTRACT THE 2012 OLYMPICS And they lit an imaginary torch from the fake fireplace NBC used in Salt Lake City.

My time is up. You've been great. Enjoy Scandal.

THE **NOTES**

(Taptaptap…) Last appearance. Try to get over it.

(Fox went a little nuts with the stats…) Bo Belinsky pitched a no-hitter as a rookie for the Angels in 1962 and dated Mamie Van Doren, Ann-Margret and Connie Stevens. I think he would have laughed.

(Elsewhere, Tampa Bay infielder…) Barabbas was the man who came off the cross at the crucifixion of Christ. He will make an appearance in a later column. There's something wrong when this guy gets more mentions than Jesus.

(A miss and Andy…) Zeke Mowatt was one of the New England Patriots who allegedly sexually harassed *Boston Herald* reporter Lisa Olson in 1990. A few months later, in the middle of the first Gulf War, Patriots owner Victor Kiam was caught on videotape at a dinner delivering this icebreaker: "You know the similarity between the Iraqis and Lisa Olson? They've both seen Patriot missiles up close." Do you see the value of an editor?

THE **CUTS**

The Cardinals almost had to sacrifice a roster spot. However, U.N. inspectors found no biological weapons in Steve Kline's hat. I think this was cut because my editors were worried they'd actually find biological weapons in Iraq that week. Sure, *now* it's funny.…

In other baseball news, Royals first base coach Tom Gamboa has been switched to the bullpen. Great. Now that means the shirtless father and son can take a leak on him. I guess this was too cruel, as if I was giving the father and son ideas.

THE **HIT(S)**

"The Warrior"

Sorry I'm late. I was waiting for my ranking from the BCS.

WORLD SERIES: SOMETHING WILD Barry Bonds is finally on a grand national stage. You think his head looked big before....

Baseball in San Francisco is a little different. You've heard of the Rally Monkey? The Giants have a Rally Florist.

And don't miss the seventh inning costume change.

Fox is taking some liberties with that Virtual Manager. I saw one: "Would you like to see a pitching change, or another shot of those three babe lawyers on *Girls Club*?"

In other baseball news the Mariners gave manager Lou Piniella permission to talk to other teams. He can't decide whether he wants to spend next season kicking a Mets or a Devil Rays cap.

NET GAIN FOR NHL RINKS So far, the only complaint about the safety netting is from Thrashers fans in Atlanta. They'd like it to block out more action.

DOLPHINS LURE CRIS CARTER AWAY FROM *INSIDE THE NFL* Wow. Jackie Jr. had a longer run on HBO.

They've agreed on a one year deal with juicy incentives. Cris, if you need a pen, I think Terrell Owens has one.

Meanwhile, are you like me? Are you waiting for Terrell to score a touchdown and pull a telestrator out of his sock?

The league fined Owens $5,000 after the Niners-Seahawks game...for having his shirttail hanging out. Hey, what about another $10,000 because the cap on his Sharpie wasn't made by Reebok?

In other NFL news the Jets have moved their business offices into Manhattan. I believe they're located on Fourth and Long.

The Redskins are thinking of adding seats to FedExField. They need a place to put all the guys Steve Spurrier is trying out at quarterback.

The Falcons are selling season tickets for $100. Well, it's $100, provided you buy four sets of louvered doors at the Home Depot before Dec. 31.

Meanwhile, McDonald's was forced to recall its Brian Urlacher bobblehead dolls. Embarrassing. Turns out the dolls had a higher nutritional content than the Big Mac.

KARL MALONE BEGINS 18TH SEASON IN UTAH Eighteen years for the Mailman. Shouldn't he at least be up to Mail Supervisor by now?

Despite injuries to Antonio McDyess, Latrell Sprewell and top draft choice Frank Williams, many experts say the Knicks are good enough to finish as high as sixth in the East. The Big East.

Stephon Marbury signed a lifetime endorsement deal with AND 1. Marbury's line will be known as AND 1 for the Road.

Yao Ming finally received a visa from the Chinese government, three months after the draft. And he would have had to wait another 24 hours, but he canceled his side order of Peking duck.

FOX SPORTS GRILL TO OPEN IN SCOTTS-DALE Try the Steve Lyons Hero: ham on a stale b-roll.

FORMER DOLPHINS KICK RETURNER FULTON WALKER JR. FOUND GUILTY OF SELLING MARIJUANA OUT OF HOME, SENTENCED TO SIX MONTHS' HOME CONFINEMENT Sometimes, you don't have to come up with a joke.

My time is up. You've been great. Enjoy The Cyrkle.

THE **NOTES**

(In other NFL news…) This is a layup. Thank God they were bad that season.

(The Falcons are selling season tickets…) Falcons owner Arthur Blank was the founder of Home Depot. And what's funnier than louvered doors? Window treatments? I don't think so.

(Try the Steve Lyons Hero…) B-roll is the background footage they shoot on remote pieces. "Ham" and "stale" are comedy truths I hold to be self-evident. I was so proud of this joke, until Steve Lyons e-mailed me and thanked me for the shout-out.

THE **CUTS**

Pac Bell Park is gorgeous, but do they have to blast Judy Garland records between innings? Here is a list of things straight people can make gay jokes about: 1) Show tunes; 2) costume changes; 3) Judy Garland; 4) Liza Minnelli; 5) Judy and Liza singing show tunes after a costume change.

I can't wait for Game 5 in San Francisco. Mike Piazza will throw out the first denial. And 6) Mike Piazza's press conference.

THE **HIT(S)**

"Red Rubber Ball"

"Turn Down Day"

I missed the Country Music Awards. Help me out here. Did David Eckstein win for Best Banjo Hitter?

PATS ROUT BILLS IN BALLYHOOED BRADY-BLEDSOE MATCHUP Tom Brady threw for 310 yards, four touchdowns and completed passes to everyone except Tara Reid.

Elsewhere, Bengals coach Dick LeBeau delivered on his guarantee of a win over the Texans. LeBeau's getting cocky. He's predicting there won't be a sequel to *I Spy*.

The Seahawks signed quarterback Jeff George. Mike Holmgren is confident that by Week 10, George'll be able to disregard an entire game plan.

Did you hear that the field at Giants Stadium is being resodded? Last month, during the Browns-Jets game, the turf was so thin Jimmy Hoffa downed a punt at the one.

KNICKS BUILDING FOR THE FUTURE They just extended the contract of coach Don Chaney. That's Step 1. Step 2: Schedule three games a month against the Washington Generals.

Cavaliers coach John Lucas served a two-game suspension after he included the nation's top high school player, LeBron James, in a workout at Gund Arena. Are you like me? Are you thinking one day in Cleveland might drive the kid to college?

Telemundo announced its NBA broadcast team. Bit of a shocker: Dan Issel and John Calipari.

The Hornets have tweaked their logo slightly to reflect the team's move to New Orleans. Now the hornet is shirtless, drunk and staggering down Bourbon Street holding a pitcher of stingers.

MAPLE LEAFS OFF TO A BAD START If they give up any more goals, Ed Belfour will have to change his name to Bel4.87.

In other hockey news fans at Madison Square Garden have begun chanting "Refund!" when the Rangers fall behind. You know, if this works, Latrell Sprewell might try it with Scott Layden.

Tom Hicks has put the Stars up for sale. The club is valued at $207 million, but he'll take $150 million from ARod.

ANGELS VICTORY PARADE DRAWS 100,000 Actually, it was 60,000, plus the people standing in line for Space Mountain.

All your favorite Disney characters showed up: Snow White, Donald Duck, Mickey Hatcher.

And meanwhile, the man who attacked Royals first base coach Tom Gamboa called a local newspaper and apologized. Yeah, he said he's sorry he didn't wear one of those tattoos for Goldenpalace.com.

NEW YORK CITY IS U.S. PICK TO HOST 2012 OLYMPICS New York edged out San Francisco to make the finals. The two cities are still battling for the rights to open a Liza Minnelli theme park.

WILLIAMS SISTERS SIGN LUCRATIVE PACT WITH McDONALD'S As part of the deal their dad, Richard, gets to serve a four-year term replacing Mayor McCheese.

A.C. GREEN REVEALS HE LOST HIS VIRGINITY LAST APRIL And I don't understand this, but his agent, Mark Fleisher, had wanted him to hold out until the second week of training camp.

My time is up. You've been great. Enjoy Thin Lizzy.

THE **NOTES**

(Did you hear that the field at Giants Stadium is being resodded?) There is an urban legend that Hoffa is buried in the south endzone. Here's the sad part: In his season ticket plan, even he has to buy two preseason games.

(The Hornets have tweaked…) Logo changes are a great formula. Just be visual. Of course this might be too visual.

(A.C. Green reveals…) The original version was just *"…until the second week of training camp."* But anytime you can get a name like Mark Fleisher in, make it happen. I used to do a joke in my stand-up act about how you know a jai-alai game is fixed when you hear the P.A. announcer say, *"Post Number 5, Del Rio, serving to Post Number 2, Murray Sugarman…"* It killed in Bridgeport, and Haifa.

THE **CUTS**

Sergei Fedorov auctions Porsche on eBay. The car was once driven by his former girlfriend Anna Kournikova, which means it can't get out of third. This is a rewrite of a joke I wrote for Dave when the show went to L.A. in 1995: *"CBS gave me a company car. Which means it can't get out of third."* Did I say rewrite? I meant Xerox.

BC-yes! Upsets galore. The Eagles handed Notre Dame its first loss. Luckily, before the game, the Irish broke out the green jerseys. That way, they can give the loss to Tulane. Loved the bold headline, but not much else. By the way, put Notre Dame on the list right after Rick Pitino.

THE **HIT(S)**

"The Boys Are Back in Town"

You know, I don't need this job. Anytime I want, my frat buddies can hit a Pick Six for me.

TAX PROBLEMS FOR DUSTY BAKER The former Giants manager owes $1 million as a result of investments made during the early 1980s. This, of course, was way before he got heavy into Bonds.

There were a lot of red flags for the IRS about Dusty. During his second season in San Francisco he tried to write off Darryl Strawberry as a dependent.

In other baseball news Yankees owner George Steinbrenner has threatened to cut off dental benefits for 150 employees. Not only that, he's thinking of charging for the cable picked up by the plate in Don Zimmer's head.

Rockies starter Jason Jennings won the NL Rookie of the Year award. He'll spend the off-season in the Coors Field humidor.

The Red Sox hired Bill James as a special adviser. Do you really want a guy who's going to say, "Forget Tom Glavine. You know who's available for nothing? Rube Waddell."

MICHIGAN BANS BASKETBALL TEAM FROM POSTSEASON Thanks a lot, guys. My March Madness brackets were due in *last* week.

As part of its self-inflicted punishment for NCAA violations, the school will remove four championship banners hanging in Crisler Arena. And I don't get this: The banners will then be laundered by former booster Ed Martin.

KNICKS' SELLOUT STREAK ENDS AT 433 It's sad. Spike Lee is now sitting courtside next to a guy who was the 10th caller.

The last nonsellout at Madison Square Garden was on Feb. 4, 1993. Which, coincidentally, was also Louis Farrakhan Bobblehead Doll Night.

Between injuries and suspensions, the Lakers bench is really short. Before the Wizards game they had to suit up three of the guys who are trying to sign Kobe Bryant to a shoe deal.

THE NHL IS NOW SELLING GAME-WORN JERSEYS Make sure you get an authentic one. I paid $400 for a Rangers number 11 sweater with MESSIEST on the back.

The league is running the Sabres. O.K., but that still doesn't explain Buffalo's new power-play specialist: Vladimir Guerrero.

PAUL TAGLIABUE IS NOT KIDDING AROUND He's going to fine *Monday Night Football* $40,000 every time a helmet-to-helmet collision graphic is shown.

The Steelers are 4-0-1 since former XFL MVP Tommy Maddox took over at quarterback. In a related story He Hate Me was named Co-Employee of the Month at Outback Steakhouse.

The Lions are offering tours of Ford Field. For $5 you get to see the locker rooms, the luxury suites and the field. Sadly, the tour stalls when it gets inside the red zone.

The Steelers and the Falcons played the NFL's first tie since '97. Here's the shocker: Bud Selig had nothing to do with it.

FORMER NEBRASKA COACH TOM OSBORNE WINS REELECTION WITH 93% OF THE VOTE Who was his opponent, Kansas?

NEXT MONTH TNT WILL PREMIERE ITS ORIGINAL FILM *SECOND STRING*, ABOUT BACKUP PLAYERS FOR THE BILLS WHO TRY TO WIN THE SUPER BOWL AFTER THE STARTERS FALL ILL I prefer the original title, *The Fall and Rise of the Frank Reich.*

My time is up. You've been great. Enjoy Sam the Sham and the Pharaohs.

THE **NOTES**

(The Steelers are 4-0-1...) ESPN Magazine will always have a fond place in my heart. I used to love when they would open all the windows in the office and get that good cross-promotion going. Seriously, though, the fact that they hired me to write the type of column that had never appeared in any legitimate sports publication, a column that was as far from journalism as Rush Limbaugh is from Atkins, shows a breadth of tongue-in-cheek vision. But forget that. Whatever happens to me from now on, *ESPN Magazine* will always be the place that published one of my favorite jokes of all time.

In the last five years, the greatest gift to sports humor was, no question, the XFL. This demon spawn of the WWF and NBC was so ill-conceived, so disastrous from the outset, you couldn't help but pile on and stay on. During Week 2 of its only season, I wrote: *"The XFL has cameras everywhere. Next week, the halftime show is Vince McMahon's colonoscopy."*

Let me explain something I may have left out. There are some jokes I just write for myself, or for "the room" (fellow writers and editors). I am fully aware that they will never make it into print. I don't care. I'm just trying to brighten a colleague's day. You know, like sending porn over the Internet, which is wrong, and not just because they end up getting your credit card number. O.K., so I send this joke with my column. Steve Wulf was my editor at *ESPN Magazine* and the man most responsible for hiring me there. A nicer, savvier writer-editor they haven't made. He calls me and says, "That Vince McMahon colonoscopy joke? My computer was still laughing when the child block came up and cut it." O.K., so it's gone. Fine.

The next day, Steve calls me. I'm on the phone, but he sounds ashen. "John Papanek (then the editor in chief at *ESPN Magazine*) saw the McMahon colonoscopy joke..."

Now, when I say for "the room"? That "room" should not include people such as one's boss. My blood was draining like a Bird jumper as Wulf continued.

"...You won't believe this, but he wants to run it!"

And that is why I'll forever be indebted to *ESPN Magazine.*

THE **CUTS**

In last week's loss to the Cavaliers, the Lakers scored the least number of points since they moved to L.A. Phil Jackson is desperate. He called the Dalai Lama and yelled, "I said big toe, not big tao!" I just wanted to show you that 99% of the time Kostya Kennedy cuts the right jokes. Jesus, who wrote this, Mark Russell?

THE **HIT(S)**

"Wooly Bully"

"Little Red Riding Hood"

Welcome to the column. Do you prefer Jeff Smoker, or non–Jeff Smoker?

AUGUSTA NATIONAL POLL REVEALS 74% BACK ITS MEMBERSHIP POLICIES The poll was conducted among a random sampling of 1,000 guys named Hootie.

While 74% said they like the status quo, the other 26% responded, "You go, girl!"

Meanwhile, Hootie Johnson has begun his own p.r. campaign. Last week he was photographed buying a copy of *Redbook*.

BINGO LONG AND HIS TRAVELING EXPOS? The Expos will play 20 games in Puerto Rico—but only if they come up with gas money for the plane.

There was a rumor that the Expos would share Fenway Park next season with the Red Sox. The Sox got excited when they did the math: 1918 is 2003 Canadian.

Elsewhere, Alex Rodriguez picked up $300,000 in incentives by winning a Gold Glove and finishing second in the MVP voting to Miguel Tejada. Great. Now A-Rod can finally afford that 22nd car.

NFL CRACKS DOWN ON OVERWEIGHT OFFICIALS You know what's really scary? Vertical stripes are supposed to be slimming.

They have to come up with some guidelines. It's gotten out of hand. Last week a back judge grabbed Johnny Grier's microphone and tried to order some nachos.

The Giants, down to two healthy receivers, were forced to sign veteran Herman Moore. And that was only because Angie Harmon wanted a two-year deal.

Oh, come on, like she hasn't worked routes with Jason Sehorn.

The Colts denied that owner Jim Irsay is being investigated for prescription drug fraud. He may face a lesser charge: possession of Bill Romanowski's phone number.

NASCAR TAKING EVEN MORE SAFETY PRECAUTIONS Next season the HANS device will be mandatory on all photographers within 50 feet of Tony Stewart.

The Cowboys may sponsor a car. To me, it won't really be a Cowboys car unless Michael Irvin is handcuffed in the backseat.

I'M STARTING TO WORRY ABOUT PETE WEBER His new bowling ball looks a lot like Ralphie on *The Sopranos*.

JURY AWARDS LEIGH STEINBERG $44.6 MILLION IN SUIT AGAINST EX-PARTNER Sounds high, but don't forget, 10% goes to his agent, Leigh Steinberg; 15% to his manager, Leigh Steinberg; and then he has to pay his lawyer, Leigh Steinberg.

My time is up. You've been great. Enjoy Little Lulu.

THE **NOTES**

(Augusta National poll reveals...) I had waited two months to make fun of the man's name, which in some countries would get me thrown out of the joke writers union.

(Jury awards Leigh Steinberg...) I think we all learned our lesson with the A.C. Green virginity joke about adding an agent to make it at least 10% funnier. Let's learn it again, three more times.

THE **CUTS**

(re: NFL overweight officials) This is serious. If it gets any worse, the league may be forced to add gravy to its list of banned substances. Kostya Kennedy told me, "You can have three out of the five overweight jokes." As I mentioned, we try to stay away from the gratuitous fat stuff, but "gravy" is a funny word. Come on. Say it. You're laughing. Don't lie to me.

THE **HITS**

"To Sir with Love"

Good to be here. Anybody need tickets for the next seven Arturo Gatti–Micky Ward fights?

BIGGER COURT FOR MICHAEL? A woman accused of extortion by Michael Jordan is now suing him, claiming that in 1991 he offered her $5 million to keep quiet. That's ridiculous. Five million dollars in 1991, and she wasn't even a lottery pick?

Come on. Nobody takes money from Michael Jordan. Except the house.

The woman claims she had an oral agreement with Michael. An oral agreement. Isn't that what got Clinton impeached?

In other NBA news the Nets are trying to get point guard Chris Childs to lose weight. So far the best they've come up with is having Dikembe Mutombo give him the finger wag every time Childs orders pie.

The Dallas Mavericks are now 13–0. And I don't get this. David Stern is thinking about fining Mark Cuban for not complaining.

In two games last week Yao Ming scored 48 points on 17-for-23 shooting from the field. Are you like me? Are you thinking Charles Barkley should change the name of his show from *Listen Up* to *Pucker Up*?

MAJOR LEAGUE BASEBALL CONSIDERING A MINIMUM AGE FOR BATBOYS You must be at least 16, or really adorable.

And only two batboys will be allowed in the dugout at any time. Although J.T. Snow will be allowed to bring a carry-on item.

In other baseball news Mets catcher Mike Piazza went to Italy and had an audience with the pope. And this was nice. The pope taught him how to say "I'm not gay" in Latin.

The Padres signed relief pitcher Jesse Orosco. He'll be placed on their way-over-40-man roster.

The man who knocked out David Wells's teeth in a diner was found guilty of assault. However, he was acquitted on weapons possession because the butter knife he was holding was registered.

TOMMY MADDOX IS O.K. The Steelers QB was released from the hospital after recovering from head and neck injuries. However, Troy Aikman is being held for observation after watching the replay.

Because of a design flaw, Gillette Stadium does not have nearly enough men's rooms. On Sunday three Patriots fans were arrested in the stands for trying to go on fourth down.

Hamilton County, Ohio, is being urged to sue the Bengals for not fielding a competitive football team in taxpayer-funded Paul Brown Stadium. I'm no Alan Dershowitz, but isn't this "breach of contact"?

THIS JUST IN: TIGER WOODS HAS ANNOUNCED HE WILL NOT ENTER THIS YEAR'S BASSMASTERS In related news *The New York Times* urged Augusta National to change its membership policies. Not to be outdone, Hootie Johnson told *The National Enquirer* he was abducted by aliens working in the clubhouse kitchen.

In other golf news, Smith & Wesson announced it will introduce its own line of golf clubs. This should give new meaning to the phrase "shotgun start."

You think Sergio García's over the ball too long now, wait till he starts having to adjust his telescopic sight.

OHIO STATE NO. 1 IN BCS That's BCS—Burning Car Standings.

BOB KNIGHT SUES INDIANA OVER FIRING You know, if he loses, he might give the judge the chair.

My time is up. You've been great. Enjoy Spandau Ballet.

THE **NOTES**

(Come on. Nobody takes money from Michael Jordan…) Michael Jordan has two solid fertile fields of joke vegetation: minor league baseball and gambling. Believe me, I tried, but I could not make the comic connection between Karla Knafel and the Birmingham Barons. So we went with gambling.

(And only two batboys will be allowed…) J.T. Snow pulled Dusty Baker's 3½-year-old son, Darren, out of harm's way during a play at the plate in Game 5 of the World Series. And yes, he was adorable. J.T., that is. Darren was O.K. A little pushy.

(In other baseball news, Mets catcher Mike Piazza…) Let me reiterate, I always thought it was terribly unfair that Mike Piazza felt he had to hold a press conference to announce he was not a homosexual. But then he went to see the pope, and hey, I gotta feed my family.

THE **CUTS**

Look, if anybody's owed money by MJ for keeping quiet and staying out of the way, it's Jack Haley. Jack Haley enjoyed a long career in the NBA by being Michael Jordan's version of Jilly Rizzo. Unfortunately, nobody knows this. So, if they're really hip, they think I'm talking about the guy who played the Tin Man in *The Wizard of Oz*.

A *Wizard of Oz* reference? Maybe I owe Piazza an apology.

THE **HIT(S)**

"True"

THE SHOW

For those who watched the Macy's Parade, there was no Butterbean balloon this year. That was Butterbean.

GIANTS ROOKIE RECEIVER TIM CARTER VICTIM OF CARJACKING He surrendered all his valuables, was held against his will for 3½ hours, then given $40 in cash and forced out onto the street. You know, outside of the $40 rebate, it sounds like the Giants' season ticket plan.

Meanwhile, NBC aired the National Dog Show opposite the Lions-Patriots game. I kept flipping back and forth, and at one point I could swear I saw the back judge checking Tom Brady's teeth.

John Madden had a quiet Thanksgiving. It was just him, the Ace Hardware Man and the six-legged turkey.

Minnesota has lost 16 straight away from home. So Randy Moss isn't the only Viking who has trouble on the road.

NEBRASKA FINISHES WORST REGULAR SEASON IN 41 YEARS The Huskers went 7–6. They aren't even allowed to watch the Fiesta Bowl.

In other college news USC routed Notre Dame 44–13. But don't worry, the Irish can remain BCS eligible by crediting the loss to Bob Davie.

And FSU quarterback Adrian McPherson was suspended from the team and was arrested for stealing a blank check. Not only that, he tried to reopen Peter Warrick's shoplifting account at Dillard's.

JORDAN SAYS THIS WILL BE HIS LAST YEAR However, under league rules, you can still try to extort money from him until 2005.

In other NBA news Allen Iverson says he's now afraid to stay in Philadelphia. Turns out six members of his posse had sinus problems and moved to Arizona.

Are you like me? Are you thinking if two more Blazers get arrested, they'll have enough for a lineup?

METS MIGHT OWE NEW YORK CITY $1 MILLION IN BACK RENT ON SHEA STADIUM They insist it's not their problem anymore. They put the lease in Art Howe's name.

The Red Sox dropped out early in the running to sign free agent Tom Glavine. The deal fell through when Boston couldn't guarantee him a fourth year as Joe Thornton's left wing.

COMPAQ CENTER IN SAN JOSE RENAMED THE HP PAVILION By Christmas the Zamboni will be redesigned to look like a giant inkjet printer.

In other hockey news I'm not sure if this will attract more fans, but the Mighty Ducks are running a new promotion: Come as Your Favorite Disney Cruise Stomach Virus Symptom.

MODERN PENTATHLON REMAINS IN OLYMPICS, FOR NOW It was very close to being dropped from the Games. The IOC's problem: too many events, not enough bribe money.

The modern pentathlon consists of cross-country running, swimming, fencing, shooting and horseback riding. Originally the Olympic committee wanted to eliminate fencing and replace it with shopping.

George Michael has been tapped to compose a theme song for the 2004 Games. Good for him. Nice to see George tapped by someone other than a cop in a public restroom.

LENNOX LEWIS TO DEFEND WBC TITLE AGAINST VITALI KLITSCHKO Vitali is the No. 1–ranked contender. And the No. 2–ranked Klitschko.

CURTIS STRANGE IN CAST AFTER ELBOW SURGERY Sounds like God lost a bet on the Ryder Cup.

My time is up. You've been great. Enjoy David Soul.

THE **NOTES**

(In other college news USC routed Notre Dame...) Finally, I make the Tulane "green jersey" joke from a month ago work.

(George Michael has been tapped...) Children under 16, ask your dad to explain this.

(Curtis Strange in cast after elbow surgery...) Hey, if Jordan can have a gambling problem, why not the Almighty?

THE **CUTS**

Brian Griese will be out 2–3 weeks with a sprained knee. The Broncos are thinking of signing his dog as a pass rusher. Griese injured his knee when he claimed he tripped over his dog in the driveway. Come on, was that before or after the dog ate his gameplan?

Try not to laugh too loud at that one. You'll wake the Sox new general manager. Theo Epstein was 28 when he was named the Red Sox G.M. Anyone who says they're not jealous is lying. Not lying at the level of "I tripped over my dog in the driveway," but close.

THE **HIT(S)**

"Don't Give Up on Us, Baby"

Let's move this along. I have less than two weeks left to get an undeclared gift for Chris Webber's father.

NFL ENTERS WILD STRETCH RUN Dan Reeves has finally adjusted to Michael Vick's reckless style of play. He now stands on the sideline, hooked up to a Zocor IV drip.

Houston's Reliant Stadium has an on-site jail. Go ahead and laugh, but it may be the closest thing to protection David Carr gets all year.

Panthers defensive end Julius Peppers was suspended for the rest of the season for violating the league's substance abuse policy. He's not allowed to participate in contact drills, other than film session fights with Steve Smith.

Smith was suspended for a game after breaking a teammate's nose during a film session. Apparently the guy wouldn't shut up, and Smith couldn't hear half the things Adam Sandler was saying.

Colts WR Marvin Harrison is on pace for 145 receptions, which would obliterate the league record. In a related story, Randy Moss has a streak of 45 consecutive games with at least one complaint.

JIM THOME GETS HIS PHIL The All-Star first baseman left the Indians to sign a six-year, $85 million deal with the Phillies. It sounds like a lot, but he has to pay medical insurance for the Phanatic.

The Mets won the Tom Glavine Sweepstakes. All that's left is the press conference at which he announces his sexuality.

The Canadian Baseball League will begin play next May in eight cities. And you know what's sad? In that league the Expos would still be considered a small-market team.

JAZZ RETIRES JEFF HORNACEK'S NUMBER 14 Hornacek was the fourth player to be honored, joining Darrell Griffith, Mark Eaton and Pete Maravich. This is all so political. Griffith and Eaton, sure, but Maravich?

Jazz owner Larry Miller might sell the team's nickname back to New Orleans. He hasn't named a price, but he'll subtract a couple of zeros if they take Greg Ostertag.

And this just in: An unidentified NBA player came home to his wife, had dinner and went to sleep.

WINSTON CUP CHAMP TONY STEWART VISITS THE WHITE HOUSE It went well. He shook hands with President Bush and shoved only three Supreme Court judges.

FLORIDA PANTHERS ENFORCER PETER WORRELL SENTENCED TO 10 DAYS AFTER PLEADING GUILTY TO DUI Of course, Worrell likes to think of it as 2,880 five-minute majors.

It's not all bad news for the Panthers. At least Mike Keenan's doghouse has an ocean view.

FORMER CBS TOP EXEC QUITS AUGUSTA Thomas Wyman called his ex–fellow members "rednecks" for not admitting a woman. I'm no Jeff Foxworthy, but when the guy who green-lighted the *Dukes of Hazzard* reunion movie calls you a redneck, you are.

In other golf news, St. Andrews has changed its famous Road Hole bunker on 17. The wall was lowered two feet, and a Starbucks was put in.

Traditionalists are furious. What's next, they're going to allow women in there?

NAVY CRUSHES ARMY 58–12 Everyone saw it coming. Before the game Hans Blix inspected the Cadets' offense and found no weapons.

NOMAR GARCIAPARRA AND MIA HAMM ENGAGED Sadly, Nomar has to wait until the honeymoon before he's allowed to use his hands.

My time is up. You've been great. Enjoy The McCoys.

THE **NOTES**

(Houston's Reliant Stadium...) Do you see that "Go ahead and laugh"? Some people call that a setup. I call it begging.

(Jazz owner Larry Miller might sell...) Ostertag wore number 00 for years, before switching to number 47 and becoming completely irrelevant.

(And this just in: An unidentified NBA player...) This is my favorite kind of joke. You know, other than ones that end in "Viagra."

*(**Navy crushes Army...**)* Everybody saw this joke coming, except the U.N.

THE **CUTS**

The Rockets' Steve Francis has an inner ear disorder. It's causing a very painful side effect—Yao Migraines. Technically, this is not a pun. But it qualifies on strength of groan potential.

Meanwhile, I'm starting to worry about the New York Times. *Its latest college football poll has USC No. 1, Miami No. 2 and then two at-large picks from Martha Burk. The* Times *had like 12 reporters covering this case, all bashing Augusta. You can't make this stuff up, unless you're Jayson Blair.*

THE **HIT(S)**

"Hang on Sloopy"

I forgot to get the Sunday papers. Help me out here. How many Heisman votes did Carson Daly get?

RETURN OF THE ROSE? Pete Rose met with Bud Selig three weeks ago. They could only agree on one thing: The J.Lo–Ben Affleck marriage won't last.

Insiders believe there's been some progress. Now Pete can get reinstated if he admits he's been dyeing his hair.

When Rose met with Selig he was accompanied by former Phillies teammate Mike Schmidt. Well, sure. He needed someone to drive him in.

In other baseball news the Red Sox have added two sock-shaped mascots for next season, Lefty and Righty. Theo Epstein signed them out of his play group.

The Reds were desperate. General manager Jim Bowden flew in Michael Jackson to dangle Ken Griffey Jr.

NFL EXTENDS DEAL WITH DIRECTV FIVE MORE YEARS Gee, I don't know if the wire I attached to my neighbor's dish will last that long.

In other NFL news, Rich Gannon is nearing a slew of records. However, none of them will be recognized until he does a lame commercial for Isotoner gloves.

Giants receiver Ron Dixon was suspended for one game without pay for conduct detrimental to the team. He missed a couple of team meetings and microwaved Jim Fassel's two-point conversion chart.

By the way, who came up with that two-point chart, Casey Kasem?

The league has moved the starting times of the Jan. 19 conference finals up to 3 p.m. and 6:30 p.m. Great. Now schoolkids will have to stay up till 10:00 to watch *60 Minutes*.

Arizona tight end Justin Levasseur awaits trial after being busted with 87 pounds of marijuana. Eighty-seven pounds. Or as Nate Newton calls it, an appetizer.

Why 87 pounds? Don't hold me to this, but I believe the NFL has strict rules on this: Tight ends can only be caught with an amount between 80 and 89.

GRIZZLIES WIN FOUR STRAIGHT Memphis fans are excited. Elvis just bought four seats on the floor. For him and one guest.

The woman suing Michael Jordan for $5 million claims she was introduced to him in 1989 by NBA referee Eddie F. Rush. That explains why before every date MJ had to check in at the scorer's table.

The Trail Blazers are on pace to lose $100 million this season. And it could get as high as $115 million if players start jumping bail.

TIGER WOODS GETS KNEE SCOPED Of course, *The New York Times* urged him to skip the surgery and boycott his meniscus.

In a related story, Senate majority leader Trent Lott is out with a torn ACLU.

Elsewhere, Suzy Whaley has officially announced that she'll compete in the Greater Hartford Open this summer. It will make her the first woman to play in a men's tournament in 65 years. Don't confuse her with Martha Burk, who's the first woman to play *with* a men's tournament.

ESPN TELEVISES LEBRON JAMES'S HIGH SCHOOL GAME You know you're something special when you beat the No. 1 high school team and two of its starters sign letters of intent to be in your posse.

KEYSHAWN JOHNSON WANTS TO SPLIT WITH HIS WIFE Same complaint as always from Keyshawn: Not enough touches.

My time is up. You've been great. Enjoy Orleans.

THE **NOTES**

(The Reds were desperate...) Can't believe I made it this long without a Michael Jackson joke. Oh, wait. The Jimmy Johnson line about Jerry Jones. Never mind....

(Giants receiver Ron Dixon...) Fassel, the Giants' coach, had made a questionable decision the week before. Not as questionable as the decision to hire him, but still...

(Why 87 pounds? Don't hold me to this...) Love uniform number jokes, especially those that make fun of the NFL's sphincter-tight set of rules. This has Greg Ostertag beat by a mile.

(Keyshawn Johnson wants to split...) Remember what I said about jokes after famous people die? Divorce works even better, because you can go straight to the bedroom, rather than the formaldehyde.

THE **CUTS**

A federal judge has ruled Chris Webber's perjury trial can wait until after the season. Great. That means he doesn't have to use a timeout he doesn't have. Whenever Kostya wants me to cut a joke, he says, very subtly, "This is something the funny guy at the *L.A. Times* would have come up with." Works every time.

***MGM begins preproduction on* Rocky VI.** *Pretty good plot. Sylvester Stallone beats a dead horse for the title.* And this is something the film critic at the *L.A. Times* would have come up with.

THE **HIT(S)**

"Dance with Me"

"Still the One"

Boy, you can tell it's the holiday season. I saw Pat Riley at the NBA Store, trying to exchange his XXL fine for a medium.

JEFF KENT, 2000 NL MVP, SIGNS WITH THE ASTROS And the Giants are now scrambling to find a second baseman who can hit for power and alienate Barry Bonds.

The Yankees want to acclimate Japanese slugger Hideki Matsui to New York as quickly as possible. Next week he'll fly into the city and be sucker punched in a coffee shop.

You can tell Godzilla is coming to the Big Apple. There's a guy in Times Square screaming, "Run for your lives!"

Oh, wait a minute. That guy's in Times Square every day.

Big off-season for the Yanks. Godzilla and Todd-zeilla.

Also in baseball the Red Sox acquired Jeremy Giambi. What, Ozzie Canseco wasn't available?

With the Giambi acquisition, new G.M. Theo Epstein shows he's serious about upholding Red Sox tradition. The tradition that gave you Dom DiMaggio, Billy Conigliaro, Mike Maddux....

JERRY JONES MEETS BILL PARCELLS FOR FIVE-HOUR "PHILOSOPHICAL DISCUSSION" You know what this means. Parcells is very, very interested in turning down the Cowboys' coaching job.

They met secretly in New Jersey. Jerry showed up wearing a disguise. His original face.

In other NFL news Priest Holmes is out with a hip injury. Is that all? I thought he'd been transferred to another parish.

FLORIDA STATE QUARTERBACK CHRIS RIX TO MISS SUGAR BOWL He overslept and missed a final exam. Remember the good old days when a college player could pay another guy to sleep through an exam for him?

Rix had a lame excuse. He claimed Adrian McPherson stole his blank blue book.

So it looks as if Bobby Bowden will have to go with his third-string QB, 27-year-old true freshman Chris Weinke Jr.

Elsewhere, Texas A&M explained why they fired long-time coach R.C. Slocum. The Aggies had no choice. He refused to turn all recruiting over to Tom Berenger.

There are a record 28 bowl games. That means Division I-A played a full season to eliminate Rutgers, Army and Buffalo.

BET FOUNDER ROBERT JOHNSON NAMED OWNER OF CHARLOTTE FRANCHISE His first order of business: getting Trent Lott to apologize to Charlotte for losing the Hornets.

In other NBA news Michael Jordan submitted court papers claiming that the woman who's suing him for $5 million agreed to take $250,000 to keep their affair quiet. And I think we can all agree: She did a bang-up job keeping quiet.

Actually the offer was $250,000 to keep quiet, $375,000 if Jordan got blackjack.

And $250,000? That's just bad business. Didn't she know she could have made much more money having a kid with Shawn Kemp?

Karla Knafel. Didn't she try to jump 12 NBA team buses and Snake River Canyon in 1974?

AVALANCHE AXE BOB HARTLEY It was sad at the end. He had only one supporter: Mr. Carlin.

HARRY HOLLINGSWORTH, WHO POPULARIZED USING A COMPUTER TO MAKE FOOTBALL PICKS, DIES AT 77 The computer had under 78.

My time is up. You've been great. Enjoy the Royal Guardsmen.

THE **NOTES**

(The Yankees want to acclimate Japanese slugger...) A few months before, David Wells had been sucker punched by a 5' 4" guy Wells claims came at him with a butter knife. A friend of mine said, "Well, sure. You see David Wells, you want to butter him."

(They met secretly in New Jersey. Jerry showed up...) You can actually buy software for Microsoft Word that automatically turns "Michael Jackson" into "Jerry Jones." Mac users, you're on your own.

(Karla Knafel. Didn't she...) This is a formula I copped from Mulholland and Barrie where you purposely confuse someone's name. When Rick Lazio ran for Senator against Hillary Clinton, they wrote, "*Rick Lazio. Wasn't he the host of* Dance Fever?"

(Avalanche axe Bob Hartley...) And here is another version of that, except Bob Hartley really was the name of Bob Newhart's shrink character.

THE **CUTS**

Rix was suspended under a Florida state law, named the "Deion Sanders Rule." Wait a minute. I thought the Deion Sanders Rule was that you can't call for a fair catch by waving jewelry. This was tragically cut for space. From then on, all my Deion Sanders cracks were about suits.

Ted Williams to remain in cryogenic chamber. *Okay, everybody sing: "Buy me some Freon and crackerjack...."* When I was putting this book together and I was planning to include jokes that had been cut, this was one I had in mind. Not because it's great, just to show that you need people, mature people, to tell you, "Ah, no."

THE **HIT(S)**

"Snoopy vs. the Red Baron"

"Snoopy's Christmas"

Before we begin, congrats to Shaquille O'Neal, who married his longtime girlfriend. Are you like me? Are you thinking that's the only ring he'll get this year?

WILD WILD-CARD WEEKEND The Giants still have not gotten over blowing a 24-point lead to the 49ers. For the last three days Jeremy Shockey has been taunting himself.

You don't want to use the word collapse, but after the game the entire defense had to be treated by a seismologist.

In the Steelers' comeback win, the Browns played it a little safe in trying to protect the lead. Dwayne Rudd didn't take off his helmet until Tuesday.

The Jets routed the Colts 41–0. Am I the only one who saw this connection? The actress who plays Meadow Soprano sang the national anthem, and the next thing you knew, Peyton Manning's arm had mysteriously disappeared.

The New Jersey Sports and Exposition Authority spent about $120,000 to put in a new field at Giants Stadium for the playoffs. In a related story the first three fairways at Sawgrass are missing.

And Bill Parcells entered Week 2 as coach of the Cowboys. That means I already lost the office pool.

Jerry Jones followed league guidelines before hiring Parcells. He saw Denzel Washington's reel from *Remember the Titans*, and his plastic surgeon interviewed Dennis Green.

OHIO STATE OT'S CANES FOR NATIONAL CHAMPIONSHIP Miami coach Larry Coker learned his lesson. Next season he's going back to parolees.

Tough start to 2003 for the Hurricanes. First their undefeated streak ends at 34, and now they head into spring practice $5 million over the cap.

O.J. Simpson showed up at a USC practice before the Trojans routed Iowa in the Orange Bowl. And this is sweet: He told Heisman Trophy winner Carson Palmer, "This is something nobody can take away from you. Unless you lose the civil trial."

EIGHT IS ENOUGH: PITCHING-RICH YANKEES RE-SIGN ROGER CLEMENS Clemens can't wait for his first start, on April 9. And his second, on June 6.

Clemens is five shy of 300. No, I'm sorry. He needs seven wins for 300. I was thinking of his weight during his last season in Boston.

In a recent interview, Yankees owner George Steinbrenner blamed Derek Jeter's declining stats on his off-the-field activities. This is Step 1 in George's meddling. Step 2: He replaces Jordana Brewster with Billy Connors.

MARIAN HOSSA SETS SENATORS TEAM RECORD WITH FOUR GOALS IN 8–1 WIN Sadly, three days later all the scores were returned because of insufficient funds.

Serious financial problems in Ottawa. First the Senators failed to meet the team payroll, now it turns out they haven't paid the red-light bill since August.

ATLANTA FIRES HOCKEY, HOOPS COACHES ON SAME DAY It wasn't supposed to happen that way. The Hawks were going to wait on Lon Kruger, but Trailways was running a two-for-one sale.

JEFF GORDON TO HOST *SATURDAY NIGHT LIVE* ON JAN. 11 All audience members will be equipped with the HANS device to keep them from nodding off.

My time is up. You've been great. Enjoy Gerry & the Pacemakers.

THE **NOTES**

(Ohio State OTs Canes for national championship…) The "parolees" line launched a giant pit-bullish column from the *Miami Herald*'s legendary Edwin Pope, in which he said, "There's nothing personal," then mentioned me by name 17 times. His major point was the word "parolee" implies a conviction, and there had never been a Miami player convicted of a felony. This, of course, reminds me of the scene at the beginning of *Stripes*, when Bill Murray is at the Army recruiting office and the guy behind the desk asks him if he's ever been convicted of a major crime. "Convicted?" Bill Murray says, "No. Not convicted."

(In a recent interview, Yankees owner…) Here is an update: Billy Connors is still on the Yankee payroll, while Jeter has replaced Jordana Brewster with a five-babe rotation.

THE **CUTS**

This just in: Al Qaeda is now taking credit for blowing up Cinergy Field. Sixteen months later, this was still not funny.

O.J. at a USC practice. This now explains why, when they dumped the Gatorade on Pete Carroll, a knife fell out. Eight years later, it was still funny.

Shaq and his longtime girlfriend were married last month in a private ceremony. And this is encouraging. He hit on over 60% of his vows. I like this better than the "ring" opener. If Shaq ever learns how to shoot free throws, that will be like a fire in the warehouse for me.

THE **HIT(S)**

"Don't Let the Sun Catch You Crying"

"Ferry Cross the Mersey"

Good to be here. Sorry I'm late. I was out clubbing with Livan Hernandez.

NFL DOWN TO FINAL FOUR And by final four, of course, I mean the number of controversial calls.

Did you catch the end of the Titans-Steelers game? Did I miss a meeting? Is overtime now best-two-out-of-three field goals?

Tampa Bay routed San Francisco. Now the Buccaneers have two objectives before Sunday's NFC championship: 1) Make sure Brad Johnson is healthy, 2) Bribe God to heat Veterans Stadium to at least 41 degrees.

Forty-Niners cornerback Ahmed Plummer left the game with a dislocated shoulder. The trainer said he hadn't seen a separation like that since Plummer tried to cover Amani Toomer.

Oakland easily took care of the Jets 30–10. By the end of the third quarter there were only 10,000 guys left in Network Associates Coliseum dressed like Darth Vader.

Meanwhile, more bad news for the Saints. They had such a poor finish, New Orleans lost home field for Mardi Gras.

Denver's Clinton Portis was named the AP's NFL Offensive Rookie of the Year. And Giants TE Jeremy Shockey received a new honor, Most Likely to End Up Working for Vince McMahon.

DENNIS RODMAN ARRESTED IN NEWPORT BEACH A woman accused Rodman of assaulting her. Which means he either faces a trial or a 10-day contract with the Blazers.

Also in basketball, Kobe Bryant set an NBA record with 12 three-pointers, including nine in a row, in the Lakers' win over Seattle. It's all part of Phil Jackson's new trey-angle offense.

All players still on an NBA roster after Jan. 10 get paid for the entire season. This is why Jan. 9 is known around the league as "Dwayne Schintzius Eve."

A game between the 76ers and the Jazz last month was delayed when someone threw a rat on the floor. Which raises the question: Was this someone a fan, or a vendor with bad touch?

EDDIE MURRAY AND GARY CARTER GET ELECTED TO THE HALL OF FAME Not only that, the writers voted to allow Pete Rose to use the men's bathroom at Cooperstown Mobil.

The Tigers are moving the left centerfield fence at Comerica Park 25 feet closer to home. Experts believe this will increase home runs by 50. Fifty-two if you count homers by the Tigers.

SENATORS FILE FOR BANKRUPTCY Desperate fiscal situation in Ottawa. Last week at the Corel Centre they had to pass the hat to raise gas money for the Zamboni.

In other NHL news the Maple Leafs have introduced a "Kids' Night Out with the Leafs" program. Pretty good deal. For $99 you get two tickets, two small sodas, a popcorn and your choice of a face wash from Tie Domi or Darcy Tucker.

ITALIAN COURT ORDERS ALLEGED RUSSIAN MOBSTER WHO WAS AT CENTER OF OLYMPIC FIGURE SKATING SCANDAL EXTRADITED BACK TO U.S. While he awaits trial, ABC wants him to fix the results of *American Idol*.

ESPN WILL LAUNCH 24-HOUR *ESPN DEPORTES* Which raises the question: What's Spanish for "Boo-yah!"?

My time is up. You've been great. Enjoy Brownsville Station.

THE **NOTES**

(Good to be here. Sorry I'm late...) That week, then-Marlins pitcher Livan Hernandez had gone after someone with a golf club. Ah, the off-season....

(All players still on an NBA roster...) Dwayne Schintzius, doubly blessed by being 7′ 2″ and white, had a wonderfully leisurely NBA career. Seven years, more than 24 total minutes.

*(**ESPN will launch 24-hour** **ESPN Deportes**...)* When I left *ESPN Magazine* to come to *SI*, Dan Patrick called me and said, "Now, when you go over there, play nice." This is nice, isn't it?

THE **CUTS**

Miami tailback Willis McGahee took out a $2.5 million insurance policy two weeks before he was injured in the Fiesta Bowl. I don't think this is what the folks at Allstate had in mind when they offered coverage for "hurricane damage."

Comprehensive policy. The only way McGahee wouldn't have been paid off is if he'd injured his knee running away from a Miami booster. These were cut as part of our "Let's not have Edwin Pope write another column" campaign.

THE **HIT(S)**

"Smokin' in the Boys' Room"

THE **SHOW** | January 27, 2003

Good to be here. By applause, how many of you think we should be able to challenge two Super Bowl ads per half?

BUCS DON'T STOP HERE Tampa Bay upset the Eagles in Philadelphia 27–10. And what are the odds of this? The Bucs' point total, the game-time temperature and Donovan McNabb's QB rating were all the same number.

It was the last football game at the Vet. But they've booked fights in the stands until the end of the month.

I kept flipping back and forth between the Golden Globes and the AFC Championship. Help me out here: Was Kim Cattrall called for roughing the passer?

The price for a 30-second Super Bowl spot is $2.1 million. And $2.3 million if the ad performs well enough to make the Pro Bowl.

The NFL is refusing to run ads for Las Vegas tourism during the Super Bowl because it feels the ads would promote gambling. And frankly, the league doesn't need to promote gambling during the Super Bowl. Weeks 1–3 are where it needs help.

YAO BESTS SHAQ IN FIRST MEETING Great matchup. The 7′ 5″ rookie blocked O'Neal's first three shots and deflected a couple of derogatory remarks.

O'Neal has apologized to Yao for his ethnically insensitive comments. Hey, it could have been worse. Shaq could have rapped them.

Big month for Yao. The Shanghai Sharks retired his number 15. Be honest. How many of you thought the Shanghai Sharks were in the Campbell Conference?

MOM GIVES LEBRON JAMES $50,000 HUMMER FOR 18TH BIRTHDAY You're right. There must be a better way to phrase that.

Ohio state high school officials are investigating the gift. If there's any impropriety, LeBron will lose his amateur status. I think I speak for fans everywhere when I say, "What amateur status?"

KELLOGG'S FROSTED FLAKES NAMED OFFICIAL BREAKFAST CEREAL OF THE NHL Only they had to change Tony the Tiger's catchphrase to "They'rrrre solvent!"

Two weeks ago there was one bankrupt team in the NHL. Now there are two. I'm telling you, this cloning thing really works.

There were hints the Sabres were in trouble financially. Former owner John Rigas's autobiography begins on Chapter 11.

The Sabres may be forced to relocate. Isn't this a little like saying Diana Ross may be forced to get a designated driver?

But wait. A last-minute buyer for the Senators has emerged. Maybe you know him—Joe Millionaire?

RUMORS SAY STEVE LAVIN THINKING OF RESIGNING AT UCLA Apparently he only has enough mousse to last through nonconference games.

The rumor mill also says Lavin could be headed in the direction of Toledo. Bob Toledo.

MIKE TYSON'S DIVORCE IS FINAL Tyson agreed to pay Monica Turner $6.5 million in future earnings. However, the purse may be withheld by the state of Nevada.

WNBA MAY AWARD FRANCHISE TO MOHEGAN SUN Oh, I hope I'm not too late with a name. The Casino Bouncers.

My time is up. You've been great. Enjoy Eddie Money.

THE **NOTES**

(O'Neal has apologized to Yao...) Here are the areas you can make fun of Shaq: 1) free throws; 2) rapping; 3) *Kazaam*.

(Mom gives LeBron James $50,000 Hummer...) This is the kind of quip that makes you proud of the First Amendment.

THE **CUTS**

Troy Aikman says he may be interested in playing for Bill Parcells. I'm worried. You know those new concussion-prevention helmets by Riddell? If Troy came back, he'd have to wear one inside another. Steve Wulf, my editor at *ESPN Magazine*, loved concussion jokes. Kostya Kennedy does not. Something about brain fluid and potentially life-threatening blahblahblah. Killjoy.

And congratulations to Rangers legend Mark Messier, who turned 42 January 18. Unfortunately, because of the new rules, his colon has already been called three times for obstruction. And did I mention he's not thrilled about the lower GI, either?

THE **HIT(S)**

"Two Tickets to Paradise"

"Baby Hold On"

"Take Me Home Tonight"

(I know that's three hits, but it's essentially one song.)

Before we begin, anybody need tickets for Jimmy Kimmel IV?

BUCS TURN RAIDERS INTO GROUND CHUCKY Are you like me? Did you get a lump in your throat when after the game Jon Gruden yelled, "I'm going to Disney World—to pick up my car!"

Bit of a rout. Halfway through the third quarter the guys in the ABC truck had switched over to *Becker*.

Speaking of ABC, I don't want to tell anyone their business, but who was in charge of on-field audio, Michael Strahan's orthodontist?

Online fan poll results accounted for 20% of the final Super Bowl MVP vote. Which explains why the Miller Lite catfight girls finished fourth.

Rich Gannon set a Super Bowl record with five interceptions. He was picked off by everyone except Terry Tate, Office Linebacker.

Come on. Shania Twain had more success in the air than Gannon.

Raiders fans were not allowed to wear or carry the following items at the game: shoulder spikes, skull masks, scream masks, spike-covered wristbands, broadswords, light sabers and battleaxes. And the list was even longer for the guys.

Secretary of Homeland Security Tom Ridge declared Qualcomm Stadium a no-fly zone for the Super Bowl, which prohibited aircraft from coming within seven miles on game day. Basically, it's the same restrictions that apply to Ryan Leaf the rest of the year.

SERENA SLAMS VENUS DOWN UNDER Come on. This was the most predictable thing to come out of Australia since the plot for *Kangaroo Jack*.

It was the fourth consecutive time the sisters have met in a Grand Slam final. It's getting a little out of hand. During the final all the linesmen were named Williams.

In her semifinal Serena was trailing Kim Clijsters 5–1 in the third set. And you know it was tense. For a few minutes the guy actually stopped engraving Serena's name on the championship trophy.

Andre Agassi easily dispatched Rainer Schuettler to win the men's singles. It was Agassi's fourth Australian title. His third without hair.

And this is odd. Because of the time change the tournament actually ended *before* Andy Roddick and Younes El Aynaoui finished their quarterfinal match.

NEWS CORP. LOOKING FOR BUYERS FOR DODGERS That sound you hear is a million people in Brooklyn trying to come up with four hundred bucks apiece.

The asking price for the team started at $400 million. And if you make an offer before Feb. 15, the Dodgers will throw in unlimited hat blocking for Mike Brito.

According to reports, Pete Rose is willing to admit he bet on baseball. And that was only after Johnny Bench asked him, "What would you do for a Klondike Bar?"

CAVALIERS FIRE COACH JOHN LUCAS Management felt he'd lost touch with his players. Well, sure. LeBron James hasn't called him in weeks.

IOC INVESTIGATING CHARGES THAT IRAQI OLYMPIC CHIEF ODAI SADDAM HUSSEIN TORTURED ATHLETES Of course, Odai claims he gave the torture contract to his brother, Luca Brazzi Hussein.

My time is up. You've been great. Enjoy the Spiral Staircase.

THE **NOTES**

(Bucs turn Raiders into ground Chucky...) The Super Bowl is the biggest sporting event of any year, and the biggest vein of raw material. Nine hours of hype, commercials, halftime and then the game. And when all is said and done, you make a joke with *Becker* because the "K" sound is funny. Sad.

(Come on. Shania Twain...) During the halftime show, Shania Twain came in on a wire. No wait. I'm thinking about Donnie Brasco.

(Raiders fans were not allowed...) Here is a case, rare, where the longer the setup, the better the misdirection at the end. And that was just in the lobby....

(IOC investigating charges...) At the time, there was a patronage scandal involving the USOC president. But you really don't need that context when you have Luca Brazzi, the buttonman from *The Godfather*.

THE **CUTS**

Michael Jordan passed Wilt Chamberlain for third on the NBA career points list. However, he still trails Wilt in all-time scoring by 19,000 dates. Strangely, and don't ask me to say why, "dates" sounds much funnier than "sexual partners."

Last week, the Knicks-Nuggets game was held up nine minutes after forward Rodney White vomited on the court. It was the biggest offensive output by a Denver player this season. But not funnier than "vomit."

THE **HIT(S)**

"More Today than Yesterday"

All right, a couple of jokes, but then Jerry Sloan and I have to shove off.

100,000 ATTEND BUCS VICTORY CELEBRATION And this may be rubbing it in. Jon Gruden even stole the Raiders' parade route.

Al Davis is taking the loss hard. He's gone more than a week without suing anyone.

Keyshawn Johnson says he is finished talking to the media. And he will continue to hold press conferences until he's satisfied everyone knows.

FREE CLOTHES THROW BACK LEBRON JAMES'S AMATEUR STATUS Help me out here. Does this mean he's now free to accept a Cavaliers jersey?

LeBron had a busy week. An 88-year-old woman claimed he hit her car with his new Hummer H2. LeBron, of course, thought he still had a foul to give.

Meanwhile, are you like me? Are you wondering if Ron Artest will have to be restrained by his teammates from attending the All-Star Game?

In other NBA news, the Celtics have added premium sideline seats next to the team bench. And this is exciting. Instead of paying $1,000 a game per ticket, fans will just hand their money to Vin Baker.

ARIZONA HOOPSTERS DENY STEALING $80 WORTH OF CANDY FROM VENDING MACHINE All-America Luke Walton was allegedly just a lookout while the machine was vandalized. But of course the media gave him all the credit for the break-in.

In the players' defense, it is the last half of the season. You know, Crunch time.

Oddly, the same thing happened 10 years ago at Michigan with the Fab Five. But they only took six 100 Grand bars.

NHL ALL-STAR GAME RETURNS TO EAST-WEST MATCHUP We're lucky. The league was very close to adopting a brand-new format: teams in the red against teams in the black.

The Rangers fired coach Bryan Trottier and replaced him with team president and general manager Glen Sather. But don't kid yourself. Sather had to first be approved by the team president and general manager.

PETE ROSE MAY BE INDUCTED INTO CANADIAN BASEBALL HALL OF FAME But first he has to admit he never bet on curling.

The Canadian Baseball Hall of Fame, or, as it's more commonly known, Ferguson Jenkins's rec room.

Elsewhere, the Mets unveiled bright orange jerseys. Great. That should make it easier for arriving flights at LaGuardia when the control tower says, "Make a right at Mo Vaughn."

The man who assaulted Yankees starter David Wells got 45 days in jail. But he can be released early if he promises to sucker punch a Red Sox pitcher.

The Red Sox are installing 280 seats on top of the Green Monster. Tickets will cost $50, with a $35 rebate if you can hit Bernie Williams with your beer.

MIKE WEIR FIRES 330 TO WIN BOB HOPE CHRYSLER CLASSIC The courses played a little easy this year. Seriously, when was the last time you heard David Feherty say, "Alice Cooper...for eagle"?

ARENA FOOTBALL DEBUTS ON NBC It's much more civil than the XFL. The AFL's big star is "He Dislike Me."

My time is up. You've been great. Enjoy Mott the Hoople.

THE **NOTES**

(In other NBA news, the Celtics have added…) I'm not a fan of criticizing players strictly for making money, but some contracts just beg for it. This one does, and so does Jose Offerman's, which, if you were paying attention, was eaten by Rich Garces a few months before.

(The Rangers fired coach Bryan Trottier…) This is a blatant switch on a line I heard Marv Albert do when Celtics general manager M.L. Carr appointed himself coach. Marv, never more droll, said, "I hear he did well in the interview with himself."

(Arena Football debuts on NBC…) Former NBC Sports p.r. maven Ed Markey, who used to feed the less-droll stuff to Marv, sent me this line. It's so perfect, I couldn't take credit for it. Man, was I tempted.

THE **CUTS**

Arizona hoopsters caught stealing $80 worth of candy from vending machine. *This is no way for student-athletes to behave. Everybody knows knocking off a vending machine is a job for a booster.* I liked this line the best because of the double meaning of booster. But we went with pretty boy Luke Walton.

A replica of the Stanley Cup made with 6,000 pieces of Lego was stolen from a sports show in Las Vegas. Police spent four hours questioning Bob Probert's seventh grade teacher. His current one. Years ago, I was on a radio show in Detroit. The host, former Pistons P.A. announcer Ken Calvert, asked me to throw out a trivia question to the listening audience for a T-shirt. I came up with an impossible one: "Who is the only Harvard graduate to play for the Red Wings?" The answer is my friend Danny Bolduc. Not important. The first guy who called in said, "I'd like to answer the trivia question. Bob Probert?" We gave him the T-shirt. Too funny.

THE **HIT(S)**

"All the Young Dudes"

Attention moviegoers: *How to Lose a Guy in 10 Days* has nothing to do with the Red Sox and Bartolo Colon.

JUDGE CLEARS LEBRON JAMES He's free to rejoin his high school team despite accepting gifts. However, he is not allowed to become president of the USOC.

LeBron was cleared to play in last weekend's Prime Time Shootout in Trenton. Although he was forbidden to use the phrase "new jersey."

You know the saddest part of this whole story? Wes Unseld and Gale Sayers would have had to pay retail.

LIONS NAME STEVE MARIUCCI COACH Mariucci, of course, was let go by the 49ers over "philosophical differences." He wanted to run the best Coast offense, and management preferred a game plan based on the works of Hegel.

In another recent coaching move, the Vikings promoted George O'Leary to defensive coordinator. Although on his résumé he claims he's been promoted to Senate majority leader.

WHITE SOX SELL STADIUM NAMING RIGHTS TO U.S. CELLULAR However, the fans will still be free to call it Comiskey Park…for 300 anytime minutes a month.

U.S. Cellular Field. I can't wait for "Pocket Vibrator Night."

Umpire John Hirschbeck was suspended for 10 days for using inappropriate language in a conversation with a major league executive, reportedly Rob Manfred. However, the suspension can be reduced to three days if he carpools to sensitivity training with Bruce Froemming.

In other off-season news, the Angels lost Alex Ochoa and Orlando Palmeiro to free agency. Well, there goes that dynasty.

CAROLINA TRADES ALL-STAR SAMI KAPANEN TO THE FLYERS Immediately after the deal, the Hurricanes were downgraded to a tropical drizzle.

With Kapanen gone, the Canes' best skater is now Kristi Yamaguchi Hedican.

Meanwhile, *Hockey Night in Canada* continues to make changes to try and lure new viewers. So far the best idea is a version of *The Bachelor*, when Don Cherry's bull terrier chooses among 25 bitches.

NBC CHANNELS TO AIR 806½ HOURS OF 2004 SUMMER GAMES Not only that, NBC is increasing the amount of total live-event coverage 45%—to 23 minutes.

The Games will air somewhere on TV 24 hours a day, including 13 hours a day on Bravo. Here's the breakdown: An hour of actual events, 12 hours of that *Inside the Actor's Studio* guy asking three questions.

MARTHA BURK NOW HELPING WNBA PLAYERS' ASSOCIATION What does this mean? She'd like to see them admit 70-year-old Southern men?

Meanwhile, Spalding's Infusion is now the official ball of the WNBA. Perfect. They can use it to pump up attendance figures.

MILLER LITE OFFERS FANS FREE SIX-PACK IF RUSTY WALLACE WINS DAYTONA 500 Are you like me? Are you wondering what Viagra will offer if Mark Martin wins?

EAST BEATS WEST IN ALL-STAR GAME I missed the opening. Help me out here: Did Martina McBride step aside so Jordan could sing the national anthem?

My time is up. You've been great. Enjoy C.W. McCall.

THE **NOTES**

(Meanwhile, Hockey Night in Canada...*)* What a relief to write a joke about the NHL that has nothing to do with solvent teams or labor. Not to mention having a chance to use the word "bitch" correctly.

(NBC channels to air 806½ hours...) Actually, it turned out to be 1,120 hours, which makes the payoff 50% cattier.

(Meanwhile, Spalding's Infusion...) The Infusion comes with a pump already in the ball. Be honest. How many of you read this joke and thought, "Wait. There's still a WNBA?"

THE **CUTS**

In other NFL news, our long national nightmare is over. The Peyton Manning–Mike Vanderjagt feud has ended. Manning had called Vanderjagt an "idiot kicker" in response to disparaging comments Vanderjagt made about him. I'm confused. I thought an "idiot kicker" was that guy who throws people off American Idol.

(OR...) I thought an "idiot kicker" was what they call the bouncer on Jerry Springer.

Vanderjagt make his remarks on Canadian television. You know the best thing about Canadian television? The 15-yard endzone. (OR...) Everybody can be in motion. Sometimes we cut stuff because the story will be too old when the magazine comes out. So here's my question. Why, almost three years later, does it seem fresher?

THE **HIT(S)**

"Convoy"

Sorry if I seem a little down. My editor put me on probation. He found out I had my picture taken with the ref who worked the game with the ref who had his picture taken with LeBron.

PITCHERS AND CATCHERS REPORT All the Yankees' starters arrived, and Tampa's population grew enough to get another congressman.

The Mets signed David Cone, 40, to an AAA contract. Or is that an AARP contract?

Their rotation will be set when Jerry Koosman gets out of his assisted-living facility.

Trouble at the White Sox training camp. They held their first mandatory workout, and the shirtless father-and-son team were no-shows.

In other baseball news the Red Sox will wear red socks this season. If this doesn't tell you the new owners aren't serious about putting a championship team on the field, you're just not paying attention.

The commissioner's office has laid off 26 full-time employees, including the guy who used to say, "Would you mind filling this up, Mr. Canseco?"

ANNIKA SORENSTAM ACCEPTS INVITATION TO PLAY IN THE COLONIAL She'll have to play from the back tees. But, on the bright side, if she makes the cut, she'll be allowed to run into the woods to take a leak.

Sorenstam would be the first woman to play on the PGA Tour in 58 years. Wait a minute. Didn't Jan Stephenson play a round in the mid-'70s? No, that's right. She played around in the mid-'70s.

Annika got into the tourney on a little known exemption. The "Let's drive Hootie Johnson nuts" exemption.

Speaking of which, Martha Burk recently visited the town of Augusta. She checked out some potential sites for an anti-Masters demonstration, then crashed a special stag screening of *The Hours*.

SI POLL SAYS FAN INTEREST IN NBA DOWN 40% IN LAST FIVE YEARS It's not all bad news. In the last five years Michael Jordan retirements are up 200%.

David Stern dismissed the poll as "junk science." Junk science. Was that Shawn Kemp's major?

The NBA All-Star Game was the most watched basketball game in cable-TV history. Not only that, it was the second-highest rating ever for TNT, just behind its one millionth showing of *The Shawshank Redemption*.

The Lakers are finally above .500. And, according to Stern, they've already locked up the No. 9 seed.

I'm starting to worry about Pat Riley. Now he's complaining about the officiating on *The Bachelorette*.

FORMER COWBOYS QUARTERBACKS ROGER STAUBACH AND TROY AIKMAN START WINSTON CUP TEAM Are you like me? Are you thinking this will be the first car to leave a race with a concussion?

Meanwhile, Domino's is now the "official pizza" of NASCAR. And the two most popular toppings are pepperoni and R.J. Reynolds tobacco.

NFL CONSIDERING NEW PLANS FOR DECIDING OVERTIME So far, the two best ideas are a) the first team to score six points wins or b) three rounds of Pictionary with the assistant coaches.

CBS DEVELOPING SITCOM BASED ON LIFE OF TONY KORNHEISER I believe the tentative title is *Everybody Loves Rogaine*.

My time is up. You've been great. Enjoy Vanilla Fudge.

THE **NOTES**

(Annika Sorenstam accepts invitation…) Oh yeah, like you never did that.

(Meanwhile, Domino's is now the "official pizza…") I miss not being able to make tobacco jokes about NASCAR. If I'd known they were going to change corporate sponsorship, I would have made more. Something like… *the pit crew took 11 seconds to change all the tar.* Damn.

(CBS developing sitcom based on life of Tony Kornheiser…) Hey, have you seen this show? It's not too late to change the title. Uh, maybe it is. My deadline was October.

THE **CUTS**

The San Diego City Council unanimously approved to name the Padres' new stadium Petco Park. Please accept my apology for the following line: Petco Park. The House that Woof Built. If this joke doesn't prove I have the mind of a fourth grader, well then, I'll find you some more.

THE **HIT(S)**

"You Keep Me Hanging On"

THE **SHOW**

O.K., I've read all the post–Swimsuit Issue letters, and you've made your point. From now on, there will be less cleavage in this column. (Les Cleavage. Wasn't he a backup tight end on the 1972 Raiders, behind Raymond Chester?)

TYSON KO'S ETIENNE IN 49 SECONDS In a related story, Showtime has changed its motto from No limits to No refunds.

Big night for Showtime. Jay-Z, followed by JV.

Poor Clifford Etienne. Forty-nine seconds. On the bright side, Peter McNeely finally has someone he can make fun of.

Quite a week. Tyson didn't show up at the gym for three days; he missed a scheduled flight to Memphis; he got a tattoo on his face; he canceled the fight; then he changed his mind. Well, at least his behavior wasn't erratic.

During the time Mike had backed out of the fight, promoters in Memphis scrambled to get a new opponent for Etienne. Unfortunately, Mitch (Blood) Green couldn't get the day off at Bed, Bath & Beyond.

On the undercard, former Olympic figure skater Tonya Harding lost in her pro boxing debut. But seriously, after you've danced topless in a wedding dress, isn't everything else anticlimactic?

PISTONS TOPS IN EAST It's the first time they've led this late in a season since 1990. Or 11 Grant Hill ankle operations ago.

This year, the Pistons made extensive improvements to The Palace at Auburn Hills. Each rest room is now manned by an attendant. Of course, if there are two attendants, they play a zone.

Maybe I made this up. I was watching an old episode of *The White Shadow*, and I swear halfway through, Kobe Bryant shows up and hits for 42.

Not to be outdone, Michael Jordan became the first to score 40 points after his 40th birthday. Am I wrong, or is he playing well enough to retire two more times?

SPRING TRAINING BEGINS Call me a baseball traditionalist, but it just isn't spring training until Jose Canseco is in handcuffs.

Canseco was locked up for numerous probation violations, including leaving Florida for more than 30 days. He had no choice. He was a character witness for the Texas woman who ran over her husband.

Elsewhere, Barry Bonds underwent minor surgery on his left elbow. No big deal. He had it removed, covered in polyurethane, then grafted over his right elbow so he can really lean over the plate.

The most exciting part of the procedure was when the surgeon dropped his scalpel and two guys wrestled for it before being dragged into court.

Dodgertown in Vero Beach has undergone a $7 million renovation. Isn't it nice to hear about the Dodgers spending $7 million on something that won't wind up on the disabled list?

Unfortunately, the Dodgers still need Rupert Murdoch to come up with another $5 million to build a state-of-the-art apology to Sandy Koufax.

LEBRON JAMES TO HAVE JERSEY RETIRED Of course I'm happy for the kid. But I just hope St. Vincent–St. Mary can somehow make a little dough off this.

CART UNVEILS NEW CORPORATE LOGO FOR 2003 SEASON It's three open-wheeled cars leaving to go to the IRL.

My time is up. You've been great. Enjoy Billy Joe Royal.

THE **NOTES**

(During the time Mike had backed out of the fight...) Mitch "Blood" Green, who Tyson had gotten into a 3:00 a.m. street fight with in 1988—gold. Bed, Bath & Beyond—uranium. Together—nuclear comic fusion.

(On the undercard, former Olympic figure...) After cutting "allegedly danced topless at her husband's bachelor party," this was all the legal department let me make up. (That sound you hear is me sighing.)

(Unfortunately, the Dodgers still need Rupert Murdoch...) A blind item in the Murdoch's *New York Post* had implied Koufax was gay. The pitcher cut off all contact with the Dodgers until Murdoch's News Corp. sold the team. I know, I know. The *Post*? Reckless debasement of an icon? Doesn't sound like them.

THE **CUTS**

You know it's a short fight when Michael Buffer only has time to say, "Let's get ready to rum—" This joke does not track, because Michael Buffer does his thing before the fight. Still, it made me laugh. I was doing it around the house all Sunday, until my wife said, "All right, we get it." So, three times.

NFL scouting combine ends. *You'll never guess who graded out the best. Zora.* Zora was the winner on the first *Joe Millionaire*. Is that better?

It's tough to get news out of the combine. The only thing I heard was a Hoosier Dome rat did 4.3 in the 40. But keep in mind, that's without pads. If you don't have the "without pads" tag, this is what comedy professionals call a "sentence."

THE **HIT(S)**

"Down in the Boondocks"

THE SHOW

Good to be here. Be honest, how many of you still think John Deere makes a scouting combine?

LEADER OF KU KLUX KLAN SPLINTER GROUP SAYS HE'LL PROTEST IN SUPPORT OF AUGUSTA MEMBERSHIP POLICIES A KKK splinter group? What does that mean, they burn kindling on your front lawn? Or do they wear fitted sheets?

Don't kid yourself. Klansmen are big golfers. But they'll only hit a hooded seven-iron.

NFL FREE AGENTS ROAM THE EARTH Dallas released Emmitt Smith. Which raises the question: Does the Cowboys' Ring of Honor have a hard salary cap?

In other NFL news, the Steelers released quarterback Kordell Stewart. The move will save them $6.3 million. They'll use the money to pick up a free agent, or buy the Penguins.

The Colts got kicker Mike Vanderjagt to restructure his contract. It was either that or have Peyton Manning designate him a "franchise idiot."

PHIL JACKSON HAS KIDNEY STONE REMOVED Finally, a rock Kobe Bryant didn't want.

He had a lot of trouble passing it. Oh, wait a sec. I'm still talking about Kobe.

Laker Nation is really grateful. Jackson's urologist is now dating Lara Flynn Boyle.

LEAGUEWIDE LOSSES IN THE NHL THIS SEASON ALLEGEDLY $250 MILLION Do you know what that's called in this economic environment? A rousing success.

The league is a mess. Nashville is thinking of changing the team's name to the Creditors.

Also in the NHL, the Bruins may be sending a message. March 4 at the FleetCenter is Robbie Ftorek Bobbleheadless Night.

THOUSANDS OF NIKE SHOES ADRIFT AFTER SPILLING FROM CONTAINER SHIP It's part of Nike's new Air Valdez line.

Water damage caused the shoes to shrink so much they fit the kids who made them.

In other sneaker news, Pony hired adult-film stars for its new ad campaign. Too bad Just Do It is already taken.

You thought you saw a lot of tongue on the old Ponys....

IN NEW BOOK DAVID WELLS SAYS HE WAS "HALF DRUNK" WHEN HE THREW HIS PERFECT GAME Boomer wanted to get rid of his hangover, but six innings into the perfecto everyone was so superstitious, the beer vendors wouldn't go near him.

Wells says he'd gotten drunk at a *Saturday Night Live* cast party. I know he's just trying to sell his book, but you don't hear Don Zimmer bragging about hitting fungoes after being out all night at the *Golden Girls*' wrap party.

Wells says he was pretty blitzed. All he recalls about the SNL party is that he shook off Molly Shannon three times.

Elsewhere, the Devil Rays have 33 nonroster invitees in camp. The breakdown: 18 pitchers, seven position players and eight guys to shag caps thrown by Lou Piniella.

COLLEGE OFFICIALS HAVE SUMMIT ON FAN MISBEHAVIOR Not much happened. They agreed to limit replays of controversial calls and to double the number of Ritalin vendors at Cameron Indoor Stadium.

USA TODAY PUBLISHES TOP 10 HARDEST THINGS TO DO IN SPORTS Big surprise at No. 1: Getting former USOC CEO Lloyd Ward to fly coach.

My time is up. You've been great. Enjoy The Troggs.

THE **NOTES**

(Phil Jackson has kidney stone removed…) The first joke is a little cheap. The second one saves it. Of course, this was back in the day when the only thing you could hit Kobe with was not making a pass.… You know, there's probably a better way to put that.

(Thousands of Nike shoes…) If you are not old enough to remember the *Exxon Valdez*, you're thinking, "Why is he making fun of the Dodger pitcher? That's not right."

(Wells says he was pretty blitzed…) Sometimes, you write a joke and think, "Wait a minute. This might not be a joke. This might have actually happened." There is a happy ending. A year later, Molly Shannon was married, and did not dance topless in her wedding dress.

THE **CUTS**

Do you think when he finally passed the stone, Phil yelled "ee-Yao!!!?" I had a choice between this and the urologist joke. I'm Jewish, almost 50. I need to see the urologist.

In other college news, the University of Miami baseball program was placed on probation. Despite the probation, Miami will be able to compete in postseason. The Canes received a special dispensation from Edwin Pope. Kostya Kennedy's very sensitive response to this: "O.K., you got it out, we laughed, let it go." Hence, the title "editor."

THE **HIT(S)**

"Wild Thing"

"Love Is All Around"

THE SHOW | March 17, 2003

Good to be here. See if you can figure out which jokes are still on the bubble.

MLB FEELS NEED FOR SPEED Managers, coaches and umpires must watch a video produced by the commissioner's office with suggestions on how to speed games up. The video is 20 minutes long. Here's what I don't get: It took Steve Trachsel 33 minutes to get through it.

Not only that, Tony La Russa and Dave Duncan made four trips to the VCR before starting the tape.

Despite moving to the Cubs, Dusty Baker will still get to manage the NL in this year's All-Star Game. Baker's thrilled. He already has a tie picked out.

Pete Rose may be reinstated as early as June 1. It depends on 1) how fast Major League Baseball can complete its ongoing review and 2) how well he does on the Pick-Six at the Preakness.

Are you like me? Are you waiting for David Wells to claim that his Hooters VIP card was taken out of context?

The Reds are having trouble trying to move Ken Griffey Jr. So far the best offer is from the Orioles. They're willing to give up Milt Pappas.

FRESNO STATE BANS HOOPS TEAM FROM NCAA TOURNAMENT The school confirmed allegations of academic fraud. What happened to the good old days, when boosters used to pay off teachers?

A team statistician revealed he'd written papers for three players. Fresno State has a no-nonsense policy about this. If you're caught having someone else write your papers, that's it, you get sent to Minnesota.

It's not all bad news for the Bulldogs. The investigation revealed that the towel Jerry Tarkanian used to chew on was clean.

NBA EXPECTED TO IMPLEMENT MINIMUM-AGE RULE FOR DRAFT Starting next year you have to be at least 20. Or 18 with a shoe deal and a Hummer.

In other basketball news, a Celtics-Clippers game was held up for nine minutes when fans sprayed a macelike substance behind the Boston bench. Players were coughing, gagging, their eyes watering. You know, the same reaction as if they'd been told Rick Pitino was coming back.

The Celtics got guard Bimbo Coles off waivers. I'm no Elias Sports Bureau, but I think he's the first bimbo to play in Boston since Margo Adams.

FEDOROV CONFIRMS BRIEF MARRIAGE TO ANNA K The Red Wings star wouldn't say how long they were married, because they're still fighting over custody of the cake.

This may explain things: Turns out Kournikova is Russian for "Jennifer Lopez."

Things just didn't work out. Same old story. Sergei wanted a stay-at-home wife, and Anna wanted to concentrate on blowing her tennis career.

In other NHL news, the league is instituting a $1,000 fine for flagrant divers. And it's $2,000 if you dive and come out of the tuck position.

But this is nice. For every $1,000 fine for diving, a $50 royalty goes to Bill Barber.

GIANTS LET JASON SEHORN GO Management just couldn't get around his contract. Which makes it the only thing in two years that couldn't get around Jason Sehorn.

LANCE ARMSTRONG AND WIFE SEPARATE She'd had enough. He kept finishing 46 minutes ahead of her.

My time is up. You've all been great. Enjoy Bread.

THE **NOTES**

(The video is 20 minutes long…) When you need a slow worker for a reference, Trachsel's your man. Frank Castillo is also good, but Trachsel has a more phlegmy "K" sound in his last name. Which is one more "K" than Castillo had in the big leagues last season.

(In other basketball news, a Celtics-Clippers game…) Are you beginning to detect a theme?

(The Celtics got guard Bimbo Coles off waivers…) Margo Adams was Wade Boggs's road Annie for years. I bet he used to wait until he was 0 and 2 before hitting on her.

(Lance Armstrong and wife separate…) What did I tell you about divorce and separation? It's gold, Jerry. Gold.

THE **CUTS**

Martha Burk files two permit applications with Augusta police. She wants to hold demonstrations at different locations on Magnolia Drive during the last two rounds of the Masters. Of course, the Sunday protest placement is much more difficult. Smart joke that was cut because the situation would be resolved after we came out. And I thought Martha was bitter. How about me for bringing this up two years later?

Meanwhile, Reverend Jesse Jackson has thrown his support behind Martha Burk's crusade. It took a while, but he finally came up with a rhyme for "misogynism." I guess this was mean. Why can't Johnnie Cochran have supported her? It would have made it so much easier.

THE **HIT(S)**

"Make It with You"

"Baby, I'm-a-Want You"

"Diary"

"Guitar Man"

"It Don't Matter to Me"

(Way way too successful, but that week, I did Mark Patrick's radio show, and he closed the segment by saying, "Bill, you've been great. Enjoy Bread," and I loved the way it sounded.)

Sorry I'm late. I was tending the pin for Scott Hoch.

MARCH MADNESS BEGINS Big weekend at ESPN: Selection Sunday, which came the day after Sanction Saturday.

Thirty-two teams automatically made the dance. Thirty-one conference winners and an at-large berth for Rick Majerus.

I screwed up my office pool. I had Georgia with ineligible players and St. Bonaventure with academic fraud.

Help me out here. Is IUPUI an actual school or Tony Cole's last report card?

Are you like me? You don't care who wins or loses the NCAAs, you just hope that Coca-Cola makes some money off this.

Coca-Cola will be sponsoring this year's tournament. They'll start with a 64-ounce bottle, then 32, then 16....

THIS JUST IN: JOSE MESA TESTS POSITIVE FOR DANGEROUSLY HIGH AMOUNTS OF CAFFEINE In an interview Mesa said if he faced former teammate Omar Vizquel 10 times, he'd hit him 10 times. Do you know what that means? His control is back.

Vizquel ripped Mesa in his autobiography. Otherwise the book was tame. The most scandalous revelation: In the famous '96 game against the Red Sox when Omar had six RBIs, he did it with a hangnail.

SUNS TRY TO MAKE UP WITH BARKLEY After Sir Charles claimed he was denied an opportunity to buy season tickets, the team offered him two courtside seats. They'll be ready in three weeks, they just need to install the heavy-duty shocks.

The average age of a Suns season-ticket holder is 51. Which explains the P.A. guy coming on during timeouts and yelling, "Make some noise if you have acid reflux!"

The average age is 51. But it's a dry 51.

NFL ASKS EIGHT OFFICIALS TO RESIGN Asking them to resign? Who's behind that strategy, Richie Phillips?

In other NFL news the Patriots acquired coveted free-agent linebacker Rosevelt Colvin and former All-Pro safety Rodney Harrison. In a related story the Redskins stole three blocking sleds from the Jets.

The Patriots have increased the handling fee on season-ticket accounts by 150%. Although, they prefer to call it the "tuck rule."

MARTHA BURK SUES AUGUSTA FOR PROTEST PERMIT Not to be outdone, some Klan members have filed a request to have holes 11 to 13 renamed Amen KKKorner.

Town sheriff Ronnie Strength tried to appease Burk by offering her an alternative protest site: Augusta, Maine.

NOTHING BUT ACTION AT NHL TRADING DEADLINE Forty-six players changed teams last week. Unfortunately, Jaromir Jagr had under 45½ and dropped a hundred grand.

I don't want to tell anyone their business, but Penguins G.M. Craig Patrick should pitch a show to ABC: *Who Wants to Dump a Millionaire?*

Sad what's happened in Pittsburgh. Last week they wanted to pull the goalie but they didn't have an extra skater.

VILLANOVA ENDS UCONN WOMEN'S STREAK AT 70 The Wildcats celebrated by NOT making unauthorized phone calls to everyone they know.

BOB UECKER NAMED TO HALL OF FAME And this is official: On his plaque he'll be wearing a cap from *Mr. Belvedere*.

My time is up. You've been great. Enjoy the Beau Brummels.

THE **NOTES**

(Help me out here. Is IUPUI an actual school...) I desperately wanted to do something with IUPUI, and then Georgia star Tony Cole showed up. Or didn't show up.

(The average age of a Suns season-ticket holder...) Had this line in the stockroom for months. It only works in between these two jokes, and it only goes away with proper diet and Zantac.

(The Patriots have increased the handling fee...) I am a degenerate Patriots fan. Have been since 1970. But like another patriot fan, Captain America, I fight evil wherever I see it.

THE **CUTS**

CBS may move NCAA tourney if war begins. *Until then, please secure all your brackets with duct tape.* Too sensitive, given the time.

Good news out of Tampa: The George Steinbrenner Terror Alert has gone from orange back to yellow. No wait. I'm sorry. George Steinbrenner's turtleneck has gone from orange to yellow. See "duct tape, brackets."

THE **HIT(S)**

"Laugh, Laugh"

"Just a Little"

Good to be here. I don't know about you, but for me, nothing says March Madness like a Final Four in April.

NCAA DOWN TO ONLY 16 That is, only 16 in-game promos for *Survivor*.

Butler stunned Louisville in the second round of the tournament. And I don't get this: Rick Pitino said it would have never happened if he'd been able to get Tim Duncan.

In other college hoops news, Bob Knight refused to accept his salary this season because the team fell far short of his expectations. Oh, my God, he still thinks he's at Indiana!

A'S-MARINERS JAPAN SERIES CANCELED Great. Now what are they going to do with the 500,000 passes Ichiro left at Will Call?

What a shame. Just when the citizens of Tokyo had come up with enough money to put a down payment on Miguel Tejada.

The Devil Rays' equipment bus was severely damaged after it hit a cow. Here's the sad part: Before the accident, the cow had the inside track to be the Rays' fifth outfielder.

Jose Canseco was sentenced to two years' house arrest. Which means he and brother Ozzie can only start bar fights in his den.

The Yankees acquired Bubba Trammell in a trade for Rondell White. This fills the team's need for a righthanded designated driver for David Wells.

CAVALIERS FINE LEADING SCORER RICKY DAVIS FOR TRYING TO PAD STATS Davis deliberately took a shot at the opposing basket in an attempt to get his 10th rebound and a triple-double. It could have been worse. He could have grabbed the rebound, then stolen the ball from himself 10 times.

The Cavs' front office was furious. They felt his behavior completely detracted from the team's 12th win, which put them only 19 games out of a playoff spot.

You know, this kind of nonsense never happened when John Lucas was the coach. Back then Ricky only took shots at his own basket and his own teammates.

NFL CONSIDERS EXPANDING PLAYOFF FIELD If the proposal is approved, two additional teams will be added to the postseason. A wild card from either conference and the winner of the Fiesta Bowl.

Elsewhere, the Falcons have updated their logo. Pretty clever. It's a bird who's building a nest entirely out of stuff he bought at The Home Depot.

MORE THAN 3,000 PAIRS OF AIR JORDAN XVIIIs STOLEN Police describe the thieves as "armed and extremely fly."

Three thousand pairs of Nikes. Wow. That's almost four square feet of real leather.

So the Jordans never got to where they were supposed to go. Watch them blame this on Kwame Brown.

JOHN DALY WILL TRY TO DRIVE A BALL ACROSS THE MONONGAHELA RIVER And if he makes it, he'll still be a one-iron and a wedge away from the 5th fairway at Oakmont.

SARAH HUGHES WINS SULLIVAN AWARD Very prestigious. It goes to the nation's top amateur athlete without a Hummer.

My time's up. You've been great. Enjoy Yes.

THE **NOTES**

(Butler stunned Louisville in the second round…) O.K., five more and we'll call the Pitino thing an obsession. Right now, it's still a hobby.

(More than 3,000 pairs of Air Jordan XVIIIs stolen…) This is me pathetically reaching out to the young people. One problem: The young people stopped using "fly" in 1993.

(Three thousand pairs of Nikes…) My apologies. I was all out of child labor jokes that week.

THE **CUTS**

Elsewhere, the Harlem Globetrotters signed seven-foot center Stanley Roberts. Great. I hope this means the Globetrotters are bringing back that trick where they attach a rubber band to a vial of clean urine. You have my word. If the Trotters ever sign another player who was kicked out of the NBA for four years for drug use, this is in.

Phoenix touring pro trying to play in U.S. Women's Open. *His point is that if a woman can play in a men's tournament, why can't a man play in a women's tournament? And our point is, Who are you again?*

That's what's great about America. One day, you're working at The Wigwam telling some 18 handicapper, "Hey, we just got the new Pinnacles in," the next day you're thinking, "How can I get Martha Burk's attention?" (OR…) "I'm gonna hit from the red tees and make some real money." I loved this story, if for no other reason than to give a shout out to The Wigwam, a wonderful resort in nearby Litchfield Park, and to myself, an 18 handicapper buying the new Pinnacles.

THE **HIT(S)**

"Roundabout"

Good to be back. Had a bad week. I was kicked out of Iraq for giving away the location of the Bowl Coalition.

NCAA REACHES CLIMAX Surprising week in college basketball. Marquette was routed, Texas was upset and Matt Doherty was eliminated.

Doherty's been gone a week, and already he's received an offer from Georgia—to teach Jim Harrick Jr.'s 8 a.m. class.

Doherty may have seen things coming last fall. The Tar Heels' slogan was "Wait till the year after next!"

Michigan State students caused $40,000 worth of damage after the Spartans were ousted by Texas in the Elite Eight. According to Big Ten bylaws, you're not allowed to overturn cars and start fires unless you win a national title.

RED SOX AGAIN HAVE TOP TICKET PRICE IN MAJORS The average is $42.34. Coincidentally, 4234 is when experts predict the Sox will win their next World Series.

Derek Jeter may be lost to the Yankees for only six weeks with a dislocated shoulder, not two to four months as originally thought. But George Steinbrenner is still furious. Especially since he found out that Jeter's shoulder went out at night.

The Yankees say Jeter may avoid surgery and be treated "conservatively." Treated conservatively. What does that mean? He has to see Trent Lott's orthopedist?

Jeter has been replaced by 25-year-old Erick Almonte. If that name sounds familiar, he's Danny Almonte's son … from his first marriage.

San Diego has an interesting catchphrase this year. "Padres baseball: Deal with it."

And congratulations to Sammy Sosa, who became the 18th player to hit 500 home runs. Rafael Palmeiro is still nine away from 500. But his streak of consecutive games on Viagra is alive at 169.

Palmeiro didn't want to be a pitchman. In fact, the first time he bought Viagra, he told the pharmacist it was for Rusty Greer.

I don't want to tell people their business, but wouldn't a more natural spokesman for Viagra be A-Rod?

NBA TO AIR DRAFT LOTTERY IN PRIME TIME ON ABC And they've renamed it *8 Simple Rules for Dating LeBron.*

Last Wednesday, during a Trail Blazers practice, Zach Randolph punched teammate Ruben Patterson in the face. Things got so out of hand, players rushed over from two other fights to break it up.

Ron Artest was fined $20,000 for making an obscene gesture to Cleveland fans on April 2. Austin Croshere was injured trying to restrain Artest's finger.

PENGUINS' LEMIEUX MAY RETIRE THIS SUMMER I think he's just trying to show up the owner.

Mario feels good physically, but he's desperate to keep pace with Michael Jordan's career retirements.

Red Wings assistant Joey Kocur was suspended for throwing a chair onto the ice during a game against the Blues. On the bright side, every time a coach throws a chair, Bob Knight gets a $50 royalty.

MIKE TYSON COHOSTS *JIMMY KIMMEL LIVE* And this isn't surprising. The show's ratings shot up in the coveted 18–34 sociopathic felon demographic.

ANNIKA SORENSTAM GETS CALLAWAY TATTOO She's calling it Big Berthmark.

My time is up. You've all been great. Enjoy Kansas.

THE **NOTES**

(Jeter has been replaced by 25-year-old Erick Almonte...) This is cruel, until you add "first marriage." Then it rockets to "mischievous."

(Palmeiro didn't want to be a pitchman...) Let me stress: Rusty Greer does *not* have a problem. You know, other than being a grown man named Rusty.

(I don't want to tell people their business...) I am extremely proud of this joke, but even prouder some marketing guy at Pfizer was reamed because he *didn't* think of A-Rod.

THE **CUTS**

Doherty resigned as North Carolina coach after two straight years of failing to make the NCAAs. In his honor, UNC will name the cellar of the Dean Dome after him. I liked this better than "Wait till the year after next," but knowing how nice Dean Smith is, he probably gave the guy an office in the basement of the building.

The league announced it will not fine Mavericks owner Mark Cuban for an April Fools' prank in which he pretended to pick a fight during a Mavericks game with a man dressed as a referee. Wait a minute. Is this David Stern's idea of April Fools? Because it doesn't count after April 1. I think I know why this was cut. At the end, I seem very angry.

THE **HIT(S)**

"Dust in the Wind"

Good to be here. Quite a finish at Augusta. Who would have thought that by Sunday afternoon there'd be more people in the hunt than in the protest?

TOUGH FINAL ROUND FOR TIGER WOODS He finished at two over par, which put him in a tie with Jeff Maggert's chest.

Third-round leader Maggert incurred a fluke two-stroke penalty when a shot out of the bunker ricocheted off the lip and hit him in the chest. And speaking of flukes, he caught two retrieving his ball out of Rae's Creek.

Mike Weir was trying to become the first lefthander in 40 years to win a major... if you don't count Tiger hitting out of the trees on the 3rd hole.

The opening round of the Masters was postponed for the first time since 1939. Of course, in 1939 Martha Burk was on the set of *The Wizard of Oz*, trying to get the Lollipop Guild to admit women.

It rained so much the first day, Hootie Johnson actually thought about giving a membership to Mother Nature.

CBS stayed away from the controversy. Although on one of the promos for *Survivor*, I could have sworn I saw Hootie wearing the immunity necklace.

It took me a while to adjust to the commercial-free broadcast. But once I moved the TV into the bathroom, I was fine.

BREAK UP THE ROYALS! Despite the hot start, Kansas City is still a little desperate with marketing. Its 2003 media guide lists Runelvys Hernandez as "the alltime winningest pitcher named Runelvys."

And the page on Carlos Beltran is attached with Velcro.

In other baseball news, the Devil Rays signed reliever John Rocker to a minor league deal. Apparently he's developed a changeup to go with the straight bigotry.

LEBRON JAMES NOW SAYS HE MIGHT GO TO COLLEGE That means the Cavaliers have less than a month to build a campus.

LeBron? College? Come on. Next week TNT is televising a draft lottery to determine the selection order for his endorsements.

Last week, LeBron was named Ohio's Mr. Basketball for an unprecedented third straight year. Not only that, it's the first time the award was given to a corporation.

STANLEY CUP IN FULL BLOOM We started with 30, we're down to 16 and soon we'll be down to two. No, wait. I'm thinking of how many teams will be left next year after the NHL doesn't settle its labor problems.

The Mighty Ducks took a 2–0 lead over the defending champion Red Wings. That sound you heard was the Rally Monkey grilling octopus.

Congratulations to the Minnesota Wild, which won its first playoff game. Help me out here. The Minnesota Wild? I thought the XFL folded.

HALL OF FAME CANCELS ANNIVERSARY SCREENING OF *BULL DURHAM* DUE TO ANTIWAR SENTIMENTS OF SUSAN SARANDON AND TIM ROBBINS Does that mean in its place the Hall will show a few bombs starring Kevin Costner?

MARION JONES AND TRAINING PARTNER TIM MONTGOMERY ARE EXPECTING They must have met in the same heat.

My time is up. You've been great. Enjoy Count Five.

THE **NOTES**

(The opening round of the Masters was postponed…) This story does have a happy ending. Three years later, Martha did get four gals into the Flying Monkeys.

(It took me a while to adjust to the commercial-free broadcast…) This raises an interesting philosophical question: If I actually did move the TV into the bathroom, but no one heard me, does this joke count?

(Stanley Cup in full bloom…) Would Miss Voyant, Miss Claire Voyant, please pick up the courtesy phone…

THE **CUTS**

The top three picks in the lottery should be James, Carmelo Anthony of Syracuse and Darko Milicic. Wait a minute. Darko Milicic. Didn't he fight Sylvester Stallone for the title in Rocky IV*?* When I was a comic, I had a line in my act about the Dyslexic Theater Company performing "Annie Get Your Nug." Ivan Draco…Darko Milicic. Can a brother get a little love?

Mattiace was playing Augusta National for the first time since 1988. He qualified for the Masters by winning the Nissan Open, and resigning from the Gary McCord Fan Club. CBS golf analyst Gary McCord was banned from the Masters years ago after saying the greens had been "bikini waxed." He should have known Augusta National does not admit women's depilatories.

THE **HIT(S)**

"Psychotic Reaction"

Before we begin—if you don't like any of these jokes, my caddie chose them.

FAN GOES AFTER UMP A man jumped onto the field during a White Sox–Royals game and tried to tackle the first base umpire. Here's the good news: He wasn't shirtless.

And you know what's really sad? This whole thing could have been easily avoided if Geraldo hadn't given away the umpire's exact location.

The man was charged with aggravated battery. I feel so foolish. I thought "aggravated battery" meant someone catching Rick Ankiel.

In response to the incident, the White Sox have upgraded security. From now on, fans have to run through a metal detector before going onto the field.

In other baseball news, the Angels may be sold to Mexican-American multimillionaire Arturo Moreno. The deal needs to be approved by 23 owners and the Rally Monkey's accountant.

According to *Forbes* the Yankees are worth $849 million. And that figure jumps to more than $850 million once David Wells returns his empties.

Curt Schilling had an appendectomy. He's expected to miss one start, and after that he'll be on a strict stitch count.

Dusty Baker seems very comfortable in his new job as the Cubs' manager. Meanwhile Dusty's four-year-old son, Darren, no longer allowed to be a batboy, is still getting adjusted to his new job in a Nike shoe factory.

RAIDERS $1 BILLION FRAUD TRIAL BEGINS I'm no Alan Dershowitz, but technically, isn't every legal action involving Al Davis a fraud trial?

Davis is suing the NFL, claiming the Buccaneers' logo is too similar to the Raiders'. That explains why Rich Gannon kept throwing to their players in the Super Bowl.

NBA PLAYOFFS BEGIN The Nets routed the Bucks in Game 1 of their series. Gary Payton scored only eight points, but to be fair, he was double-teamed all game by Jason Kidd and a Toronto cop.

Payton, Jason Caffey and Sam Cassell turned themselves in to Toronto police after the game on assault charges stemming from an incident at a local strip club. As I understand it, the ruckus started when they tried to stuff 68.5 cents into a G-string.

In other basketball news, call me a cynic, but this latest retirement by Michael Jordan doesn't even make my top three.

MICHIGAN STATE'S CHARLES ROGERS FLAGGED AT NFL SCOUTING COMBINE FOR "DILUTED URINE" Experts believe he drank a large amount of water before his drug test. On the bright side, he ran a 4.23 40 to the men's room.

Diluted urine? Help me out here. Does this mean his pro contract will be negotiated by a masking agent?

Barry Sanders was a presenter at the Sports Emmy Awards in New York City. He showed up, but he left the stage too soon and did not explain why.

DETROIT IN DENIAL The Red Wings have their work cut out for them. No team has lost the first four games in the first round of the playoffs and gone on to win the Stanley Cup.

Come on. Even the Tigers got a victory in April.

FORMER *SNL* STAR WILL FERRELL RUNS BOSTON MARATHON He ran for 90 minutes, then was replaced by two guys who are much less talented.

HOOTIE JOHNSON DECLARES THERE WILL NEVER BE A FEMALE MEMBER AT AUGUSTA NATIONAL Martha Burk says her protest will now "move off the sports pages and onto the financial pages." Is that before or after it makes a stop in the obituaries?

My time is up. You've all been great. Enjoy Henry Gross.

THE **NOTES**

(Payton, Jason Caffey and Sam Cassell turned themselves in...) The exchange rate is perennial gold. And it need not be money. Peter Gammons one night described the announced attendance at Olympic Stadium as "3400 Canadian."

(Former SNL star Will Ferrell runs Boston Marathon...) And then he shook off Molly Shannon twice.

THE **CUTS**

Payton, Sam Cassell and Jason Caffey turned themselves in to Toronto police after the game on assault charges stemming from a recent incident at a local strip club. What is going on here? Bucks players cause a scene at a strip club, and Anthony Mason isn't involved? Too long, and not as good as the exchange rate line. Once again, Jason Caffey doesn't get in the game.

Secretary of Defense Donald Rumsfeld showed up for Michael Jordan's last home game. He presented MJ with an American flag, and a rocking chair looted from Saddam Hussein's bunker. Ah, memories....

THE **HIT(S)**

"Shannon"

Good to be here. See if you can tell which of these jokes have "upside" and which are "need picks."

DID YOU FEEL A DRAFT? Five defensive tackles were taken with the first 13 picks. I hadn't read or heard this much about DTs since Max McGee before Super Bowl I.

This is so embarrassing. Until last week I thought a "mock draft" was when you made fun of Chris Berman's comb-over.

I think Mel Kiper Jr. may have too much time on his hands. I mean, do we really need a list of the 30 Best Available Loads?

Buffalo was very busy. The Bills selected running back Willis McGahee in the first round, then they traded their third and fifth picks to get the rights to his orthopedic surgeon.

NBA HEADS INTO SECOND ROUND OF PLAYOFFS … EVENTUALLY Going on Week 3 of TNT's coverage, or as it's known to Charles Barkley, "Forty games in 40 orders of nachos."

Jazz forward Deshawn Stevenson was suspended one game for conduct detrimental to the team. As I understand it, during the flight to Sacramento he didn't wait for John Stockton and Karl Malone to be pre-boarded.

Sad days at Madison Square Garden. Spike Lee is now heckling circus elephants.

BUD SELIG SAYS HE PLANS TO STEP DOWN AS COMMISSIONER WHEN HIS TERM ENDS Selig's tenure ends in December 2006. Which gives Pete Rose only 31 more months to kiss his ass.

In other baseball news, a Chicago alderman has proposed raising the fine for trespassing onto a field during a White Sox game, from $100 to $1,000. That sounds high, but it includes parking.

After 23 games the Tigers are hitting .179 as a team. Things are so bad that manager Alan Trammell had the phone company come out to the park and install a Mendoza Line.

Rickey Henderson signed with the Newark Bears of the independent Atlantic League. Tough league. They don't allow you to refer to yourself in the third person.

Rickey said he signed with the Bears because he was looking forward to finally playing for their manager, Walter Matthau.

FAVORITES FALL IN STANLEY CUP PLAY-OFFS I hope I'm not too late with a TV slogan. "The NHL Playoffs: Win or Go Broke."

Despite what you've heard, the Anaheim-Dallas series is not best of seven overtimes.

The Ducks' 4–3 win in Game 1 was the fourth-longest game in history. There were so many intermissions and studio breaks that by the fourth OT, Barry Melrose had gone through his supply of mousse and started dipping into Mel Kiper Jr.'s.

I have to study up on the Wild. Right now, I recognize more guys on *Mr. Personality*.

WARNER BROS. OPTIONS SCRIPT FOR MOVIE ABOUT A SPORTS ANCHOR Wait a minute, isn't there already a film called *Dumb and Dumber*?

DICK VITALE AND RICK PITINO JOINT OWNERS OF 2-YEAR-OLD RACEHORSE The thoroughbred will stay in Kentucky for three years, then leave for a better job.

My time is up. You've been great. Enjoy the New Seekers.

THE **NOTES**

(Did you feel a draft?) I love the draft, almost as much as getting a refer-ence to *delirium tremens* into the column. Even now, I'm shaking.

(After 23 games, the Tigers are hitting .179...) The "Mendoza Line" is the demarcation point when a hitter's average slips below .200. It was named for the late 1970s shortstop Mario Mendoza. The cruel fact is Mendoza's lifetime average is a comfortable .215. Jeez, who was his agent, Reuben Kincaid?

(Dick Vitale and Rick Pitino joint owners...) Let me get this straight. I pass up a Dick Vitale opportunity to hammer Pitino again? O.K., here's one: *Vitale can't wait to enter the horse in the Diaper Jim Dandy....* Happy?

THE **CUTS**

Tough questions on the Wonderlic Test: If Booster A has $5,000 cash and a Lexus, and Booster B ten grand and a tricked-out Caddy, who will arrive at the University of Miami campus first? Apparently, the Edwin Pope retaliation embargo was still in effect.

Bud Selig says he'll step down as commissioner when his term ends. And when an ex–used car salesman tells you he'll walk away without a deal, you have to believe him. Selig is now signed through 2009...and he'd like to put you in a preowned LeSabre.

THE **HIT(S)**

"I'd Like to Teach the World to Sing"

"Look What They've Done to My Song, Ma"

Good to be here. Just saw a riveting new sports movie, *Bend It Like the USOC Drug Policy.*

RUN FOR THE ROSES NOTHING BUT LAUGHS

Funny Cide became the first gelding to win the Kentucky Derby since Clyde Van Dusen in 1929. Clyde wasn't a horse, just a guy who had run screaming onto the track out of surgery.

Favorites are now 1 for the last 23. Or, as the Tigers would call it, a hot streak.

Domestic Dispute was 10th. He got three calls, but no one pressed charges.

I guess this isn't surprising. Immediately after the race Domestic Dispute was claimed by the Hawks' Glenn Robinson.

MAVS STAVE OFF HISTORY AND WIN GAME 7

Call me sentimental, but it would have been nice to see the Blazers win something this year other than an adjournment.

Portland lost despite 16 points from ageless Arvydas Sabonis. It was Sabonis's best game ever following a Michael Jordan retirement.

In the other Game 7, Detroit completed a comeback from 3–1 down. I bet things turned around when they benched Cujo.

In the last two games the Pistons got offense from rare sources: 77 points from Chauncey Billups and 25 from the Pine Artist formerly known as Tayshaun Prince.

STEVE BOWDEN, BOBBY'S SON, PLEADS GUILTY TO SWINDLING INVESTORS, INCLUDING $1.6 MILLION FROM HIS DAD

How come I think Steve Bowden probably tried to recruit Adrian McPherson?

Steve sold unregistered securities with former Alabama quarterback Brian Burgdorf. This explains why the scam worked. They kept telling people they were with the SEC.

FIFTY MILLION VIEWERS IN JAPAN WATCH FIRST U.S MEETING BETWEEN ICHIRO AND MATSUI

The game was available on cable as part of George Steinbrenner's new "HAI Network."

The first pitch aired live at 8 a.m. local time, preempting Japan's most popular morning show, *Sadaharu and Kathie Lee.*

Also in baseball, the Rockies have distanced themselves from recent comments made about homosexuality by their pitcher Todd Jones. That's good. Usually they just blame the altitude.

Jones said if there was a gay player, "he shouldn't walk around proud." You know, if it doesn't pan out for Jones in Colorado, he's got a job waiting as a righty setup man for Pennsylvania senator Rick Santorum.

In response to the threat of SARS, the Blue Jays offered $1 tickets to a game against the Rangers last week and drew more than 48,000. Of course SkyDome is covered by the retractable surgical mask.

Pretty scary. These days, the only person in Canada who's not wearing a mask is Gump Worsley.

CYNTHIA COOPER RETURNS TO HOUSTON COMETS

Cooper is 40 years old. She plans to play one season, retire, play minor league baseball, come back for one last season of basketball, retire, become part owner of a team, divest her ownership, come back for one last season, then try to make it on the celebrity golf tour.

PRESIDENT CLINTON TO ATTEND INDIANAPOLIS 500

O.K. now, everybody together: "Gentlemen, start your interns!"

My time is up. You've been great. Enjoy Looking Glass.

THE **NOTES**

(Run for the Roses nothing but laughs...) I think I saw this, the guy running on the track out of surgery, in a Jerry Lewis movie, *The Errand Gelding.*

(Domestic Dispute was 10th...) I love this joke because no one got hurt.

(Pretty scary. These days, the only person in Canada...) The last NHL goalie to play without a mask was Andy Brown. But if you've learned anything from me about what sounds funny, you go with "Gump."

THE **CUTS**

Carl Lewis subject of DUI investigation. *Luckily, if he's found guilty, it goes on Ben Johnson's driving record.* Lewis won gold in the 100 meters in Seoul when Canadian Johnson set a world record before testing positive for steroids. But that was 17 years ago. Thank God nothing like that could happen today.

Touching scene at the end of the game. Mark Cuban put his arm around Portland coach Maurice Cheeks and taught him the words to the Dairy Queen theme song. Earlier in the series, Cheeks had helped a little girl sing the national anthem. Earlier in the year, Cuban had worked at a Dairy Queen for a day. You're right, not funny.

THE **HIT(S)**

"Brandy (You're a Fine Girl)"

Sorry I'm late. I had to drop Bob Ryan off at sensitivity training class.

BRAVES AGAIN LEADING NL EAST Meanwhile, what do you say we cut the formalities and just declare the Mets Wilpons of Mass Self-Destruction?

The Mets are dying to attract customers. Last Saturday at Shea Stadium was Mo Vaughn bobblehead giveaway. And thanks to state-of-the-art technology, Mo's bobblehead comes with a jigglegut.

And you can fill the right knee with your choice of fluid.

The Royals won their first 11 games at home, falling one short of the major league record, set by the Tigers in 1911. Of course, that's when the Tigers were still using major leaguers.

MIKE SHULA NAMED NEW HEAD COACH AT ALABAMA All that's left is the contract signing and the gelding procedure.

I don't want to give anyone career advice, but if I were that stripper, I'd change my stage name from Destiny to Bare Bryant.

PHIL JACKSON UNDERGOES HEART PROCEDURE His angioplasty took two hours, and there were no complications—except when security had to warn Jack Nicholson about getting too close to the anesthesiologist.

The Pistons are 4–0 when Anita Baker sings the national anthem. Not only that, she's the only one who can post up Ben Wallace in practice.

Meanwhile, everybody's still criticizing the NBA referees. The other day David Stern had to fine himself $50,000.

People may actually have a point about the questionable officiating. The other night I was watching the Nets-Celtics, and Bennett Salvatore called a foul on Wally Szczerbiak.

It gets worse. During Game 4 of the Lakers-Spurs series, a ball went off Tim Duncan out-of-bounds, and I swear I heard a ref yell, "Our ball!"

FORMER ABC SPORTS PRESIDENT HOWARD KATZ NAMED COO OF NFL FILMS The big transition for him, of course, will be getting used to doing everything in slow motion.

Tough negotiation. Katz didn't take the deal until NFL Films promised to give him a recording of the late John Facenda for the outgoing message on his answering machine.

THERE GOES MR. JORDAN Michael started getting a little bit suspicious when he walked into Wizards owner Abe Pollin's office and his secretary was wearing a pink slip.

Call me an optimist, but I believe Jordan will return to the Wizards' front office. With boxes and bubble wrap.

WILD AND DUCKS BATTLE IN CUP SEMIFINALS There's a lot at stake. They're playing for the right to be considered the fifth-best team in the West.

In the East the Senators will net $600,000 for every home playoff game. If they go all the way, they could make as much as $5 million, plus whatever the Cup will bring in when they sell it on eBay.

U.S. HAS WORST SHOWING AT WORLD HOCKEY CHAMPIONSHIPS IN 14 YEARS Do you believe in the "B" pool? Yes!

INDIANAPOLIS 500 MAY HAVE FEWER THAN TRADITIONAL 33 CARS Apparently, many of the drivers are having trouble getting their inspection stickers.

My time is up. You've all been great. Enjoy Bobby Vee.

THE **NOTES**

(Sorry I'm late. I had to drop Bob Ryan off at sensitivity training class...) Bob Ryan has been writing for the *Boston Globe* since I was adding jokes to my haftarah. I grew up devouring his stuff along with that of his formidable colleagues, Ray Fitzgerald, Peter Gammons and John Powers. But Bob had a bad day that week. He made some comments about Jason Kidd's camera-loving wife, Joumana, on a Celtics postgame show. His cracks were at first over-the-top, but only talk-radio out of line. Unfortunately, he closed his rant with the line, "I'd like to smack her." His cohost, Bob Lobel, gave him a couple of chances to recant his remarks, but Ryan held fast. The problem was that two years before, Joumana had filed domestic abuse charges against her husband, which were later dropped. Ryan was suspended by the *Globe* for a month without pay. The story has a happy ending. Mike Barnicle did not steal any of his material.

(Tough negotiation. Katz didn't take the deal until...) In my first column for *ESPN Magazine*, I was writing about Oliver Stone's muffed punt of a film, *Any Given Sunday*. One of the jokes was: *Oliver Stone never got NFL approval for the film. You can't blame Stone for being paranoid. He believes the league has it in for him ever since he tried to hire John Facenda to narrate the Zapruder film.* Of course, that was back when I could channel Dennis Miller.

THE **CUTS**

During the ninth inning of a recent Mets loss, shortstop Rey Sanchez was in the clubhouse getting his hair cut by Armando Benitez. Benitez denies this. Of course. Who'd want to see him in the ninth? If you've followed Benitez's career, you know this line only works in the Mets clubhouse.

NBATV is now available in high definition seven days a week. So, all the action none of us can see now, we'll be able to see it that much clearer. I don't want to say this line is a tad existential, but I think I heard Kierkegaard laughing. By the way, Tad Existential was my junior proctor at Deerfield Academy.

THE **HIT(S)**

"Rubber Ball"

"Take Good Care of My Baby"

"The Night Has a Thousand Eyes"

"Come Back When You Grow Up"

(Again, too many hits, but the "Q+A" column, which runs next to me every week, featured Bobby Valentine that week, and Kostya and I couldn't resist the hip insideness.)

Good to be here. I just got off the phone with Phil Jackson's cardiologist. He says the Spurs' series win cannot be considered a bypass.

FUNNY CIDE ROUNDS SECOND, HEADS FOR BELMONT The New York–bred routed the field by almost 10 lengths and could become the first Triple Crown winner in 25 years. I have a racing etiquette question: When a gelding is this big a favorite, is it bad form to use the expression "in the bag"?

This just in: Photographs after the race revealed the only thing Jose Santos had in his right hand was a middle finger for the stewards.

MARLINS TAKE "SENIOR CIRCUIT" LITERALLY The new Florida manager is 72-year-old Jack McKeon. He's four years older than the next oldest manager, five years younger than the average Marlins fan.

McKeon's old. He's the only manager to use a designated hip.

The previous Marlins skipper, Jeff Torborg, knew his job was in jeopardy a week ago when *Baseball Tonight* called and asked for his earpiece size.

Elsewhere, the Tigers have a promotion going at Comerica Park, Motown Mondays. Are you like me? Are you thinking Junior Walker will be the only one playing with All-Stars there this season?

ACC "INVITES" MIAMI, BC AND SYRACUSE TO JOIN CONFERENCE The Big East stands to lose three of its top teams. But now that we know Miami is involved, do you have a feeling this thing will end up being decided in court?

The addition of Syracuse makes sense. When I think of the Atlantic Coast, I remember all my summers on the ocean in central New York.

PISTONS ADVANCE TO EASTERN CONFERENCE FINALS Did you have a chance to see that Game 6 overtime thriller? Afterward Brent Musberger needed to be treated for hype-tension.

Detroit is now 10–0 in overtime this season. Who wants to break the news to rookie Tayshaun Prince that he doesn't get paid time and a half?

The Nets weren't expecting to play Detroit. Byron Scott had only prepared incendiary remarks about Philly fans.

New Jersey swept Boston in four. On the bright side the Celtics lasted a game longer than Antoine Walker's personal heckler.

VIJAY SINGH WINS BYRON NELSON CLASSIC Now it's on to the Dinah Shore....

Citing fatigue, Singh pulled out of this weekend's Colonial a week after saying Sorenstam should not be allowed to play there. You know, remarks like that will get him in trouble...and 50% off his dues at Augusta National.

LEBRON JAMES TAPS AARON GOODWIN TO BE HIS AGENT Goodwin is based in Seattle. He represents Bucks star Gary Payton and 500 countermen at Starbucks.

Big job ahead for Aaron. I don't want to say LeBron comes with a lot of baggage, but his posse has a skycap.

GIANTS COACH JIM FASSEL REUNITED WITH SON AFTER 34 YEARS The kid's first words: "How tough can it be to find a decent long snapper?"

***NEW YORK TIMES* FORCES OUT REPORTER WHO FABRICATED INFORMATION** Here's the shocking part: It wasn't the guy who came up with the formula for its college football poll.

My time is up. You've been great. Enjoy the Raspberries.

THE **NOTES**

(Elsewhere, the Tigers have a promotion going at Comerica Park...) Junior Walker and the All Stars had such hits as "Shotgun," "Pucker Up Buttercup" and "What Does It Take to Win Your Love." Which makes them much too successful to be included at the end of the column.

(Big job ahead for Aaron...) I wish, oh I wish I had written this joke. I will always give credit, but the guy who wrote it would be, ah, conflicted, if I gave away his identity. If you guess Paul Silas, you're very close.

(Giants coach Jim Fassel...) The Giants had blown a 28-point lead to the 49ers in the playoffs and still had a chance to win when the game ended on an errant field goal snap by Trey Junkin. All fodder for a tearful father-son reunion.

THE **CUTS**

Meanwhile, the commissioner's office is furious the Marlins did not follow its hiring guidelines. Of course, Florida claims the two over-70 minority candidates couldn't make it up the stairs for the interview. Close your eyes, then imagine Redd Foxx and Morgan Freeman climbing the stairs, then tell me I'm wrong.

Ducks walk over Wild. After rising to national prominence, Minnesota managed one goal in four games. Another victim of the notorious Sports Illustrated *"nine pages from the cover" jinx. SI* does not like it when we refer to the jinx. Why? Are they afraid it'll jinx things?

THE **HIT(S)**

"Go All the Way"

"I Wanna Be with You"

Good to be here. Unfortunately, the *American Idol* people are still angry with me because I phoned in 200,000 votes for Rocco Baldelli.

PERRY AND LEONARD TIE RECORD AT COLONIAL WITH 61s Are you like me? Are you wondering if they put the red tees back in?

ANNIKA DRAWS CROWDS BUT HAS NO PLANS FOR WEEKEND The media attention early in the week was wild. *The New York Times* sent six reporters, and more than half of them actually showed up.

Of course, Jayson Blair filed three stories from Colonial Williamsburg.

FOR THE FIRST TIME MAJOR LEAGUE BASEBALL ALLOWS FOX TO MIKE POSITION PLAYERS Which raises an interesting question: What's Spanish for "Hey, check out that blonde five rows behind the dugout"?

The Brewers have employees going door-to-door trying to sell tickets. The results are not good. So far, 500 people have tried to order those Thin Mint cookies.

Elsewhere, New York City police arrested a man who was allegedly harassing Mets general manager Steve Phillips. According to prosecutors the guy was hanging out every day at Shea Stadium. On the bright side, he's been showing up more than Mo Vaughn.

Sad days in San Diego. The Padres lost nine in a row and are playing so poorly they're thinking of wearing the camouflage jerseys all the time so no one can see them.

The Reds are on pace to challenge the National League record for home runs in a season. And this is with Ken Griffey Jr. spending most of the season on the Great American Disabled List.

The new stadium helps. The ball really carries. Every fifth inning the grounds crew has to drag the upper deck.

CLEVELAND WINS NBA DRAFT LOTTERY The Cavaliers showed up to the lottery prepared for LeBron James. They brought a personalized team jersey and a personalized, extra-wide parking pass for the Hummer.

The Cavs are not allowed to use James as a promotional tool until the draft, on June 26. So enjoy the last four weeks of the Smush Parker Era.

DE FERRAN TAKES INDY 500 His teammate, Helio Castroneves, finished second, just missing an unprecedented third straight Indy victory. Helio still climbed the chain-link fence after the race, but this year it was just to escape being kissed by Jim Nabors.

SENATORS IMPEACHED The Devils won Game 7 in Ottawa 3–2. Jeff Friesen scored the winner for New Jersey, on an assist from Jason Kidd.

The Ducks had 11 days between the semis and the finals. And I don't know how this happened, but Jean-Sébastien Giguere got five more shutouts.

I gotta tell ya, Giguere has put up more zeroes than that house on *Big Brother*.

HBO CUTS TRAINING CAMP SERIES *HARD KNOCKS* They're thinking of replacing it with another NFL-related show, *Curb Your Ephedrine*.

JAYSON WILLIAMS, OUT ON BAIL, TO OPEN A CAR WASH IN NEW JERSEY It's an extra five dollars if you want the hot alibi.

My time is up. You've been great. Enjoy R.B. Greaves.

THE **NOTES**

(The new stadium helps. The ball really carries…) This is a blatant switch on the old joke, *The pitching staff was so bad, they had to drag the warning track.* My point is, why settle for a double?

(Jayson Williams, out on bail…) During the O.J. trial, I wrote a similar joke: *According to one deposition, O.J. claimed at the time of the murder he was out buying ice cream. I believe it was Baskin-Robbins's new flavor, Rocky Alibi.*

THE **CUTS**

Annika draws crowds, but has no plans for weekend. *CBS came this close to canceling its coverage of the final two rounds and replacing it with an eight-hour "Hack-athon."* Love the use of the word "hack." The only problem is that the show was never watched by more than two foursomes.

During Friday's press conference after failing to make the cut, a grateful and emotional Sorenstam said she was going back to her own tour. You know what would have been great? If Vijay Singh had burst in right at the end and said, "You complete me." (Answer to myself: No it wouldn't have been great.)

De Ferran takes Indy 500. *Unfortunately, the next day, 100,000 spectators sued Marlboro Team Penske over secondhand smoke.* Tobacco jokes. They're not just for NASCAR.

THE **HIT(S)**

"Take a Letter, Maria"

Good to be here. Am I wrong, or does the oversized head on Tiger Woods's new Nike driver look like LeBron James?

WORLD CHAMPION ANGELS MEET PRESIDENT BUSH IN ROSE GARDEN Unfortunately, the Secret Service kept dragging David Eckstein back to the T-ball field.

People who raise more than $200,000 for Bush's reelection campaign will be known as Rangers, in apparent tribute to the team the President once co-owned. Of course, those who cough up $70 million and have nothing to show for it will be known as New York Rangers.

Rumor is Ted Turner may buy the Braves. It all depends on if he can lock up Andy Messersmith to a long-term deal.

After a recent loss, Curt Schilling took a bat to a QuesTec camera used to evaluate umpires. It was the first time the machine registered a high strike.

Jack McKeon is still adjusting to managing at the age of 72. Last week he left the "take" signal on for 15 minutes.

NBA PLAYOFFS END HIATUS. FINALS BEGIN ON JUNE 4 Come on. The last thing stretched out this much in the NBA was Mel Turpin's waistband.

In other basketball news Larry Brown resigned from the Sixers. In a related story, Allen Iverson says he's willing to show up late for practices run by Jeff Van Gundy, Mike Fratello or Mike Dunleavy.

Miramax Books will pay Yao Ming a reported $1.5 million for his autobiography. Pretty catchy title: *Everybody Wang Zhizhi Tonight.*

Earlier today Yao released this statement: "Please don't tell the Chinese government I'm getting $1.5 million."

NFL AGENT DREW ROSENHAUS SAYS BRIAN GRIESE WILL UNSEAT JAY FIEDLER AS DOLPHINS QUARTERBACK Not only that, Rosenhaus also has Willis McGahee on the phone, pretending to accept deals from Reebok, Gatorade and Buick.

Note to the Vikings' front office. You're on the clock: 320 days, 23 hours and 45 minutes.

SERENA BREEZES IN FRENCH OPEN EARLY ROUNDS The other night I saw what I thought were two minutes of highlights. Turns out it was her entire match.

In other tennis news, Wimbledon has eliminated the mandatory curtsy to the Royal Box. Unless, of course, Queen Latifah is in the house.

NHL COMMISSIONER GARY BETTMAN DELIVERS ANNUAL STATE OF THE GAME ADDRESS It was five minutes of excitement, followed by an hour and a half of clutching and grabbing.

TV ratings for hockey continue to slide. ABC was seriously thinking of renaming this year's finals *Who Wants to Be a Niedermayer?*

Patrick Roy retired after 18 seasons. His pads will now be turned into affordable housing for three families.

NIKE GIVES $1 MILLION CONTRACT TO 13-YEAR-OLD Are you like me? Before you found out he was a soccer player, were you thinking, "This kid must be some kind of genius gluing those insoles"?

JOUMANA KIDD BEING CONSIDERED FOR *MONDAY NIGHT FOOTBALL* SIDELINE GIG Not to be outdone, Eric Dickerson has the inside track on becoming TJ's nanny.

My time is up. You've been great. Enjoy Spooky Tooth.

THE **NOTES**

(Jack McKeon is still adjusting to managing at the age of 72…) This was handed to me by the brilliant syndicated sports radio host Mark Patrick. My reward: an angry letter to the editor, published with a photo, and McKeon winning the World Series. That's part of the gig I hadn't anticipated when I got the column. Maureen Dowd once told me that half her e-mail begins, "Dear Liberal Slut…" I don't know. That I could live with.

(Miramax Books will pay Yao Ming a reported…) Wang Zhizhi was the first Chinese player in the NBA. Not, as some people think, a disease Dennis Rodman picked up in Vegas.

THE **CUTS**

Ted Turner buying the Braves again? Yeah, that'll happen right after Jane Fonda says, "O.K., let's give the marriage another shot." This reminds me of a monologue I wrote in 1993: "You knew the NLCS was over when Jane Fonda started making out with the Philly Phanatic."

Not quite as easy on the other side. By Day 3, the only American men left in Paris were Andre Agassi and David Sedaris. Here's the problem. Most *SI* readers think David Sedaris is either: a) the shortstop for the Angels, or b) the guy who worked with Alvin and the Chipmunks.

THE **HIT(S)**

None. (Here's the deal. I was going to use Gary Wright, the keyboard whiz who sang "Dream Weaver." But who cares? Gary Wright sounds like some guy who got 14 at-bats as a September call-up for Texas. So I went with his previous band, the very underrated Spooky Tooth, who were huge in Europe in the mid-'70s and never got any real attention here. Kind of like Harvey Glance.)

THE **SHOW**

Good to be here. I missed the Tony Awards. Help me out here. Did the Mighty Ducks win for Best Revival?

FUNNY CIDE'S VISA DECLINED AT BELMONT Empire Maker spoiled the New York–bred's bid for the Triple Crown. Now, I guess all that's left for the gelding is to be put out to stag.

Still, it was a great five weeks, and in his honor, Funny Cide's owners renamed themselves No-Sackatoga Stable.

They say the gelding process can have a calming effect. Hey, it worked for Richard Simmons.

SAMMY SOSA: BULLETIN BOARD MATERIAL? Cork was found after Sosa's bat broke in Tuesday's game at Wrigley against the Devil Rays. And what are the odds of this? Royals pitcher Jason Grimsley flew in from Los Angeles to steal the bat out of the umpires' room.

Sammy says he only uses a corked bat in batting practice. Yeah, and Gaylord Perry only used K-Y jelly on English muffins.

According to an ESPN poll, 80% said the incident would severely hurt Sosa's reputation. And the other 20% said, "If I answer this poll, do I get a fleece?"

After the incident Major League Baseball X-rayed 76 of Sosa's bats. And I don't get this. They also X-rayed Kerry Wood.

Meanwhile, interleague play is in full swing. All week Edgar Martinez can be reached at Club Med.

A COUPLE OF PEOPLE WIN FRENCH OPEN Here's how little interest there was in the Justine Henin-Hardenne–Kim Clijsters women's final: People in Belgium were switching to Arena Football.

Serena Williams felt the crowd at Roland Garros was unduly hostile toward her during her upset loss to Henin-Hardenne in the semis. Rude, hostile and unsupportive to an American? I'm sorry, that just doesn't sound like the French.

DAVID STERN BITTERLY CONTESTS CLAIMS OF LAGGING TV RATINGS FOR NBA PLAYOFFS Or something like that. I wasn't watching.

Don't forget the winner of the NBA Finals gets home field advantage in next year's All-Star Game.

GATTI WINS RUBBER MATCH WITH WARD Not only that, the epic third battle between the two junior welterweights delivered a huge audience for HBO's new X-rated boxing show, *G-string Duvas*.

In other boxing news, a torn chest muscle has forced Kirk Johnson to pull out of his scheduled June 21 bout with heavyweight champion Lennox Lewis. That's less than two weeks away. Does anybody have Peter McNeely's phone number?

O.K., how about Roy Jones Sr.?

Lewis recently filed a $385 million lawsuit against Don King. Help me out here. If Lennox wins the suit, isn't King entitled to half?

RICK NEUHEISEL TRYING TO KEEP JOB AMID ACCUSATIONS OF GAMBLING The Washington football coach allegedly won $20,000 in the 2002 NCAA basketball tournament pool. However, Neuheisel claims he had a Husky booster come in to install his brackets.

MARIAH CAREY TO DESIGN SEXY GOLF CLOTHES FOR WOMEN All the shirts will have a plunging neckline, to match her career.

My time is up. You've been great. Enjoy Bobby Goldsboro.

THE **NOTES**

(They say the gelding process can have a calming effect...) O.K., you've been good. You deserve a Dave Letterman story. The first year at CBS, Richard Simmons was on the show. We came out of commercial for the second segment, and Richard, greased up in the tank top and shorts, was playing around with one of Dave's cigars. This exchange followed:

RICHARD: Dave, would you teach me how to smoke a cigar?

DAVE: Uh, Richard, I'm sure you've already got the hang of it.

(Sammy says he only uses a corked bat in batting practice...) Not just sarcasm. Well-lubricated sarcasm. Speaking of well-lubricated sarcasm, anybody seen Richard Simmons?

(Gatti wins rubber match with Ward...) The setup is complete and utter illogical nonsense. I don't like to do that. It ruins the credibility you've earned with your readers. But I had to get to *"G-string Duvas,"* so forgive me.

THE **CUTS**

I don't want to start a witch hunt, but lately, Dusty Baker's toothpick has been looking a little too chewy. Let me explain. After the success of the Kerry Wood X-ray line, I got cocky and was just looking for any wood at Wrigley.

Cleveland Indians games are an average 30 minutes shorter than a year ago. Big deal. The average outing by a starting pitcher is 45 minutes short-er. Once again, the actual facts turn this joke into a sentence. Why don't they sign Steve Trachsel?

THE **HIT(S)**

"Honey"

"Watching Scotty Grow"

Help me out here. Who do I call to get Roger Clemens's family to stop following me around?

TIGER'S FORMER CADDIE CARRIES BAGS FOR GUY WHO WINS U.S. OPEN For those of you unfamiliar with Jim Furyk, he is a less dynamic, lower-key version of Scott Simpson.

Before Furyk hit his birdie putt at the 11th hole, a topless woman ran out of the gallery onto the green. And, in Furyk's honor, she covered herself cross-handed.

Tom Watson, 53, led after the first round with a five-under 65. Then he threw his backswing out.

During his record second-round 63, Vijay Singh was heckled by a man in the gallery about Annika Sorenstam. The fan was removed by Chicago cops and immediately thrown into the audience at *Jerry Springer*.

NBC really lost interest once Tiger Woods dropped back. Midway through the final round, it cut away for 15 minutes for a live tour of the empty Arena Bowl pregame show set.

I don't want to say Tiger's game went south, but he played the last 27 holes at Doral.

SOSA SITS SEVEN GAMES After an appeal, Major League Baseball reduced its suspension by a game. Originally, Sosa wanted them to cut it in half, but he was afraid of what they might find.

Bob DuPuy reduced the suspension because he believed Sosa's explanation about picking up the wrong bat by accident. Why can't the IRS send a guy like this to audit me?

Last week Bill Clinton called Sosa and told him to "hang in there." And then urged him to get all his bats dry-cleaned.

The incident may cost Sammy millions in off-the-field earnings. Fortunately, he just got a new endorsement: "Cork: The other white meat."

Elsewhere, the Yankees were no-hit by six different Astros pitchers. By the seventh inning a desperate George Steinbrenner hired three steroid vendors.

And the Mets promoted pitcher Jason Roach from Triple A. Roach turned up at Shea Stadium in Tony Tarasco's glove compartment.

SPURS DOWN NETS Jason Kidd had strong stats in the Game 6 loss in San Antonio. And that was after being out all night with a local real estate agent.

The Nets got permission to wear their ABA retro jerseys for Game 5. And it would have been great, except for the Tim Duncan matchup with Billy Paultz.

As the series wore on, the New Jersey fast break really slowed down. Come on. Martin Brodeur moved faster in the Stanley Cup handshake line.

In other NBA, news Kobe Bryant underwent surgery for a torn labrum. He injured his shoulder trying to suddenly grasp the logic behind LeBron's $90 million shoe deal.

And an Illinois judge ruled that Michael Jordan does not have to pay former girlfriend Karla Knafel $5 million in hush money. What a relief. For a minute there I was worried he wouldn't have enough cash to buy the Bucks.

FORMER UNIVERSITY OF MIAMI RUNNING BACK JAMES STEWART PLEADS GUILTY TO FELONY DISTRIBUTION OF COCAINE He'll be sentenced in October, and the following month at the Orange Bowl he'll be inducted into the Hurricanes' Drug Ring of Honor.

MANCHESTER UNITED TRIES TO SELL DAVID BECKHAM TO BARCELONA The deal fell through after Man U was unable to get Beckham's approval and his wife, Victoria, refused to change her name to Picante Spice.

My time is up. You've been great. Enjoy the Cuff-Links.

THE **NOTES**

(Tiger's former caddie carries bag for guy...) I asked Kostya to ask Jim Herre, the editor of *Sports Illustrated*'s Golf Plus, if there was anyone on the tour duller than Scott Simpson, who I had come up with. His reply: "Uh, no."

(Last week, Bill Clinton called Sosa...) This answers the question: Is there an expiration date on Monica Lewinsky jokes? Uh, no.

(And the Mets promoted pitcher Jason Roach...) Tarasco had been caught with pot during spring training, which helped this joke a lot. But if you remember anything I tell you, remember this: Drugs sound much funnier when found in a glove compartment.

THE **CUTS**

The Mets fired General Manager Steve Phillips. In a related story, Mike Piazza's groin called a press conference to confirm his injury was baseball-related. Is there anything better than body parts talking? Yes! Body parts calling a press conference!

For an open course, Olympia Hills played a little easy. Three members finished in the top 20. I had to put this joke in as a tribute to my parents, a couple of formidable single-digit handicappers. I can't tell you how many times I'd be watching the Open with them and my dad would say, "Remember how I used to hit the one-iron?" And before I could answer, my mother would say, "When?"

During his record second-round 63, Vijay Singh was heckled by a man in the gallery about Annika Sorenstam. The fan was removed by Chicago cops and immediately thrown into the audience at Jerry Springer. In 1998, I wrote a piece for the *New Yorker* entitled "Jerry Springer's Voice Mail," after the host claimed he got 2,000 calls a day from people who wanted to be on his show. Here's an excerpt: *"Hello? Does your show do makeovers anymore? My name is Eunice Manheim. My son, Eunice, is a skinhead. I'd like him to be transformed into a Republican congressman. It should take about 20 minutes. He's a size 42 husky."*

THE **HIT(S)**

"Tracy"

Good to be here. Just finished a new book about Wizards: *Harry Potter and the Vanishing Season-Ticket Base.*

NEXTEL TO REPLACE WINSTON AS CORPORATE SPONSOR OF NASCAR The deal becomes effective next January, at which time the Winston Cup will be turned into the Bodine Family Spittoon.

Are you like me? I bet you can't wait for next season's Talladega 500 Minutes.

O.K., one more....NASCAR driver concussions will each feature their own distinctive ring.

LENNOX LEWIS CUTS AND RUNS WITH HEAVYWEIGHT BELT When the fight was stopped after six rounds, Lewis was behind on all cards at the Staples Center. Help me out here. Nobody could find any staples for Vitali Klitschko's eye?

In other boxing news, Mike Tyson was arrested in an early morning brawl in New York City. (I know what you're thinking, but no, this is not a repeat of The Show from 1988.)

FINALS EXIT: NBA RATINGS TUMBLE Sad. Just when you thought the low scoring was over.

The ratings were the worst since 1981. But to be fair, the 1981 Finals occurred just after President Reagan had deregulated Brent Musburger.

To give you an idea how few people were watching, Chris Berman offered to come up with nicknames for each viewer.

Elsewhere in the NBA, the New Orleans Hornets named Tim Floyd coach. Apparently they felt his 49–190 record with the Bulls was misleading. Well, sure. The real challenge is to put up those kind of numbers with a playoff team.

JOSE CANSECO ARRESTED AFTER TESTING FOR STEROIDS Which answers the question: If you're under house arrest, is it tough finding a pharmacy that delivers?

Major League Baseball slapped Canseco with its harshest penalty for a retired player. From now on, when he's tested for steroids, he no longer gets his choice of complimentary juice.

Meanwhile, Sammy Sosa is back. During his seven-game suspension, he collected $500,000 in salary. But seriously, when you add that up against what he lost in terms of his place in the game....he's still half a mil ahead.

FORMER HARLEM GLOBETROTTER CLYDE AUSTIN ARRESTED ON FRAUD CHARGES Austin, an ordained minister, allegedly bilked churchgoers in Virginia out of $10 million. Apparently, they kept falling for that bit where he would pretend to throw holy water into the congregation and confetti would come out.

Austin has pleaded not guilty, but if he's convicted, I've got the perfect nickname for this guy: Meadowlark Felon.

RANGERS HOPE TO MEISTER JAGR The sticking point is Jagr's demand that they play home games in Atlantic City.

Saw the Stanley Cup on display the other day in a New Jersey parking lot. It looked great, except for The Club.

The Bruins traded Josef Stumpel back to the Kings. Turns out he was the player to be named later in the Josef Stumpel deal.

REFRIGERATOR PERRY TO ENTER CONEY ISLAND HOT-DOG EATING CONTEST He qualified by devouring 12 hot dogs, and Brian Bosworth.

***MONDAY NIGHT FOOTBALL* TAPS LISA GUERRERO FOR SIDELINE GIG** The Fox Sports Net reporter beat out Summer Sanders, Joumana Kidd and former producer Don Ohlmeyer's recommendation, O.J. juror number 9.

My time is up. You've been great. Enjoy Edison Lighthouse.

THE NOTES

(In other boxing news, Mike Tyson was arrested...) This is another, though unspoken, reference to Mitch "Blood" Green. But it gives me the opportunity to tell you the hippest Tyson joke I ever read. It was faxed into *Letterman* by a friend of mine named Jim Connell. Tyson had just been released from prison after serving three years for rape and had bought a house in Las Vegas. Connell's line: *Tyson is having a little problem adjusting to civilian life. The first thing he did after he bought the house was invite the Realtor to watch him go to the bathroom.*

(The ratings were the worst since 1981...) I have written many jokes using the formula "Reagan deregulated..." There was one in my novel, *The Ringer*, about a writer who left the *New Yorker* "...after Reagan deregulated the 10,000-word magazine piece." I think this is the best version of that formula, because given the ubiquity of Brent, it's kind of true.

(Former Harlem Globetrotter Clyde Austin...) Since we already did the specimen jar attached to the rubber band, the only Trotter joke premise left is this.

THE CUTS

And the Rockets hired Jeff Van Gundy. Not to be outdone, the Clippers are interested in his less talented younger brother, Jerry Van Gundy. Bill Maher originated this. He did a line about Vincent van Gogh having a brother that was just an O.K. painter, Jerry van Gogh. If the last name doesn't have a "Van," you gotta go with "Fredo." Of course, before 1972, you did Zeppo or Gummo. I had a joke in my stand-up act about Zippo Marx, the brother who used to light Groucho's cigars. And I think we now know why Bill Maher stayed a comedian and I didn't.

The Red Sox lost to the Phillies on "Steve Carlton Bobblehead Day" at the Vet. Of course, all members of the media received Tim McCarver bobbleheads. Bobbleheads, if you didn't already deduce, are easy setups. McCarver used to talk to the press for Carlton, although Lefty did occasionally grant interviews to the visiting media from Neptune.

Former Harlem Globetrotter Clyde Austin arrested on fraud charges. *I believe he worked many of his scams under the alias "Fleece Ausby."* This is hipper than "Meadowlark Felon," just not as accessible. You have to make the tough choices.

THE HIT(S)

"Love Grows (Where My Rosemary Goes)"

Before we begin, quick impression. Oprah Winfrey to Michael Jordan before his deal fell through: "O.K., I'm in. But only if you change the name to Oprah's Buck Club."

DON'T TELL ME WHAT HAPPENED IN THE NBA DRAFT, I TAPED IT Big day for the Cavaliers. They grabbed LeBron James with the first pick, then in the second round grabbed the guy who sold his mom the Hummer.

It was a moving moment when LeBron walked up to the podium, then bought it.

The star power really dimmed after the first three picks. At one point I swear I heard David Stern say, "The Phoenix Suns select…that kid over there in the giant suit."

Portland chose Travis Outlaw in the first round. Depending on how you score, he'll either be the first Outlaw to play for the Blazers or the sixth.

And finally, some good news for Pat Riley. The Miami Heat has been invited to join the ACC.

JETS DEFENSIVE TACKLE JOSH EVANS SUSPENDED INDEFINITELY AFTER THIRD POSITIVE TEST FOR MARIJUANA He faces a lifetime ban from the NFL. Of course, that can be avoided if the Jets just place him on injured reserve with glaucoma.

Evans has been suspended twice and is tested up to 10 times a month. As a matter of fact, his bathroom at home has a specimen cup dispenser. With carryout lids.

BONDS FIRST MEMBER OF 500-500 CLUB It may mean nothing to you, but it entitles him to 20% off all elbow armor.

Unfortunately the next day his 73rd home run ball fell just short of making the 500-500-500 Club.

Last week the Red Sox set a major league record by scoring 10 runs before their first out en route to a 25–8 win over the Marlins. Hey, forget that, the bullpen held the lead!

Jack McKeon was so upset after the loss, he banged back half a case of Ensure.

The Red Sox want permission from the city to hold two September concerts at Fenway Park with Bruce Springsteen and his band. Speaking of E Street, does anyone have an address for Jose Offerman?

Rangers owner Tom Hicks told his G.M., John Hart, to start dumping salaries. Here's the scary part: Martha Stewart knew this was going to happen in April.

Of course, Billy Beane is sitting patiently in Oakland, waiting for Ugie Urbina to become available with 0% financing.

Juan Gonzalez turned down a trade to Montreal. Two reasons: He's happy in Texas, and he didn't want to miss Carl Everett's annual midsummer freak-out.

LARRY ROBINSON WITHDRAWS AS RANGERS COACHING CANDIDATE Apparently, he'd like an easier challenge. Like rebuilding Iraq.

And the NHL approved the sale of the Ottawa franchise to Eugene Melnyk for $92 million. It's the first time somebody who wasn't a tobacco lobbyist shelled out that much dough for a bunch of Senators.

ANNA KOURNIKOVA SITS OUT WIMBELDON WITH BACK INJURY No one knows how she sustained the injury, but we can pretty much rule out that it came from lifting and moving trophies.

TIGER WOODS WANTS ALL PGA TOUR PLAYERS TO HAVE THEIR DRIVERS TESTED FOR CONFORMITY And cholesterol.

My time is up. You've been great. Enjoy the Outsiders.

THE **NOTES**

(The star power really dimmed after the first three picks…) Normally, I don't like making up quotes to serve as payoffs, but being as star-obsessed as Stern is, this doesn't seem all that made up.

(The Red Sox want permission from the city to hold…) This is a better, hipper version of a joke I wrote for an *ESPN Magazine* column: *eBay. Isn't that where Chuck Knoblauch has a summer home?*

THE **CUTS**

Meanwhile, I think I may have found the flaw in Tiger's putting game: way too much left hand when cupping his visor. For you beginners out there: When you have to reread a joke you wrote four times, it's too damn subtle.

Less than half the crowd at the Staples Center for the Lewis-Klitschko fight paid for their tickets. *And that doesn't include the two guys who sat for free in the space above Klitschko's eye.* There. Much better.

THE **HIT(S)**

"Time Won't Let Me"

Good to be here. Sorry I'm late, but Torii Hunter was arguing with me over a couple of jokes he thought were too inside.

SERENA HAS VENUS FOR BREAKFAST

Venus was hampered throughout the final by a painful abdominal strain. Call me old-fashioned, but I miss the good old days when the matches had to be decided by their dad.

Serena's victory was the fourth straight Wimbledon title for the sisters. I believe that ties the record set by Ivan Lendl and his less talented brother, Jerry Van Lendl.

Roger Federer won the men's title over unseeded Mark Philippoussis. Poor Philippoussis. Not only did he get routed, but he also fell six aces short of qualifying for the final table at the World Series of Poker.

Look, I don't mean to be disrespectful to the whole Wimbledon scene, but if it's called Henman Hill, people should be allowed to advance only halfway up.

VANCOUVER GETS 2010 WINTER GAMES

Figuring in the exchange rate, they had to come up with 35% more bribe money.

And this is promising. Former Grizzlies G.M. Dick Versace has agreed to let his hair be used for the freestyle-moguls venue.

HERE COMES THE NEWLY FORMATTED ALL-STAR GAME

Or, as they call it at Fox, The Best Damn Sports Ratings Ploy, Period.

For the first time, fans will get to vote online for the All-Star Game MVP. And remember, the winner gets home field advantage at a Chicagoland strip club.

The White Sox drew 15,000 walk-ups for Roberto Alomar's first game. But to be fair, it fell on the same night as Ken Harrelson's Nehru Jacket Liquidation Sale.

I'm no marketing genius, but if the Expos are looking to boost attendance at the Big O, how about turning a few concession stands into Canadian pharmacies?

TIGER WOODS SLUMPS FIELD IN WESTERN OPEN

The breakthrough came in Wednesday's practice round, when Tiger took the restrictor plate off his driver.

According to a recent poll of PGA fans, 64% say Tiger Woods is their favorite golfer. Phil Mickelson finished second, and that was without missing a putt.

In other golf news, Vijay Singh announced he'll only speak to the media if he's leading a tournament. Help me out here. What tournament was he leading when he made that announcement?

And next year, once again, the Masters will go commercial-free. Of course that could change if they get a really good offer from Hooters.

THE DOMINATOR: "I'LL BE BACK?"

Dominik Hasek may come out of retirement. Are you like me? Are you wondering how Detroit can convince Curtis Joseph the NHL work stoppage is starting a year early?

Meanwhile, legendary Soviet Red Army coach Viktor Tikhonov has been lured back to run the Russian national team. At the next Winter Games he'll be 76. Do you believe in Miracle Ears—yes!!!

In other hockey news, Colorado signed Paul Kariya and Teemu Selanne. That was only after their efforts to land Bryan Trottier and Mike Bossy fell through.

REFRIGERATOR PERRY FINISHES LAST IN ANNUAL FOURTH OF JULY HOT DOG EATING CONTEST

However, the Fridge will be invited back to Coney Island next year, based on his body of work.

BECKHAM DONS UNIFORM NUMBER 23 FOR REAL MADRID, IN TRIBUTE TO JORDAN

It's working already. Yesterday, he was served papers by Karla Knafel.

My time is up. You've all been great. Enjoy Climax.

THE **NOTES**

(Serena's victory was the fourth straight…) Never give up. Never ever give up.

(And this is promising. Former Grizzlies G.M. Dick Versace…) Dick Versace used to have a curly blond Afro that looked like high-tech insulation. Go download a photo from the '80s. I'll wait.

(The White Sox drew 15,000 walk-ups for Roberto Alomar's first game…) Ken "the Hawk" Harrelson once appeared on the cover of *SI* in a powder blue leisure suit, one of several million he owned. Before he was waving pom-poms in the White Sox broadcast booth, Hawk Harrelson spent time with the Yankees and Red Sox, where he became that rarest of aviary species, the Brown-Nosed Hawk. A relentlessly unabashed homer. Most of the time you'd just let it go, but then he'd say something like, "You know, I came out to the ballpark early today and Wayne Tolleson (Doug Griffin, Craig Grebeck) put on a show in batting practice." And you'd have to shower. A couple of times.

THE **CUTS**

Vancouver beat out PyeongChang, South Korea; Salzburg, Austria; and the old set from the movie Ice Castles. Be honest. After reading this, you'll have the theme from *Ice Castles* in your head for the rest of the day.

Jan Stephenson will play in an event on the all-male Champions Tour. She received a special exemption after bringing a note from a doctor, claiming she had prostate trouble. Once again, the good taste police show up and ruin everything.

THE **HIT(S)**

"Precious and Few"

Note to reader: For no logical reason, until further notice please replace all references to Barry Zito with Roger Clemens.

THE SLIPPER FITS! BEN CURTIS WINS BRITISH OPEN! UNBELIEVABLE A year ago this kid was playing on the Hooters Tour. Of course, the big prize on the Hooters Tour is the Claret Jugs.

Tiger Woods never recovered from a triple bogie on the 1st hole last Thursday. He finished two strokes back and has not won a major in more than 13 months. O.K., I'll say it. It's time to retire and play minor league baseball.

John Daly tied for last with a final-round 80. He played so poorly he has to go to Q school next year to be one of Michael Douglas's friends.

Tough conditions the first two days in England. Or, as Tony Blair called it, "weather of mass destruction."

As usual, there were some surprise early front-runners. S.K. Ho. Wasn't that a character on *In Living Color*?

AL UNTIES NL 7–6 They're already tinkering with next year's All-Star Game. In the new format, the losing league gets custody of the Expos.

Surprisingly, National League manager Dusty Baker did not save his position players. By the end of the game the only people left on his bench were Geoff Jenkins and Amy Grant.

In other baseball news the Dodgers signed 44-year-old Rickey Henderson. In his honor, fans will not start arriving at Dodger Stadium until the third person.

Albert Pujols still has a shot at the Triple Crown. Apparently Funny Cide and Empire Maker don't have quite enough plate appearances.

This just in: The Italian sausage mascot will return after a rehab stint with the Brewers' Hickory Farm club.

RUSH LIMBAUGH HIRED FOR ESPN'S *SUNDAY NFL COUNTDOWN* Are you like me? Suddenly you want Chris Berman to talk more?

Limbaugh will contribute an opening essay, which will be followed by a short break while they refill the studio with oxygen.

Rush fits the two primary qualities ESPN was looking for: someone who can express his opinions without equivocation, and someone who can fit into Bill Parcells's old pants without alteration.

The Limbaugh hiring has had an effect. Membership in the Bristol, Conn., chapter of the NRA increased by 200%.

Also at ESPN, Deion Sanders was named host of *The New American Sportsman*. Don't miss the season premier, when Prime Time and Robert Duvall go hunting for auto repairs discounts.

Deion just won a case in court after the owner of a car-repair shop said he paid only $1,500 of a $4,200 bill on the advice of Jesus. Actually, Jesus told Deion to pay $1,500, and that He may be back in three days with the rest.

You know Deion's getting old when he can't even cover an outstanding balance.

CHRIS WEBBER COPS PLEA, AVOIDS PERJURY TRIAL AND POSSIBLE JAIL SENTENCE So, 10 years later he finally used a time out correctly.

WASHINGTON MEN'S BASKETBALL TEAM PLACED ON TWO YEARS' PROBATION Which answers the question, "Who else was in Rick Neuheisel's NCAA pool?"

MAN WAKES UP AFTER BEING IN COMA SINCE 1984 His first question: "Are the Tigers still running away with the AL East?"

My time is up. You've been great. Enjoy the Remains.

THE **NOTES**

(John Daly tied for last with a final-round 80…) ABC runs a two-hour golf special every year, *Michael Douglas and Friends*. Which answers the question: How did Michael Douglas get over his sex addiction? A question none of us asked.

(In other baseball news the Dodgers signed 44-year-old Rickey Henderson…) The only time I had to go upstairs. This joke had been resubmitted by Kostya and cut twice by executive editor Charlie Leerhsen, who is in charge of the "Scorecard" section where my column appears. Charlie is scary bright and funny. He told me he had cut the line because it was too existential. "This is the Salvador Dali melting alarm clock of jokes," he said. I told him the idea was to have the jokes no one else might think of. He relented and it was included. Three days later, I forwarded him an e-mail from my brother Tom, raving about the Rickey Henderson line, to which he responded, "Great. Now how about a rave from someone not named Scheft?"

(Man wakes up after being in coma since 1984…) Total luck. The guy goes into the coma in 1984, the year the Tigers started 26–4. He wakes up in 2003, when they're 26–84.

THE **CUTS**

You know the most surprising thing about the whole Randall Simon– Sausage Mascot incident? Nobody mentioned that the situation called for a righthanded batter. This footage, of Simon clubbing the Italian Sausage during the seventh-inning sausage race in Milwaukee, will be run forever. Unfortunately, although I liked the joke, by then the story was two weeks old.

Sportswriter Mitch Albom had been subpoenaed as a witness for the prosecution. What a break. They were planning to call him on a Tuesday. The Webber timeout joke worked better as a single. And I guess for the two people in the country who haven't read *Tuesdays with Morrie*, this ruins the ending.

THE **HIT(S)**

None. (The Remains were a legendary band from Boston that opened for the Beatles on their last U.S. tour, then disbanded when they realized they weren't going to be the Beatles. They had a couple of regional hits, "Why Do I Cry?" and "Diddy Wah-Diddy." They are the best group no one ever heard of and I promised their drummer, Chip Damiani, if this column lasted over a year, I would include them. This was Week 1 of Year 2.)

THE SHOW

If I seem a little down, bear with me. Went to see *Seabiscuit*, got shut out at the window.

TOUR DE LANCE...TAKE FIVE Armstrong won his fifth straight Tour, despite falling twice and completing stage 9 on a recumbent bike.

In his closest win yet Armstrong defeated Jan Ullrich by 61 seconds. But, to be fair, Lance could have increased his lead another two minutes if he'd been willing to fall a few more times.

Lance now has five yellow jerseys, tying him with Miguel Indurain and four others, including a guy who broke into the Padres' locker room in 1974.

Meanwhile, Tyler Hamilton became only the sixth American to win a stage of the Tour. And he did it using a spare handlebar as a collarbone.

KOBE GIVES WIFE $4 MILLION DIAMOND RING I was shocked. It's not like Kobe to give up the rock.

The ring contained an eight-carat purple diamond. Oh, I get it. Eight, to match his number. Purple, because it happened on the road.

The Lakers are standing behind their star. Not only that, Phil Jackson urged Kobe to hire a third lawyer so he could come up with a triangle defense.

This case has everybody on edge. Earlier today, Timberwolves VP Kevin McHale and his wife held a press conference to announce that their four-way deal was consensual.

The Knicks cannot get a break. Due to a clerical error, they traded Latrell Sprewell to three teams and wound up with former Bears tackle Keith Van Horne.

The T-Wolves made out great. They got Sprewell and the rights to a disoriented Calvin Klein.

NFL TRAINING CAMPS IN FULL SWEAT Which means Steve Spurrier has a little more than a month to get down to his final 53 quarterbacks.

Once again the world champion Buccaneers will train at Disney World. There's a one-hour wait to ride Warren Sapp.

The Bengals are in Georgetown, Ky. And the media attention surrounding their top pick, Carson Palmer, is so intense, he's had to check into a local hotel under an assumed name: Akili Klingler.

The Chargers moved their camp to The Home Depot Center in Carson, Calif. Which raises the question: How many two-by-fours do you need to prevent a second-half collapse?

The Jaguars placed DE Tony Brackens on the Physically Unable to Perform List. What a coincidence. Liza did the same thing with David Gest.

This just in: Lions G.M. Matt Millen has been fined another $10 for not sitting through *Bad Boys II*.

In other NFL news Seahawks tight end Jerramy Stevens served seven days in jail after pleading guilty to reckless driving. Police had discovered two open bottles of champagne in his car. Here's my question: How come the cops have an easier time finding things open than Trent Dilfer?

BUCS DON'T STOP HERE WITH SALARY DUMPING Six teams are interested in Brian Giles. Pirates G.M. Kevin McClatchy is trying to work out a time-share.

DOCTORS CLAIM GASH OVER VITALY KLITSCHKO'S EYE HEALED "EXTRAORDINARILY QUICK" Yeah, the two guys living in that space had to move out a month early.

My time is up. You've all been great. Enjoy Them.

THE **NOTES**

(The ring contained an eight-carat purple diamond...) Another color joke to accompany the yellow jersey line three graphs before. As I started to pat myself on the back, I did have this chilling thought: Maybe that was what he was thinking.

(The Lakers are standing behind their star...) Truth be told, the better version of this joke I wrote almost 11 years ago: *O.J. is shrewd. He's going to hire five lawyers and go for the prevent defense.*

(The Bengals are in Georgetown, Ky....) This refers to two first-round Bengal QB busts, Akili Smith and David Klingler. It's not the wife of the Jamie Farr character on *M*A*S*H.*

THE **CUTS**

The Texan is sponsored by the U.S. Postal Service. Which explains why it takes him two weeks to go 2,000 miles in a circle. Finally, I get it. This was cut because the U.S. Postal Service is the finest in the world. And you don't want to piss those guys off.

Tony Siragusa to appear in upcoming episode of The Sopranos.
He'll play a Sicilian. No, wait. That's wrong. He'll play Sicily. During the debate over this line, someone said, "Come on. Is he really that fat?" That was my cue to let it go.

THE **HIT(S)**

"Gloria"

"Here Comes the Night"

I feel so foolish. I thought voters in California were trying to recall Al Davis.

BASEBALL G.M.'S MOTOR RIGHT UP UNTIL TRADE DEADLINE The Yankees acquired All-Star caliber third baseman Aaron Boone from Cincinnati. So, perpetual Yankees prospect Drew Henson's future is clear: He'll go to the fall instructional league, where he'll learn to wear a headset, carry a clipboard and hold for extra points.

Tampa Bay sent righthanded reliever Al Levine to the Royals. That sets up the Devil Rays for their stretch dive.

For the third year in a row, the Mariners made no moves at the deadline. Well, sure. Heathcliff Slocumb wasn't available.

Elsewhere, the Dodgers are 48–0 when leading after eight innings. Great. Give Eric Gagne another reason not to wash his cap.

OHIO STATE NO. 2 IN PRESEASON COACHES' POLL The Buckeyes lost seven key players from last year's national champions. Four starters, and three guys Maurice Clarett said were stolen from the backseat of his car.

Also in college football, Georgia was forced to discipline nine players who tried to sell their SEC championship rings. I'm no yell leader, but I smell the makings of a great chant at Sanford Stadium: "Weeee fence.... Weeee fence.... Weeee fence...."

And somehow, the University of Florida ran a photo of a crocodile on the cover of the Gators' football media guide. Come on. Any idiot knows the difference. A crocodile has a much narrower snout than a gator and favors a run-based attack.

SUPED-UP BUCCANEERS ROUT JETS IN AMERICAN BOWL ESPN2 aired the game live from Tokyo at 5 a.m., then replayed it

that night at 8 on ESPN. And I guess this isn't surprising: Joe Theismann offered to fill in the 12-hour gap with his analysis of four key plays.

The crowd at the Tokyo Dome still isn't particularly football savvy. They kept demanding a larger portion of Simeon Rice.

As expected, everybody played in this first preseason game. Tampa Bay's Michael Pittman got one carry, and his probation officer got four.

In other NFL news the Eagles relaxed the "no outside food ban" at their new stadium, Lincoln Financial Field. The announcement came minutes after Pat's Steaks announced it had developed a working pair of hoagie binoculars.

Dennis Brolin resigned as head groundskeeper for the Patriots after 10 years, citing "philosophical differences" with coach Bill Belichick. What does that mean? Brolin believed the grass should grow vertically *and* spiritually?

It was a classic power struggle. Every time Brolin brought a mower onto the field, Belichick insisted the Turk first inform the grass it was being cut.

MARIO RETURNS FOR ONE MORE SEASON WITH PENGUINS His back feels great, but his doctors have advised him to avoid lifting anyone's hopes about a new arena.

EAGLE COUNTY PROSECUTORS GET ADDITIONAL $105,000 TO TRY KOBE BRYANT CASE Not only that, they're *this close* to getting a shoe deal for the jurors.

My time is up. You've been great. Enjoy the Swingin' Medallions.

THE **NOTES**

(For the third year in a row, the Mariners…) Heathcliff Slocumb was part of one of the three worst trades in baseball history. In 1997, just before the deadline, the Red Sox sent the erratic closer to the Mariners for Jason Varitek and Derek Lowe, who became All-Stars. Slocumb ended up bouncing around, at one point prompting Harry Caray (then alive) to say, "If he's throwing hard, I'm a Chinaman."

(And somehow, the University of Florida ran a photo of a crocodile…) I said, "favors a run-based attack." Of course, if you have a croc with an arm and a good line, go nuts, throw. Throw your brains out. See if I care.

(It was a classic power struggle…) The Turk is the name traditionally given to the member of the coaching staff who tells players they've been released during training camp. Just wondering: If Dan Turk gets cuts, does he break the news to himself?

THE **CUTS**

Clippers owner Donald Sterling named in sexual harassment suit. *The woman claims she was the victim of unwanted hugging and kissing. Unwanted hugging and kissing. Sad. Even with legal action, the Clippers aren't half as exciting as the Lakers.* This was a great story for many, many reasons, timing only one of them. Unfortunately, this got voted down in favor of the "shoe deal for the jurors" line, as it should have been.

Sterling is being sued by a former employee at his real estate company. Apparently, the trouble started when he asked her if she wanted to see his holdings. I said it was a good story. Doesn't mean they're all winners. Does anybody have Tom Dreesen's address?

THE **HIT(S)**

"Double Shot (of My Baby's Love)"

Good to be here. Maybe it's just me, but I prefer Coco Crisp right out of the box.

MIKE TYSON FILES FOR BANKRUPTCY He plans to start fighting under the name Busted Douglas.

It's serious. Next month *The Ring* magazine will start ranking his accountants.

He's so broke, his next face tattoo has to be in red ink.

Tyson has lost or blown an estimated $300 million. Wow. To put that amount in perspective, to make $300 million, Peter McNeely would have to take a dive every day for 2½ years.

KOBE DROPPED AS SPOKESMAN FOR NUTELLA I'll be honest. I never heard of Nutella. I thought it was another nickname for Mark Cuban.

The Mavericks' owner said he believes the league will benefit financially from the Bryant case. You know, he's right. That comment alone should bring in an extra million to the NBA fine office.

Seriously, maybe it's time for David Stern to start fining Cuban's psychiatrist.

SHOCKEY: PART CUBAN? In a recent magazine article the All-Pro tight end referred to Cowboys coach Bill Parcells as a "homo." First, Shockey claimed he was misquoted, then "misinterpreted," and then he apologized. Now he says the remark shouldn't count because he made it during the exhibition season.

In other NFL news the Hall of Fame Game was suspended in the third quarter due to torrential rains and lightning. (Memo to God from *Monday Night Football* producer Fred Gaudelli: Please save further stunts for bad matchups in Weeks 13–17….)

And Philadelphia running back Duce Staley continues his holdout. Apparently, he won't report until the Eagles reverse their policy on bringing outside food into the red zone.

MARLINS DEALING FOR NL WILD CARD Florida is 17 games above .500 since 72-year-old Jack McKeon took over as manager. And 14–4 since McKeon persuaded the players to start eating supper at 3:00 in the afternoon.

The Marlins have undergone a complete metamorphosis under McKeon. These days, you walk into the Florida clubhouse, the speakers are blasting Perry Como.

Meanwhile, it's August. Which means that in order to change teams, players must go unclaimed through waivers—and eBay.

Alex Rodriguez has retracted a comment he made last month, when he claimed he would consider a trade from the Rangers. So, the check cleared.

Devil Rays rookie Rocco Baldelli went 2 for 24 as his average dropped below .300 for the first time since April 2. Insiders believe the slump began when he started dating a Marilyn Monroe impersonator.

The grandson of Twins owner Carl Pohldad is working as an intern at Major League Baseball's New York City office. The job doesn't pay, just like Grandpa.

MARK PHILIPPOUSSIS REPORTEDLY DATING ACTRESS TARA REID Which means he's advanced to Tara's round of 16 boyfriends.

My time is up. You've been great. Enjoy R. Dean Taylor.

THE **NOTES**

(Mike Tyson files for bankruptcy. He plans to start fighting under the name…) I liked this better than my second choice, Mitch "Bled Dry" Green.

(In other NFL news, the Hall of Fame Game was suspended…) Fred Gaudelli produced the ESPYs for years when I worked as the head writer on the show. If he really could get in touch with God, believe me, I'm sure we would have tried to get him as a presenter. *"He's the creator of Sports Night, he's the Creator of All Things, period. Please welcome Aaron Sorkin and God…"*

(Devil Rays rookie Rocco Baldelli went 2 for 24…) He's Italian, plays centerfield, wears number 5 and is good-looking. I had to. Sue me. Aw, hell. Sue Tyson.

THE **CUTS**

Poor Parcells. When he heard about Shockey's remarks, he was so upset, he called off his engagement to Liza Minnelli. Of course, this is not true. Although I tried to argue for this joke by explaining that Parcells once referred to wide receiver Terry Glenn as "she." Which is the exact same thing Liza calls her husbands.

That's not all. In another interview, Shockey says his ultimate sexual fantasy would be "a threesome with a mother and her two twins." Forget their football program, the NCAA should investigate the University of Miami math department.

A threesome with four people. Either Shockey can't add, or he's trying to get a cheaper room rate.

A threesome with four people. Help me out here. Technically, wouldn't that be considered a "hard count"? This was a tremendous item for material, but like many items, it broke too early and all of these jokes would have looked like piling on…Liza and Miami.

THE **HIT(S)**

"Indiana Wants Me"

Good to be here. Just finished reading last week's issue of *SI*.... I'm telling you, Walt Disney must be turning over in his liquid nitrogen.

MASSIVE POWER FAILURE GRIPS CANADA, NORTHEAST 50 million people were without electricity. Although QuesTec says it was only 16.

Experts are still not certain what caused the outage, but they're pretty sure Dave Bliss will end up blaming everything on Patrick Dennehy.

The Mets-Giants game at Shea Stadium was canceled. Let me be the 200th wise-guy sportswriter to say, "It's the only time New York relievers have been lights out this season."

Come on. If the Yankees' bullpen by committee gets any more ineffective, it will be admitted to the United Nations.

Two WNBA games were called off. And attendance actually went up.

It was the first blackout in New York City since the summer of 1977. Unless you're talking about Billy Martin after a Yankees loss.

SHAUN LEAVES CHAD HANGING FOR PGA TITLE Micheel became the first player since John Daly to make the PGA his first Tour victory. Who would have bet on that? You know, other than John Daly's wife?

Strange name, Micheel. But look at the bright side. Alphabetically, it's the closest Phil Mickelson's come to winning a major.

Oak Hill was a tough layout. Tiger Woods lost three excuses in the rough.

Poor Tiger. He dropped so far out of contention in Rochester, for the fourth round he was paired with two marketing executives from Kodak.

Woods tried everything. Before Saturday's round he replaced his Titleist driver with a Nike scythe.

RAFAEL PALMEIRO REJECTS POSSIBLE TRADE TO THE CUBS Apparently the deal fell apart when team officials weren't willing to re-nickname Wrigley Field the Viagra-Friendly Confines.

In other baseball news, last week President Clinton paid a surprise visit to Barry Bonds at Shea. Clinton and Barry have a lot in common. They both go for days now without getting a chance to swing.

NFL LIFTS BAN ON PHARMACEUTICAL ADVERTISING So, figure $20 million and Eli Lilly can get the Dolphins to make their star linebacker change his name to Prozac Thomas.

In a related story, the FDA has approved the Baltimore Ravens' offense as an over-the-counter sleeping aid.

And I don't know if this has anything to do with Jeremy Shockey's recent remarks, but Bill Parcells has discontinued his training-camp tradition of making rookies stand up in the cafeteria and sing show tunes.

LANCE ARMSTRONG RECEIVES $3.2 MILLION BONUS FROM UNITED STATES POSTAL SERVICE FOR WINNING TOUR DE FRANCE Are you like me? Are you thinking that's last year's bonus check just arriving in the mail?

JIM LAMPLEY TO HOST DAYTIME COVERAGE OF 2004 SUMMER OLYMPICS This is Lampley's record-tying 12th Olympic assignment. And he plans to wear his throwback hair from the 1992 Games.

My time is up. You've been great. Enjoy the Box Tops.

THE **NOTES**

(Experts are still not certain what caused the outage...) This was an ugly story out of Baylor, where Coach Bliss admitted to trying to plant disparaging stories after the murder of Dennehy, one of his players, in an attempt to cover up illegal tuition payments he had made to Dennehy. I prefer the good old days of college basketball, with free cars, money under the table and hookers.

(Poor Tiger. He dropped so far out of contention...) Kodak has headquarters in Rochester and sounds slightly funnier than Xerox.

*(**Jim Lampley to host daytime coverage...**)* When Jim Lampley dies, Saint Peter is going to stop him at the gate and say, "Before I let you in, God needs to know the name of your conditioner." And if Lampley is hip, he'll say, "I'll have Fred Gaudelli send him a memo..."

THE **CUTS**

Barring a settlement, cameras will be allowed in the courtroom for the trial. But the shot clock will be turned off. Yeah, I know it doesn't make sense, but the jury getting a shoe deal is more logical?

Major League Baseball denied an Internet report that Pete Rose would be allowed to return to the sport next year. Actually, it wasn't an Internet report. It was a pop-up ad: "Lonely? Tired of being on the 'permanently ineligible list' for hot action?" I believe this was cut because a fact-checker said Pete never popped up.

THE **HIT(S)**

"The Letter"

"Cry Like a Baby"

Before we begin, be honest: How many of you still think the X Games are a track meet for Larry King's wives?

LEBRON SIGNS $12 MILLION DEAL TO PROMOTE SPRITE AND POWERADE It's official: If 7-Up is the "Uncola," Sprite is now the UnKobe.

In other NBA news, Arvydas Sabonis retired. He will return to Lithuania, where his legs have been living for the last two years.

Tony Massenburg signed with the Sacramento Kings. He's working on his 12th NBA roster. That ties the record held by Chucky Brown and Madonna.

U.S. OPEN UNDER WAY WITHOUT SERENA, VENUS Sad. For the next two weeks, you can find more Williamses at the Alcor Life Extension Foundation.

The USA Network hired Anna Kournikova as a correspondent. Perfect. USA never makes it to the semis, either.

The Open organizers are scrambling to generate interest. The third seed on the ladies' side is Mandy Moore.

And the men's draw is suffering as well. No Sampras, no Funny Cide, no Empire Maker…

Meanwhile, Andre Agassi is coming out with his own men's fragrance: Bald Spice.

SACRAMENTO BEE **FIRES WRITER FOR COVERING PIRATES-GIANTS GAME "LIVE" OFF TV FROM UNDISCLOSED LOCATION** Which raises a serious ethical question: What, you can't get hard liquor at Pac Bell Park?

This guy has no business calling himself a journalist. He should be calling himself a candidate for governor of California.

The writer had been with the *Bee* for 34 years. Maybe it's time to retire and pretend to go to the golf course.

MLB DECISION ON PETE ROSE REINSTATEMENT TO BE MADE SOMETIME AFTER WORLD SERIES Which is great because his hair dye doesn't expire until Dec. 1.

In other baseball news, Albert Pujols sat out his suspension. Unfortunately, he'll have to wait until next season to try and extend his hitting Gary Bennett streak.

Pujols punched Bennett in the face during an altercation on July 13. He was originally suspended two games and three Winston Cup races.

Elsewhere, the Brewers are thinking of closing the upper deck at Miller Park. If they had any sense of humor, they'd stretch a tarp across it with the words LESS FILLING.

NFL IMPLEMENTS PHONE SYSTEM ALLOWING BROADCASTERS TO CALL THE LEAGUE TO CLARIFY RULINGS ON FIELD And for an additional $4.95 a minute Paul Tagliabue will talk dirty to them.

Wait, it gets better. If the NFL doesn't deliver the ruling in 30 minutes, it's free.

Panthers All-Pro kick returner Michael Bates was acquitted of drunken driving. Apparently, he managed to convince the judge that his weaving was business-related.

PGA CHAMPIONSHIP DRAWS LOWEST RATINGS SINCE 1996 Only six million people watched the final round. Of course, CBS claims there were more viewers, but they were hidden by the rough at Oak Hill.

FORMER MLB COMMISSIONER PETER UEBERROTH ENTERS RACE FOR CALIFORNIA GOVERNOR He's worth $68 million. Not to mention $94 million in collusion coverage.

ARIZONA LITTLE LEAGUER HITS THREE HOME RUNS IN ONE GAME And thanks to ESPN, his wife and kids got to see the whole thing live.

My time is up. You've been great. Enjoy Lobo.

THE **NOTES**

(Before we begin, be honest…) Mercifully, Kostya Kennedy suspended the rule that every joke must be sports-related. Because, as we know, Larry King has nothing to do with sports. And neither do the X Games.

(U.S. Open under way without Serena, Venus…) Nice break to write a line about Ted Williams that doesn't involve the phrase "disembodied head."

(Elsewhere, the Brewers are thinking of closing the upper deck…) I loved using the expression "If they had a sense of humor" while the Selig family still owned a piece of the team. Strike while the irony is hot.

THE **CUTS**

For those of you unfamiliar with Powerade, it is similar to Gatorade, except it contains 50% less sodium, 90% less hype. Once again, shockingly close to the truth.

A recent New York Times *editorial concluded that Tiger Woods's failure to win a major this year "…is clearly not good for the overall health of golf." Are you like me? Are you thinking the* Times *should go back to making up stuff?* Apparently, they took my advice on all the Saddam Hussein/WMD stories.

THE **HIT(S)**

"Me and You and a Dog Named Boo"

THE **SHOW** | September 8, 2003

So, Mars is now the closest it's been to Earth in 60,000 years. Are you like me? Are you waiting for Bud Selig to announce that the Expos will play 22 games there next season?

EIGHT MORE THAN ENOUGH IN RACE FOR LAST NL PLAYOFF SPOT So many teams are still alive, Bob Costas twisted an ankle backpedaling from his original stance against the wild card.

The Expos drew more than 30,000 at Olympic Stadium for a game against Philadelphia. And what are the odds of this? It was Puerto Rican Appreciation Night.

In other baseball news the Yankees designated reliever Jesse Orosco for assignment. The assignment: Learn shuffleboard.

The Pirates held a Girls' Night Out on Aug. 27 at PNC Park. It came the day after Giles Night Out.

MIKE TYSON SAYS HE'S GOT ADVICE TO OFFER KOBE BRYANT What advice can he give him, other than "don't get the chicken a la king in the prison cafeteria"?

JETS ALTER POLICY IN WHICH 22,000 FANS ON WAITING LIST FOR SEASON TICKETS MUST PAY $50 TO REMAIN ON THE LIST Now, for that same $50, you get a coupon good for a 16-ounce soda.

Sure, it sounds like a rip-off, but think of all the money Jets fans have saved not having to buy Super Bowl tickets for 35 years.

To be fair, the $50 annual charge will be applied against the cost of tickets once you come off the wait list. Or against the cost of your funeral, whichever comes first.

Elsewhere in the NFL, Raiders linebacker Bill Romanowski was fined and suspended after he broke teammate Marcus Williams's orbital bone during a fight in practice. I'm going to give Romo the benefit of the doubt and say it was the glutathione talking.

Romanowski later apologized and explained the whole incident was just part of a spec script he was developing for ESPN's *Playmakers*.

Williams is contemplating legal action. And Al Davis has advised him to sue the city of Oakland because the stands were half full when he was punched.

UNIVERSITY OF MIAMI FOOTBALL GAMES AT ORANGE BOWL TO FEATURE LIMITED ALCOHOL SALES AND A LARGER POLICE PRESENCE And that's just in the Hurricanes' locker room.

Michigan State defeated Western Michigan 26–21 for the Spartans' first win under new coach John Smith. John Smith? Hey, after the way the school handled the Bobby Williams situation, I'd use an alias too.

KELLI'S PERFORMANCE AT WORLD TRACK CHAMPIONSHIPS WHITEWASHED The American sprinter may be stripped of her gold medals in the 100 and 200 meters after testing positive for the substance modafinil. Modafinil is a stimulant that makes you answer only to the name Marion Jones.

White claims the positive drug test was the result of a prescription she was taking for a sleep disorder. Well, give some of that stuff to Jon Drummond, and maybe he'll stop lying down out of the blocks.

ISIAH THOMAS FIRED AS COACH OF THE PACERS Great. This frees him up to buy and fold the WNBA.

PHIL MICKELSON FALLS SHORT IN PITCHING TRYOUT WITH TRIPLE A TOLEDO The Mud Hens are Detroit's top farm club. So, once again, Phil is not quite up to a Tiger's level.

My time is up. You've been great. Enjoy Juice Newton.

THE **NOTES**

(Eight more than enough in race for last NL playoff spot…) This is a cheap, gratuitous, patently false joke that I deeply regretted…30 seconds after Bob Costas agreed to do a foreword.

(Williams is contemplating legal action…) I don't know exactly how many times Al Davis sued the city of Oakland for nonsupport, but he went to court one time to have his name legally changed to *"People v. Davis."*

(University of Miami football games at Orange Bowl to feature limited alcohol sales…) Edwin Pope, please pick up the bitter white courtesy phone.…

THE **CUTS**

Montreal swept a four-game series at home from the Phillies to tighten things up. And after the Phils blew a 10–2 lead in the second game, the vein in Larry Bowa's head was deported. Come on. Tell me you don't have a picture in your head of Bowa's vein waiting to meet him at the border. O.K., once again, just me.

(re: Jets ticket policy) Here's what I don't get. It's $50 a year, plus an additional $4 if your check has to go through the Lincoln Tunnel. We had too many takes on this, and I forgot to include the George Washington Bridge and the Holland Tunnel, so this joke became inaccurate and irresponsible. And that's when the *New York Times* called.…

THE **HIT(S)**

"Angel of the Morning"

Bear with me, I'm still coming down from the NFL Kickoff Concert. Tell me if I'm wrong: If your team needs help against the run, you can do worse than Aretha Franklin.

RAINS END, REIGNS BEGIN AT U.S. OPEN Because of the constant showers, multimedia exhibitions on the three indoor courts at the National Tennis Center had to be taken down so players could practice. So, fans were cheated out of seeing the smash tennis musical, *Strictly Ballboy*.

So much rain at the beginning of Week 2, they had to attach pontoons to the Mac Cam.

By the way, thank God they lifted the "no outside food" ban at Flushing Meadow. The first night I thought I saw Donald Trump trying to smuggle in a tuna melt. Turned out to be his hair.

OHIO STATE NEARLY GETS KICKED IN AZTECS And now it looks as if Maurice Clarett will not be allowed to play for the defending champs this season. But here's the good news: The car he got from the local dealership still has three years of eligibility left.

Turns out that wasn't just any automobile Clarett was driving. That's the car students were going to set on fire if the Buckeyes win again this year.

Clarett's family is considering suing the NFL to let him enter the draft a year early. I think the league will probably settle out of court and give his mom title to a Hummer.

TEXANS NET DOLPHINS David Carr was not sacked in Houston's 21–20 upset over Miami. I didn't see the game. How long was he allowed to wear the red "no-contact" jersey?

Kurt Warner fumbled six times and threw an interception in the Rams' 23–13 loss to the Giants. Hey, Mike Martz, is that a Bulger in your pocket, or are you just happy to see me?

The Bengals debuted their first uniform change in 22 seasons. The new black pants are supposed to be a fashion statement. And I believe that statement is, "We got the white pants beaten off us."

Elsewhere, the Patriots released four-time Pro Bowler Lawyer Milloy. Let's hope the cap money they save will be put to good use— like psychoanalysis for Bill Belichick.

The day after he was let go, Milloy signed with the Bills in a deal loaded with incentives. For instance, he gets $100,000 for every 10 pages of the Patriots' playbook he brings with him.

CBS has changed its NFL theme music, to attract younger viewers. Not only that, the promotional spots feature hip-hop artist Ja Rule. Shouldn't that be Ja Tuck Rule?

According to *Forbes* the Redskins are valued at $952 million. And now that they have released Danny Wuerffel, it's closer to $960 million.

JOE TORRE SAYS MANAGING YANKS ISN'T FUN ANYMORE Come on. What's more fun than wasting $183 million of somebody else's money?

Big league rosters expanded Sept. 1, and the Phillies added an infielder, three pitchers and four replacement veins for Larry Bowa's head.

Juan Gonzalez has hired his third agent of the season. This sounds like something from an episode of *Arli$$*. Except it's, you know, funny.

MADDEN 2004 INCORRECTLY DEPICTS CARDINALS DT MARCUS BELL AS WHITE But on the bright side, he'll never be pulled over by a computerized cop for no reason.

The last three players to appear on the cover of *Madden* video football have suffered serious injuries. So what are the EA folks waiting for? Put Saddam on there!

CART LOSES $34.5 MILLION IN SECOND FISCAL QUARTER See, this is what happens when drivers take the $13.95-a-day collision coverage.

SKECHERS INKS DEAL WITH CHRISTINA AGUILERA The pop star will be exclusively promoting its new line of footwear, Air Hos.

My time is up. You've been great. Enjoy Toto.

THE **NOTES**

(By the way, thank God they lifted the "no outside food" ban...) A year later, I got to write jokes for the Friars roast of Donald Trump. My favorite: *"Donald, I see your hair ordered the salmon...."*

(Big league rosters expanded Sept. 1, and the Phillies added an infielder...) Never give up on a premise you like. If I had, Bowa would still be waiting at the border.

(Madden 2004 *incorrectly depicts Cardinals DT Marcus Bell as white...*) Originally, I had written "Arizona state trooper," but legal made me change it because there was no recorded incident of racial profiling among that force. (Although the state voting not to recognize Martin Luther King Day doesn't exactly move things along.)

(Skechers inks deal with Christina Aguilera...) Of course, this totally makes up for having to change "Arizona state trooper" to "computerized cop."

THE **CUTS**

Rains end, reigns begin at U.S. Open. As if CBS didn't have enough problems. First the weather, then Andy Roddick threatened to not show up for the final unless he got as much money as the cast of Everybody Loves Raymond. A reference to Brad Garrett's ongoing holdout at the time. Man, is that character, Robert Barone, funny. I'll put it up there with Ted Baxter or George Costanza or Buffalo Bill or anyone else you want to run out. One of my favorite Robert Barone lines, to his mother: *"Never lied to me? What about when you told me the ice-cream truck only plays music when they're out of ice cream?"*

THE **HIT(S)**

"Hold the Line"

"Rosanna"

Good to be here. Do I have this right? Ben Affleck broke off his engagement to Rodrigo Lopez?

OHIO STATE REMAINS UNDEFEATED The Buckeyes edged N.C. State in three overtimes. And this is nice. After the game Jim Tressel put four Buckeyes stickers on Maurice Clarett's luggage.

Clarett is being advised by Jim Brown. Hey, that's like….Yeah, like I'm gonna make a joke about Jim Brown.

TONY LA RUSSA BECOMES EIGHTH MANAGER IN MLB HISTORY TO WIN 2,000 GAMES Not to be outdone, the same night, pitching coach Dave Duncan made his 25,000th needless trip to the mound.

Last week a bomb threat delayed the opening of Tropicana Field for 20 minutes. Then, in the eighth, there was another bomb threat when Lou Piniella told Jesus Colome to get loose.

CINCINNATI IS ON THE VERGE OF BECOMING THE FIRST TEAM IN 10 YEARS TO AVERAGE FEWER THAN 30,000 IN A NEW BALLPARK Did somebody say the Big In-the-Red Machine?

Meanwhile, the Padres gave multiyear deals to announcers Jerry Coleman and Ted Leitner. Angels broadcaster Rex Hudler is still looking for a multiyear dealer.

JAMAL LEWIS JA-MAULS CLEVELAND FOR 295 YARDS RUSHING It was a dominant performance. The hardest hit Lewis received all day was an end-zone chest bump from Jonathan Ogden.

In the second quarter Jamal had a 60-yard touchdown run nullified by a penalty. Ten yards for holding … a clinic.

The real challenge for Browns fans is figuring out how to blame this on Tim Couch.

THE NFL IS INVESTIGATING CLAIMS THAT THE REDSKINS CONTACTED LAWYER MILLOY BEFORE HE WAS RELEASED BY THE PATRIOTS Milloy denied the tampering charge, then waved away reporters as he drove off in his new, tricked-out FedEx van.

The Washington, D.C., transit authority billed the NFL $64,000 for extra subway service to the kickoff festival on the Mall. That seems a little steep, but the bill was reduced to $57,000 when they figured in Aerosmith's senior citizen discounts.

Sad times for the Jets. Not only are they 0–2, but the front office is also charging Chad Pennington $50 to keep his place on the Physically Unable to Perform list.

Lambeau Field has finished its $295 million restoration. This season, when Antonio Freeman leaps into the stands, an attendant will hand him a towel and spritz him with cologne.

CAMERAS BANNED FOR KOBE BRYANT HEARING Not only that, the shot clock will be turned off.

And before being sworn in, all witnesses will first have to check in at the scorer's table.

Bryant's defense is now claiming that not only was the sex consensual, but he also had a foul to give.

MOSLEY–DE LA HOYA II TURNS OUT TO BE REPEAT De La Hoya was outraged with the scoring and is planning to hire lawyers to investigate the decision…as soon as the swelling in his face goes down enough for him to see the numbers on his phone.

Boy, you can tell the economy is bad. Yesterday, Oscar laid off 200 publicists.

DEVILS SIGN 42-YEAR-OLD IGOR LARIONOV He hopes to be the first NHL player to deliver an artificial-hip check.

IRAQI WRESTLING TEAM UNABLE TO COMPETE AT WORLD FREESTYLE CHAMPIONSHIPS Too bad. Now we'll never know if they had any Pins of Mat Destruction.

My time is up. You've been great. Enjoy Humble Pie.

THE **NOTES**

(Clarett is being advised by Jim Brown. Hey, that's like…) Loved this. The reason why it's funny is because Jim…Yeah, like I'm gonna make a joke about making a joke about Jim Brown.

*(**Cameras banned for Kobe Bryant hearing…**)* Oh, I get it. Cameras, no shot clock—not funny. No cameras, no shot clock—funny.

(And before being sworn in, all witnesses…)

(Bryant's defense is now claiming that not only was the sex consensual…) Nine months left in the proceedings, and I'm already out of hoop references. Bad clock management. See what happens when you turn the shot clock off?

THE **CUTS**

***Notre Dame embarrassed by Michigan, 38–0, for worst loss in 18 years.** The Irish looked so helpless, they may be entitled to some of that settlement money from the Boston archdiocese.* This was a sensitive issue everywhere except with Letterman. One of the better lines he did came, of course, from Mulholland and Barrie: *Now when you go into confession and say, "Forgive me father for I have sinned," the priest says, "Hah! You've sinned…"*

The Washington, D.C. transit authority billed the NFL $64,000 for extra subway service at the Kickoff Festival on the Mall. It seems a little steep, but that includes six handicapped-accessible cars for Aerosmith. Legally, the only rock band you're allowed to make fun of for being old are the Rolling Stones. Although my friend, the great comic Richard Jeni, had a monster line about opening for Three Dog Night: *"They're on Cycle 4 now."*

Kobe is currently free on a $25,000 bond. It was originally $1 million, but he reduced it by sinking the money ball blindfolded from half-court. I wrote a better version of this a couple of years ago about the bounty on bin Laden: $15 million, $25 million if you kill him and have the Powerball number.

THE **HIT(S)**

None in the U.S. (Huge in Europe, this was Peter Frampton's last band before embarking on his ridiculously successful solo career, and perm.)

Help me out here. In NFL Europe, is it true you're only allowed to drive on the left hash mark?

HURRICANE ISABEL WREAKS HAVOC Unfortunately, the rest of the Tigers' schedule remained intact.

The rain and the 100-mph winds forced the Yankees-Orioles game at Camden Yards to be rescheduled, then suspended after five innings. I have to check, but I believe this is the first time in 30 years the term *blowhard* has been used in connection with the Yankees to describe something other than Steinbrenner.

Be honest. How many of you saw that joke coming from the Bahamas?

The Twins drew their largest midweek September crowd in 12 years. And give credit to Carl Pohlad. He did not take up a collection before turning on the Metrodome air conditioner.

NO. 3 MICHIGAN UPSET The Wolverines were edged by Oregon 31–27. And the Ducks celebrated by adding nine new uniform jersey-pants ensembles.

In Vanderbilt's second game after announcing it was disbanding its athletic department, the Commodores lost to TCU 30–14. Uh-oh, beaten by the Horned Frogs. Well, there goes the biology department.

MEMBERS OF A MOUNT ENTERPRISE, TEXAS, CHURCH PROTEST "GAY DAY" AT THE BALLPARK IN ARLINGTON This raises a serious question: How gay is the name "Mount Enterprise"?

Remember, homosexuality is not a choice. Signing Chan Ho Park for $65 million— that's a choice.

Hey congregants, why stop there? You know, those two guys who were touring stadiums

in that MasterCard commercial a couple of years ago looked way too chummy.

VIKINGS PILLAGE TO 3–0 START Minnesota won its sixth straight regular-season game 23–13 over the Lions, despite losing Daunte Culpepper to an injury. The quarterback spent the second half with ice on his back … in addition to the talk-radio callers that are always there.

The NFL has a new public service ad campaign: "Stay in School, and Don't Sue Us."

This just in: According to Mike Shanahan, Jake Plummer will be listed as probable next week with a hysterectomy.

The NFL did not fine Shanahan, who originally claimed his quarterback had suffered a mild concussion when he had actually sustained a mild shoulder separation. But he may lose five yards for an illegal shift.

The league did not punish Shanahan for two reasons: 1) The rules for reporting in-game injures are vague; and 2) It was funny.

NBC MAKING HOURLONG DRAMA LOOSELY BASED ON LIFE OF LAKERS VP JEANIE BUSS I don't know if America is ready for *The Jerry West Wing.*

"Loosely based" on Jeanie Buss. What does that mean? She's dating *Tito* Jackson?

Elsewhere, Turner has hired Spike Lee to produce commercials for TNT's NBA coverage. I'm no astronomer, but do you get the feeling Mars Blackman is the closest it's been in decades?

WOMEN'S WORLD CUP UNDER WAY Big rule change this year. You cannot use your hands… to take off your shirt.

DON KING PLANS TO START 24-HOUR BOXING CHANNEL IN 2004 Ooh, I hope I'm not too late with a name: Fix Sports Net.

My time is up. You've been great. Enjoy Men Without Hats.

THE **NOTES**

(Members of a Mount Enterprise, Texas, church protest...) I am incredibly proud of these jokes. Look at them—no Liza, no Judy, no show tunes, no costume changes. It's a miracle! Praise Mount Enterprise!

("Loosely based" on Jeanie Buss...) Jeanie Buss and Phil Jackson were an item. Which reminds me. Did you hear about the Zen Buddhist who went up to the hot-dog vendor and said, Can you make me one with everything?

(Women's World Cup under way...) Be honest. How many of you saw this joke coming from Brandi Chastain's closet?

THE **CUTS**

Good to be here. O.K., who wants to leave Dr. Phil's new diet book in Mo Vaughn's driveway? Did I mention that Kostya Kennedy is a giant Met fan? As opposed to Mo Vaughn, who was a giant Met.

Time Warner sells Hawks, Thrashers. *O.K., this explains why, all of a sudden, there's two flavors of non-dairy creamer in the* SI *employee cafeteria.* There is no *SI* employee cafeteria. None that I know of, anyway. But speaking of non-dairy creamer, I wonder if the congregants from Mount Enterprise are also lactose-intolerant.

THE **HIT(S)**

"Safety Dance"

Good to be here. Is it too late to wish John Rocker a happy Rosh Hashanah?

CUBS GRAB LAST SPOT ON PLAYOFF DANCE FLOOR The NL Central champs are ready for the Braves. The rotation is in order, and Dusty Baker got his kid a fake ID.

The surprising Marlins won the NL wild card. And the Florida players dumped a bucket of Ensure over Jack McKeon.

David Szen, the Yankees' traveling secretary, was arrested for misdemeanor battery in Chicago after the team clinched the AL East. Szen allegedly pushed a security guard, then went missing. The police took a while to find him. They had a few leads, but Jeff Weaver blew them.

Szen was released on a personal recognizance bond. Funny. I assumed he'd be bailed out by Mariano Rivera.

In other baseball news the Tigers' magic number is still 1962.

The Tigers finished with 119 losses. I'm just glad Ernie Harwell retired after last season. Although it would have been fun to hear him repeatedly use the word *suck*.

GATORS SCORE 21 IN FOURTH TO BEAT KENTUCKY The Wildcats were knocked off with three minutes left when Jared Lorenzen was intercepted trying to throw the ball away. And I don't get this. After the game Lorenzen claimed he was just trying to keep the ball out of the hands of the LSU offense.

The win kept Florida in the AP Top 25 for the 226th consecutive week. And kept Ron Zook's job secure for a record 170th consecutive hour.

SEBASTIAN JANIKOWSKI SPENDS NIGHT IN JAIL AFTER GETTING IN A FIGHT AT A BAR Which makes him the only Raider who's performing the same as he did last year.

The Eagles won their first game of the season 23–13 in Buffalo. And this is promising. Next week city officials are going to lift the ban at Lincoln Financial Field and let Donovan McNabb bring in his own offense.

Speaking of new facilities, have you seen the renovation job on Soldier Field? Who did this? Queer Eye for the Stadium Guy?

Turns out that during the Browns' comeback win in San Francisco two weeks ago, QB Kelly Holcomb played with a broken bone in his leg. Not to be outdone, during the same game Tim Couch's headset was really, really tight.

The NFL fined the Broncos $25,000 for wearing their white uniforms for their Sept. 14 game in San Diego. A quick-thinking Mike Shanahan immediately listed himself as "questionable" with color blindness.

BRIAN SHAW RETIRES AFTER 14 SEASONS TO TAKE FRONT OFFICE JOB WITH LAKERS I believe his official title is Executive in Charge of Changing the Subject.

Elsewhere, the Heat cut coach Pat Riley's salary by about $500,000. Are you like me? Are you wondering whether, legally, you can sew an Armani label inside a suit from Lands' End?

CAFFEINE TAKEN OFF BANNED SUBSTANCES LIST FOR 2004 OLYMPICS Terrific. This clears the way for putting up a Starbucks next to the high jump pit.

ROUGHLY 12 MILLION PEOPLE PARTICIPATE IN FANTASY FOOTBALL LEAGUES Sure, that sounds like a lot, but if you subtract women and men who have been on a date in the last decade, it's only 11.9 million.

My time is up. You've been great. Enjoy Rick Springfield.

THE **NOTES**

(David Szen, the Yankees' traveling secretary…) This set-up was actually longer than most of Jeff Weaver's starts in 2003.

(Elsewhere, the Heat cut coach Pat Riley's salary…) I'm no psychic, but I bet a couple million guys read this joke and thought, "Hey…"

(Roughly 12 million people participate in fantasy football leagues…) I know it's exciting. I know you feel like a G.M./coach, but for the life of me, I can't see spending more time looking at box scores. I mean, Bill James told me to give it a rest.

By the way, this is a needlessly cruel putdown of all the women in fantasy leagues. All 18 of them.

A women's fantasy football league. That's a bunch of ladies who never hear a guy say, "Honey, just let me see this play…."

THE **CUTS**

Meanwhile, saw a graphic during the Florida State–Duke game: Chris Rix is 0 for 1 in the handicapped zone. There was a sympathetic piece on this item in the same issue. I didn't read it, but I hear they cited turf toe as Rix's handicap.

The Florida State QB was fined $100 for parking illegally. Rix claimed the tag he used belonged to an elderly family friend who he occasionally gets medicine for. You know, if he had just mentioned Chris Weinke by name, he could've gotten out of the ticket. Heisman Trophy winner Weinke was 26 when he graduated from FSU. That's 65 in comedy years.

THE **HIT(S)**

"Jesse's Girl"

"Don't Talk to Stangers"

Before we begin, just wondering: Is Byung-Hyun Kim eligible for the National Do Not Call Registry?

MARLINS ARE SOMETHING WILD Florida eliminated last year's N.L. champion Giants in four games. Which raises the question: What is Jason Schmidt's record on 185 days' rest?

You have to admire baseball's resiliency. Wasn't it only a year ago that Bud Selig wanted to contract two teams, and one Alex Gonzalez?

Florida is now preparing for the NLCS. They've opened up 65,000 seats at Pro Player Stadium and added 50,000 handicapped parking spaces.

The Cubs were confident they were going to win their series. Before Game 5, Sammy Sosa had ordered a case of champagne—with screw-top caps.

You know, if Andruw Jones was any shallower, he'd be dating models.

BUH-BYE WEEK FOR RUSH LIMBAUGH Limbaugh called Donovan McNabb overrated and implied the media wants him to do well because he's black. ESPN executives were livid. Rush wasn't scheduled to make his first racially insensitive remark until Week 10.

Bad week for Limbaugh. He's under investigation for illegally obtaining thousands of dollars' worth of prescription drugs. Of course, Rush will end up accusing the media of wanting the black market to succeed.

Wait a minute. If Rush is found to have used narcotics illegally, does that mean the NFL will let him return in four weeks?

Elsewhere, a federal judge recently ruled the name "Redskins" is not offensive. Okay, fine. Now how about a ruling on grown men wearing dresses and rubber pig noses?

San Diego wide receiver David Boston apologized for missing practice and fighting with a coach by issuing a 37-second statement. Damn. If he'd only spoken another 23 seconds, it would have been the most time-consuming drive by the Chargers offense this season.

Memo to Terrell Owens: I checked. Decaf is not on the NFL banned substances list. Knock yourself out.

CAVALIERS TO APPEAR ON NATIONAL TV 13 TIMES THIS SEASON Big deal. For the next six months the Lakers will be on Court TV every night.

The Nuggets hired Jim Harrick as a scout and consultant. Not only that, his son got a gig not teaching a phantom 8 a.m. class at Denver High.

NHL SHORTENS LEGAL LENGTH OF GOALIE PADS TO 38 INCHES I don't think this is the kind of cutting back the owners had in mind.

The league reported losses of $300 million last year. Man, who knew that safety netting was so expensive?

MIAMI EDGES WEST VIRGINIA TO REMAIN UNBEATEN The Hurricanes will be without starting tailback Frank Gore for the rest of the season. Some people in Miami prefer Jarrett Payton over Gore. Come on. Most people in Dade County still prefer Pat Buchanan over Gore.

JAMES TONEY BRUTALIZES HOLYFIELD FOR NINTH-ROUND TKO After the fight the 40-year-old former champ said he was "going back to the drawing board." Are you like me? Are you hoping that drawing board has a design for an Evander Holyfield Grill?

My time is up. You've been great. Enjoy the Bus Boys.

THE **NOTES**

(Florida is now preparing for the NLCS...) Why I didn't work Chris Rix into this joke is a mystery. Must have been tired.

(You know, if Andruw Jones was any shallower, he'd be dating models...) If you read this and thought, "Man, that's way too clever for him," you're right. A gift from my wife, the brilliant comedian Adrianne Tolsch.

(Wait a minute. If Rush is found to have used narcotics illegally...) This is more than a joke. It's a combination of wishful thinking on my part, and withdrawal from a scandal that died too young.

THE **CUTS**

You know what's creepy? John Ritter now has a more promising career in television than Rush. Again, I have to break out one of my brother's law books, but I believe it's 90 days before you can make a joke in print about a dead guy. That's why the Bo Belinsky line worked so well.

Rush allegedly abused the pain medication OxyContin. OxyContin is a powerful opiate derivative...or is it a vast opiate conspiracy? Once again, we could only do three takes on this. Damn.

In other NFL news, who cares? My point exactly.

Holyfield took a merciless beating at the Mandalay Bay in Las Vegas. By the seventh round, Wayne Newton had sent over two of his cut men. I wanted to say they sent over two cut men from Siegfried and Roy, but I draw the line at "extremely critical."

THE **HIT(S)**

"Boys Are Back in Town"

(Please, I'm begging you, do not confuse this with the 1976 Thin Lizzy classic, mentioned at the end of the November 11, 2002, column. The name of *that* song was "The Boys Are Back in Town." Huge difference.)

Hey, what happened? Didn't anybody tell Pedro Martinez and Don Zimmer about Separation Saturday?

RATINGS FOR THE PLAYOFFS HIGHEST IN YEARS The Cubs are drawing so many viewers, Fox is thinking about a spin-off show, *Grudzielanek in the Middle.*

In its Game 3 victory, Chicago got a two-run homer from Randall Simon. I believe he hit a hanging bratwurst.

Byung-Hyun Kim was left off the Red Sox' roster for the Yankees series because of shoulder tightness. I don't have the latest *Gray's Anatomy*, but when did the Adam's apple become part of the shoulder?

NO. 1 SOONERS LATER LONGHORNS 65–13 The game was such a rout ABC sold the rebroadcasting rights to NBC as a two-part episode of *Miss Match.*

You know a game is out of hand when midway through the second quarter Brent Musburger starts hyping the guys working the chains.

Minnesota was trying to go 7–0 for the first time in 43 years. To give you an idea of how long ago that is, in 1960 the Big Ten had only 10 teams!

GUESS WHO LEADS THE NFC EAST? The Cowboys are 4–1, yet despite the strong start, insiders still believe Bill Parcells may have trouble with Jerry Jones being on the sideline during games. No problem. Jones will just have his plastic surgeon make him look like Dat Ngyuen.

I missed the Jaguars-Dolphins game. Did Jack Del Rio get called for a chop block?

The Broncos beat Pittsburgh 17–14. See what happens when you kick away from Dante Hall?

ESPN is still recovering from the Rush Limbaugh fiasco. I'm pretty sure I heard Steve Young refer to the NFC Central as the And Blue Division.

You know, if Rush Limbaugh had a sense of humor, after he gets out of rehab, he'd show up at *Sunday NFL Countdown* with the open shirt, the sunglasses, the medallion, then start talking point spreads and referring to Chris Berman as Phyllis George.

I didn't even know they kept these statistics, but Warren Sapp's average start of possession during pregame warmups is the opponents' 35.

AL MICHAELS PREPARING HIS DEBUT AS NEW TV VOICE OF THE NBA Do you believe in acquittals? Yesss!!!!

In other NBA news, the first series of LeBron James's signature Nike shoe, the Air Zoom Generation, is modeled after his Hummer H2. Wait a minute, does that mean it can be purchased only by your mother?

Congratulations to Mavs owner Mark Cuban, whose wife had a baby girl. She's already keeping them up at night—crying about officiating.

Dallas signed a player from Iceland. Help me out here. Is that the country or the George Gervin estate?

SCOTT STEVENS AND ANSON CARTER APPEAR ON EPISODE OF *WHOOPI* Well, there goes the entire NHL advertising budget.

The producers of *Whoopi* wanted to get Martin Brodeur, but he's not used to facing that many shots.

SCIENTISTS CLAIM THEY HAVE EVIDENCE THE UNIVERSE IS SHAPED LIKE A SOCCER BALL Not only that, the Big Bang was started by God yelling, "Goooooaaallllll!!!!"

MAN KEEPS 400-POUND BENGAL TIGER IN NEW YORK CITY APARTMENT This answers the question, What ever happened to Brian Blados?

My time is up. You've been great. Enjoy the Standells.

THE **NOTES**

(You know a game is out of hand...) Kostya Kennedy said to me, "I know this is a joke, but I can hear him doing this." High praise.

(You know, if Rush Limbaugh had a sense of humor...) On Martin Luther King Day in 1988, oddsmaker Jimmy the Greek got himself off *The NFL Today* (with Phyllis George and a pre–chain gang hyping Brent Musburger) for telling reporters over lunch in D.C. his theories about black physical superiority and how slave owners would mate the strongest slaves to create a superhuman worker. If the Greek was alive today and had made those same remarks, he'd have his own show on Fox News.

(Man keeps 400-pound Bengal tiger in New York City apartment...) Brian Blados was a longtime tackle for the Bengals who came as close to 400 as anyone since Ted Williams.

THE **CUTS**

Jaguars All-Pro punter Chris Hanson opened a giant gash on his leg when he mishandled an axe Coach Jack Del Rio kept in the locker room for motivational purposes. And really, is there anything more motivational than a bunch of players screaming, "Put pressure on it until the paramedics get here!" I love the drama of this joke, but it went on too long. Meanwhile, want to hear something ironic? Hanson had a no-cut contract.

To celebrate the opening of hockey season, NHL commissioner Gary Bettman rang the closing bell at the New York Stock Exchange. Here's what I don't get. Eric Lindros is still complaining of headaches. Once again, to recap: *ESPN Magazine*—concussion friendly. *Sports Illustrated*—concussion sensitive.

THE **HIT(S)**

"Dirty Water"

(The L.A.-based Standells hit the charts for the only time with this 1965 tribute to Boston. It is cued up and blared over the Fenway Park P.A. after every Red Sox win. I was trying to get a little mojo going here. Turns out it took a year and five days to work....)

Good to be here. Just wondering. Do you think, for daylight savings, Grady Little will set his clocks back four batters?

WORLD SERIES: FISH OR CUT BABE Are you like me? Are you praying the Jeter-Steinbrenner Visa ads are best-of-three?

Marlins World Series tickets sold out in three hours. Team officials in Miami attribute that to Internet purchases and heavy walk-up sales. Or is that walker-up sales?

Game 7 of the ALCS drew a 73 share in Boston. That means 73% of the televisions in use were watching the game. I know what you're thinking, but technically a TV being thrown out a window during Aaron Boone's home run trot is still "in use."

The Red Sox were confident. They had two cases of champagne chilling in a bucket of liquid nitrogen in Arizona.

USC DEFROCKS NOTRE DAME 45–14 The Irish are now 2–4. And they're thinking of replacing Touchdown Jesus with a mural of John the Baptist making the call for holding.

I don't want to tell Tyrone Willingham his business, but it may be time to break out the lucky green booster money.

Elsewhere, Oklahoma remained unbeaten after routing Missouri 34–13. On the bright side Missouri fans did not allow a postgame sack.

Boston College president William Leahy says his school is going to the ACC "because of academics and finances, as well as athletics." And Miami is going there for all those reasons, plus the more lenient judges.

ESPN reporter Michele Tafoya apologized for purposely dropping beer on some rowdy fans while attending the Michigan-Minnesota game on Oct. 10. Apologize? Are you kidding? Finally, something we all want to see from a sideline reporter!

NBA PLANS SWITCH TO SIX DIVISIONS Let me guess: Atlantic, Central, Midwest, South,

Pacific and Special Victims Unit?

Kobe Bryant sat out the Lakers' preseason game against Phoenix. Luckily, the prosecution will not be allowed to introduce any DNP evidence.

TITANS HAND PANTHERS FIRST LOSS Just when fans in Carolina finally realized that Jake Delhomme was not the name of a top fuel dragster.

The Rams are undefeated at home. And for the last two weeks Kurt Warner's wife has been calling into local radio stations and just doing traffic and weather.

Elsewhere, the Chargers upset the Browns in Cleveland. Sounds like Marty Schottenheimer went to the wrong locker room to deliver his pregame pep talk.

Despite their 2–3 start the Eagles are sticking with Donovan McNabb. He received a huge vote of confidence from Rush Limbaugh's maid.

Rush is in a no-nonsense rehab. He's not even allowed to say, "I'll take the Vikes 10 times."

MARIO LEMIEUX SWITCHES HIS EQUIP-MENT-ENDORSEMENT DEAL FROM NIKE TO CCM It's for two years, or six retirements.

This season NHL teams are allowed to wear their dark jerseys at home. And barring an injunction, Red Wings fans will have their choice of throwing octopus or squid.

Rangers G.M.–coach Glen Sather is enforcing a new rule this season: English will be the only language spoken on the ice, the bench and in the locker room. O.K., that's it. We have to make helmets mandatory for coaches.

PATRIOTS BEAT DOLPHINS FOR FIRST SEP-TEMBER/OCTOBER WIN EVER IN MIAMI I think I speak for New England sports fans everywhere when I say, "Oh, we feel MUCH better now."

My time is up. You've been great. Enjoy Paper Lace.

THE **NOTES**

(Good to be here. Just wondering…) I'll try to be brief and dispassionate. I was at Game 7 of the ALCS. Good seats, too. First base line, two rows back, in Giuliani's comb-over. O.K., it's the bottom of the eighth, Pedro Martinez comes out. I had him at 101 pitches, but I figure he'd get a batter or two. No problem. But the first guy that gets on, he's out of there. Nick Johnson pops his second pitch weakly to short. One out. Derek Jeter comes up. Pedro goes 0 and 2 on Jeter. I have not said a word in five innings. I felt the best thing was to be quiet and not piss off fate. But I couldn't take it. I yell, "Pedro, don't throw him a strike!" He throws a strike. Double in the gap. The bullpen stirs. O.K., give him one more batter. He goes 0 and 2 on Bernie Williams. Hard single. Here comes Grady Little. Smart. Good move. Good baseball. All is right with the world. Go ahead, take the ball. Take it. Take it. TAKE IT!!! You know the rest.

(USC defrocks Notre Dame 45–14…) Not even a lousy Notre Dame team could lift my spirits that week. But I enjoyed finding a hitherto unexplored angle for Touchdown Jesus. By the way, I use a state-of-the-art version of the New Testament: 12 apostles, zero carbs.

(Rush is in a no-nonsense rehab…) Another gift from Mark Patrick, a true degenerate who knows betting lingo and the street name for Vicodin.

(Patriots beat Dolphins for first September/October win ever in Miami…) Just couldn't let it go.

THE **CUTS**

Marlins reliever Chad Fox has undergone two Tommy John elbow surgeries. He didn't need the second one, but he won a raffle at Dr. Frank Jobe's office. Dr. Jobe invented Tommy John surgery. I had this joke in my pocket for six months, just waiting for the right moment. In comes Chad Fox into the World Series. There goes the joke, back into my pocket.

*CART drivers featured in upcoming **CSI: Miami**. It's a little predictable. At the end of the episode, Tony George confesses to killing the series.* This is way too inside. Tony George is the greased monkey who runs the Indy Racing League, CART's former open-wheel racing competitor. My allegiance is to CART and Letterman/Rahal Racing. O.K., I've explained it, and I can tell by the glazed look you still don't care.

THE **HIT(S)**

"The Night Chicago Died" (which, given the Cubs-Marlins series, is beyond fitting)

Good to be back. I was at Brian Billick's yard sale. Got two VCRs for a buck.

SHAQ SAYS FEUD WITH KOBE IS OVER It must be. The other day at a shoot-around, Shaq was wearing an eight-carat diamond.

Speaking of the Lakers, technically, shouldn't Karl Malone now be known as the Subpoena Man?

David Stern begins his 20th season as NBA commissioner … and his eighth year knowing a posse is not a bunch of guys on horses.

And Scottie Pippen is back with the Bulls. However, he will still be available to the Blazers as a character witness.

MARLINS RE-SIGN JACK McKEON And thanks to Medicare, it was only an $8 copay.

The Marlins and Miami–Dade County have approved plans to fund a new ballpark that would open in 2007. Wow. That gives them less than three years to gut and rebuild the team.

If the new ballpark is built, the team promises to change its name to the Miami Marlins. O.K., but if you really want to draw some crowds, how about changing the name to Phish?

Elsewhere, the Red Sox' recently fired manager, Grady Little, is enjoying the time off. Although last night he waited too long to get take-out food.

Boston's Manny Ramirez made it through irrevocable waivers unclaimed. Now the only way the Red Sox can get rid of him is if they trade him and agree to assume 80% of his attitude.

FOUR OF TOP 10 FALL Help me out here. Does that make next week Superfluous Saturday?

Virginia Tech upset undefeated Miami. Costly loss for the Hurricanes. They have to pay the Hokies' ACC entry fee.

Michigan RB Chris Perry set a school record with 51 carries in the Wolverines' 27–20 win over Michigan State. All right, who's letting Bo Schembechler call plays?

GIANTS EDGE JETS IN OT First, the Jets were sloppy and turned the ball over. Then the Giants blew a 14-point lead and missed a field goal early in overtime. Fans at the Meadowlands didn't know who to boo… until they all settled on Jeff Weaver.

The Colts' Mike Vanderjagt is 21 for 21 in field goals. And this is sweet. Peyton Manning now calls him "our idiot savant kicker."

Are you like me? Do you think that Broncos coach Mike Shanahan is a day away from making a "name your price" call to Bubby Brister?

Corey Dillon missed the Bengals' win over the Seahawks after getting in a car accident. And now he's demanding the car be traded to Dallas.

FDA CLASSIFIES THG AS ILLEGAL STEROID So, once again, the only legal muscle-building supplement is spinach.

THG is known as a "designer steroid." What does that mean? It overdevelops your delts, pecs and sense of fashion?

You spend hours in the gym—trying to accessorize?

You get acne in the shape of the Polo guy?

U.S. SENATORS DISCUSS ELIMINATING BCS Of course, the French want to wait until the U.N. inspectors are finished.

P. DIDDY COMPLETES NEW YORK CITY MARATHON IN 4:14:54 Unfortunately, the remix runs 5:07:23.

My time is up. You've been great. Enjoy King Harvest.

THE **NOTES**

(David Stern begins his 20th season as NBA commissioner...) Which reminds me of the old joke which ends with the Lone Ranger saying, "No, Tonto. I said, 'Crazy Horse.' Not 'Crazy Whores....'"

(Elsewhere, the Red Sox recently fired manager Grady Little...) Yeah, still bitter.

(P. Diddy completes New York City marathon in 4:14.54...) The original joke had the phrase "extended dance mix," but *SI* researcher Caryn Prine was kind enough to call and tell me the correct expression was "remix." And was even kinder not to refer to me as "Grandpa."

THE **CUTS**

In a recent interview, Kobe Bryant called his Laker teammate fat, childish, unprofessional, selfish and jealous. We can argue the first four, but what's Shaq jealous about? That Kobe didn't have to pay his incidental bill at the Cordillera Spa? Love this, but after the diamond and Subpoena Man, there was no room.

The Sox insist the move had nothing to do with Grady leaving Pedro Martinez in during Game 7 of the ALCS. I believe that. And I believe Theo Epstein put Manny Ramirez on waivers to impress the producers of MTV's Punk'd. *Way way way too subtle a reference to Theo Epstein's youth.*

THG has been banned by Major League Baseball and the NFL, but not the NBA. For that to happen, it would require the approval of the players union. And the approval would have to be consensual. Still no room.

THE **HIT(S)**

"Dancing in the Moonlight"

O.K., by applause, how many of you thought the only person who could beat Tiger Woods for a money title was Oprah?

TOP-RANKED OKLAHOMA DECIMATES TEXAS A&M 77–0 It was the most lopsided loss in A&M history and would have been worse if the Sooners hadn't let the Aggies play the last 30 minutes with the 12th Man.

In a recent interview Joe Paterno said he would only leave Penn State if the White House said he was needed in Iraq. What are the odds he'd pick the only place whose rebuilding program may take longer?

NFL NETWORK GOES ON AIR It's just like the Golf Channel. Except the Golf Channel has more live football.

All NFL 24 hours a day, seven days a week. That's a lot of programming to fill. On Day Two, the first hour was just Rich Eisen sitting around, waiting for the results of his random drug test.

Warren Sapp and Michael Strahan have debuted a regular spot in which they debate various league issues. I hope I'm not too late with a title: *Pardon the Encroachment.*

WIZARDS OWNER ABE POLLIN HAS REMOVED ALL MICHAEL JORDAN–RELATED ITEMS FROM THE MCI CENTER Help me out here. Does that include 7,000 filled seats?

Kobe Bryant's next court appearance was moved from Monday, Nov. 10, to Thursday, Nov. 13, at the request of the prosecutors. Do you know what this means? They prefer *CSI: Miami* to the regular *CSI.*

In other NBA news, Kevin Garnett was fined $5,000 for throwing a ball into the stands. And this is lame. KG claims he spotted an open Wally Szczerbiak.

RAMS BEAT RAVENS 33–22 St. Louis improved to 6–3 despite four turnovers and 121 yards of total offense. The win was so ugly it was automatically added to the cast of NBC's *Average Joe.*

Elsewhere, the Falcons upset the Giants to end their seven-game losing streak and give Dan Reeves his 200th career win. And today Arthur Blank took out a full-page ad apologizing for Deion Sanders.

What a relief for Reeves. He had been stuck at 199 longer than Mario Mendoza.

Raiders defensive tackle Darrell Russell was reinstated a year and a half after testing positive for ecstasy. He was picked up by Steve Spurrier, which, coincidentally, is one of the side effects of ecstasy.

RED SOX TEAM DOCTOR ARRESTED ON DRUNK DRIVING CHARGES He failed four field sobriety tests. And Red Sox fans are blaming Grady Little for leaving him in for the last three.

Serious bust. His blood alcohol level was .1918.

Elsewhere, the White Sox named Ozzie Guillen their new manager. Guillen retired in 2000 and has spent the last three years cleaning his batting helmet.

MESSIER MOVES TO SECOND ON ALLTIME NHL SCORING PARADE The 24-year veteran scored an empty-net goal to pass Gordie Howe. Here's what I don't get. The assists went to Kovalev and Gretzky.

The NHL has hired former Al Gore consultants to do p.r. So, if they do their job, get ready for four years off.

MU'AMMAR GADHAFI'S SON, ITALIAN SOCCER PLAYER, TESTS POSITIVE FOR STEROIDS Of course the kid claims he got the stuff from his twin brother, Ozzie Gaddafi.

U.S. BASEBALL TEAM FAILS TO QUALIFY FOR OLYMPICS Great. Now Roger Clemens has to convince people he's Dutch.

My time is up. You've been great. Enjoy the Motels.

THE **NOTES**

(In other NBA news, Kevin Garnett was fined...) Wally Szczerbiak was injured at the time. Which raises the question: When is Wally Szczerbiak not injured?

(What a relief for Reeves...) See the beauty of a previous explained reference (May 5, 2003, column)? Feel free to puff your chest for getting this.

(Red Sox team doctor arrested on drunk driving charges...) Still bitter.

(Mu'ammar Gadhafi's son...) And continue puffing your chest because you know all about Ozzie Canseco.

THE **CUTS**

Deion Sanders has begun campaigning for a shot to coach the Falcons. What's he going to do? Introduce a Waistcoats Offense? That sound you hear is a standing ovation from the LPS—Lame Pun Society.

Mohammar Khadaffi's son, Italian soccer player, tests positive for steroids. *See what happens when you don't go into the family business?* Lesson #64: Just because you choose an alternate spelling of a murderous dictator's name, the "K" sound, don't make a line funny.

THE **HIT(S)**

"Only the Lonely"

Good to be here. Just heard about David Blaine's next stunt: He's going to try and survive 48 consecutive hours in Butch Davis's doghouse.

LEBRON JAMES SIGNS RECORDING CONTRACT FOR ALBUM TO BE PRODUCED BY JAY-Z This could spawn a whole new music genre: Hype-Hop.

In other NBA news, 15 teams average less than 90 points a game. Some suggest widening the rim to increase scoring. Hey, while we're at it, how about redesigning the paint to include an express lane?

New Pacers coach Rick Carlisle has implemented a 2–3 zone trap. And that's just to restrain Ron Artest.

TCU STAYS UNBEATEN The Horned Frogs have gone 10–0 for the first time in 65 years. In case you don't remember, in 1938 the BCS had TCU ranked behind Hitler, Mussolini, Stalin and Notre Dame.

Of course, the coaches' poll had Notre Dame ahead of Mussolini.

Elsewhere, Miami edged Syracuse, 17–10, behind backup QB Derrick Crudup. Brock Berlin got in for one series, and that was only after bringing a note of apology from Kellen Winslow Sr.

FIVE TO SEVEN PERCENT OF MLB PLAYERS TEST POSITIVE FOR STEROIDS The findings have a margin of error of plus/minus two Cansecos.

Dick Pound, chairman of the World Anti-Doping Agency, called baseball's policy on steroids a "complete joke." I don't want to nitpick, but if you're the head of the *World* Anti-Doping Agency, shouldn't you change your name to Dick Kilo?

All major leaguers will now be subject to testing completely random and arbitrary. Sounds like a job for QuesTec.

Here's the new punishment system: First offense, you must undergo treatment. Second offense, 15-day suspension and $10,000 fine.

Third offense, special guest appearance on ESPN's *Playmakers*.

GREEK GOVERNMENT GIVES PROSTITUTES GO-AHEAD TO WORK DURING NEXT YEAR'S OLYMPICS O.K., now that that's out of the way, we can get down to the minor stuff—like building the venues.

The prostitutes are ready. They've ordered condoms in the colors of the Olympic rings.

You know what's great about prostitutes at the Olympics? No matter what nation you're from, they let you finish first.

In other Olympic news, transsexuals will be allowed to compete in the Games. But only in pairs skating.

BENGALS MAKE CHIEFS PAST PERFECT Cincinnati gave K.C. its first defeat, 24–19. Everyone contributed: Peter Warrick scored two touchdowns, and Nick Buoniconti had six tackles.

Elsewhere, the Eagles debuted black jerseys in their win over the Giants. Hmmm. Black jerseys. Wonder if the media wants them to succeed?

Drew Bledsoe was sacked four times in the Bills' loss to the Texans. In fact, Bledsoe's been hit so much the last month, he was made an honorary Liza Minnelli husband.

Broncos RB Mike Anderson was given a four-game suspension after testing positive for marijuana. On the injury report he's listed as "doubtful, man."

Anderson claims he tested positive only because he inhaled secondhand smoke. Who's this guy being represented by, Jacoby and Snoop Dogg?

ANDY RODDICK TO STAR IN REALITY SHOW Gripping television. Every week viewers can vote off another visor.

LEVITRA TITLE SPONSOR OF SKINS GAME Maybe it's me, but I don't think I'm going to hear the phrase, "He's got about an 18-footer…" the same way ever again.

My time is up. You've been great. Enjoy Styx.

THE **NOTES**

(TCU stays unbeaten…) Whenever I see an item refer to something over 50 years old, I go back to the year and try to give the joke historical context. Thank God Hitler and Mussolini were around to bail me out.

(Of course, the coaches' poll had Notre Dame ahead of Mussolini…) Cheap, gratuitous, unfair and yet strangely satisfying.

(Elsewhere, the Eagles debuted black jerseys…) This Rush Limbaugh callback does not work unless it's Donovan McNabb's team.

(Levitra title sponsor of Skins Game…) SON: Daddy, why is this funny? FATHER: Hey, look! Here's a piece on boxing by Franz Lidz!

THE **CUTS**

In other baseball news, Royals shortstop Angel Berroa was the surprise winner for AL Rookie of the Year. Here's what happened. Two writers who meant to vote for Hideki Matsui got confused and instead of Godzilla, wrote in Reptillicus. This was cut because of the fear some people might find it offensive. O.K., but here is my defense: 1) Matsui was nicknamed "Godzilla" by the Japanese; 2) baseball writers who vote have been known to be confused; 3) Reptillicus has always been underappreciated and could use the props.

Prostitution is legal in Greece. And you know what that means: Pimps give receipts. I'd have to check, but I believe this is the first time in the history of literature that "pimp" and "receipt" have been used in the same sentence. Wait. Maybe Noam Chomsky did it.

THE **HIT(S)**

"Come Sail Away"

"Babe"

I've got to start reading the front of the newspaper. I thought "Neverland" was a reference to the Bengals' being in first place.

CANADIENS, OILERS PONDER LIFE The teams drew 57,000 at Commonwealth Stadium in the first regular-season outdoor game in NHL history. In Canada the windchill was listed as −28. Isn't it great to see −28 when it's not the line on Oklahoma?

The alumni were affected by the elements. Claude Lemieux dropped his gloves three times—to blow on his hands.

A streaker ran out in the middle of the alumni game, wearing only a shirt, a hat and an artfully placed sock, and was chased by police for several minutes. Are you like me? Are you thinking we have a new spokesman for Labatt?

NFL SAYS RAIDERS WHO TESTED POSITIVE FOR THG WON'T BE SUSPENDED What is this, Bring Bud Selig to Work Day?

The NFL Players Association was irate that the results were leaked to the media. (Note to union reps: Next time, when discussing drug tests, check *Roget's* and find another word for *leak*.)

BUCCANEERS DEACTIVATE KEYSHAWN JOHNSON Finally, they sent him on an "out" route.

Keyshawn's teammates had grown used to his complaining. In fact, two weeks ago Simeon Rice guaranteed a whine.

The former All-Pro had been dropping hints he wasn't happy. He put his Tampa home up for sale, and he changed the name of his local restaurant from Profusion to TGI Free Agency.

Elsewhere, the Lions lost their 22nd straight road game, one shy of the NFL record. Sad. No luck on the road, problems at home.... No, wait. I was thinking of William Green.

The Nov. 16 Cowboys-Patriots game on ESPN was the fifth-most-watched cable broadcast ever. Not only that, most of the viewers stuck around for the postgame open-mouth kiss between Parcells and Belichick.

WOLVERINES GNAW BUCKEYES 35–21 But don't worry about Ohio State. The team can still play for the national championship, thanks to the brand-new BCS Do-Over Bowl.

Actually, I believe it's the Xerox Do-Over Bowl.

Elsewhere, No. 3 LSU beat No. 15 Mississippi 17–14. The Tigers sacked Eli Manning three times, but a Manning family lawyer says it was *not* because he left his backside exposed.

NBA STARS PLAY FOR CHARITY ON *WHEEL OF FORTUNE* Unfortunately the hosts were Pat Sajak and Jahidi White.

The producers really blew it. How can you have NBA Week on *Wheel of Fortune* and not get Rasheed Wallace to show up and say, "Is there a *T*?"

Some people just don't know the game. Three times Bill Walton asked Sajak if he could buy an ankle.

U.S. GOVERNMENT OWES $800,000 IN DUES TO WORLD ANTI-DOPING AGENCY But the street value is closer to $4 million.

That's $800,000 overdue to an antidoping agency. You know, if Barry Bonds is really serious about changing his image, he should break out that MasterCard!

METS FIRE SCOUT FOR RACIALLY INSENSITIVE REMARKS TO DODGERS EXECUTIVE KIM NG Bill Singer blamed his actions on a chemical imbalance that resulted from his new diet combined with alcohol. Yeah, I believe it's that new Low Carb, High Slur diet.

CONVERSE DEBUTS NEW $90 SHOE, "LOADED WEAPON" Or, as they're known on the street, Glock Taylors.

NO WINNERS IN PRESIDENTS CUP Help me out here. Does that mean the Supreme Court will just give it to Bush?

My time is up. You've been great. Enjoy Foghat.

THE **NOTES**

(Actually, I believe it's the Xerox Do-Over Bowl…) UNDER 10 WORDS!! Check from God to come (see October 14, 2002, column)….

(Elsewhere, No. 3 LSU beat No. 15 Mississippi…) A story had surfaced about some crude locker room behavior by Peyton Manning while he was at Tennessee. It went away quickly. I'd rather not know what happened. Maybe we should ask Zeke Mowatt….

(NBA stars play for charity on Wheel of Fortune…) Jahidi White is such an obscure player, Jack Haley can make fun of him.

(Some people just don't know the game…) Bill Walton's NBA career was curtailed severely due to what David Halberstam called "having your grandmother's feet."

THE **CUTS**

Four Raiders test positive for THG. *Just syringe, baby.* Simple, elegant, potential lawsuit.

You can tell "Profusion" is Keyshawn's restaurant. It caters to private parties, but no reception is longer than 11 yards. I had written this joke two years before at *ESPN Magazine*, when Keyshawn was having a bad season, but never got to work it in. I tried here, but was flagged by Kostya for unnecessary mirth.

The Montreal-Edmonton game was preceded by an Oilers-Canadiens alumni game. Classic. It ended when Wayne Gretzky's mom called him in for dinner. Michael Farber, *SI*'s fine hockey writer, had a similar line in his lead. I magnanimously withdrew this joke, so I could not-so-magnanimously call attention to it here.

THE **HIT(S)**

"Slow Ride"

THE SHOW | December 8, 2003

Did you see Glen Campbell wearing a Diamondbacks jersey in his DWI mug shot? Are you like me? Were you afraid he was compensation in the Curt Schilling deal?

MICHAEL VICK RETURNS TO FALCONS LINEUP Now Dan Reeves can switch from Prozac back to Zocor.

Elsewhere, the Ravens beat the 49ers. And I don't get this. After the game Paul Tagliabue ordered Brian Billick to take 39 seconds less in the shower.

All four teams that played on Thanksgiving wore throwback jerseys. And Jerry Jones wore his original face from Super Bowl XXVII.

Fox's holiday pregame show featured a segment, *The Making of a Dallas Cowboys Cheerleader*. Jillian Barberie did the interviews, and Keyshawn Johnson gave a tour through a silicone plant.

The league chastised Chiefs coach Dick Vermeil after he promised a bottle of wine to Morten Andersen if he kicked a game-winning field goal against the Raiders, saying it constituted a performance bonus. Not only that, if you remove the cap, it's 15 yards.

And in a *60 Minutes* interview, Lawrence Taylor said that he sent call girls to opponents' hotel rooms the night before games. I'm no defensive coordinator, but I believe that's called a pimp fake.

LSU CRUSHES ARKANSAS 55–24 The Tigers have an outside shot to vault over USC and into the national title game against Oklahoma, thanks to a brand-new BCS criterion: quality Claytons.

By the way, who came up with the SEC tiebreakers, William H. Donaldson?

CURT IS NOW IN SESSION The Red Sox and Schilling were never far apart. Although QuesTec claims their first offering was way outside.

The Diamondbacks wanted Alfonso Soriano and Nick Johnson from the Yankees, but ended up dealing their ace to Boston for three unproven pitchers and another player. I think I speak for Jerry Colangelo when I say, "George Steinbrenner, you've been punk'd!"

Meanwhile, the Rangers face a dilemma. Trade Alex Rodriguez for a player of less value or get President Bush to host a fundraiser to pay the rest of his contract.

NHL FIGHTING UP 30% Things are getting out of hand. Every penalty box is now a timeshare.

The other night I saw a dozen guys pull sweaters over their heads. Turned out to be embarrassed Capitals fans.

The Rangers may acquire Jaromir Jagr. All that's holding up the deal is whether or not there's enough room behind the bench for a baccarat table.

BULLS TRADE JALEN ROSE TO RAPTORS I feel so foolish. I thought the Jalen Rose trading deadline was Jan. 15.

Disneyworld has come up with a new promotion honoring the Orlando Magic: the "L" ticket.

And the Seven Dwarfs are this close to replacing Doc with Mike Fratello.

NEW SPORTS DRINK, ACCELERADE, HITS THE MARKET Accelerade is "protein-spiked." It's available in two flavors: orange-cheese and salmon-lime.

DAVID BECKHAM AWARDED OBE BY QUEEN ELIZABETH It was a formal event at Buckingham Palace. Beckham wore a top hat and tails, and Prince Charles didn't hit on him.

My time is up. You've been great. Enjoy Redbone.

THE **NOTES**

(And in a 60 Minutes interview, Lawrence Taylor said he sent call girls…)
And if this had been in Greece, he could have gotten a receipt.

(By the way, who came up with the SEC tiebreakers…) Donaldson's the head of the Securities and Exchange Commission. Seriously, does anybody get this, besides Martha Stewart?

(And the Seven Dwarfs are this close…) A vague reference to about-to-be-fired Magic coach Doc Rivers, and a less-than-vague reference to the vertically challenged Czar of the Telestrator.

THE **CUTS**

LSU crushes Arkansas, 55–24. What a rout. The only LSU player who didn't get into the game was Dennis Quaid's character in Everybody's All-American. Great novel by *SI*'s Frank Deford, unfortunate screen adaptation. Yeah, I believed John Goodman as a 21-year-old pulling guard.

Last week, the Kings distributed free tickets in exchange for frozen turkeys. You know the proper way to prepare a frozen turkey? You have to baste it every 15 minutes with a Zamboni. Ladies and gentlemen, give it up for your headliner, Steven Wright!

THE **HIT(S)**

"Come and Get Your Love"

Finally saw *Cold Case* last week. What a ripoff. Not one word about Ted Williams.

KANSAS STATE LEAVES OKLAHOMA AT BIG 12 ... AND 1 You know, if ABC had any sense of humor, it would have renamed the BCS selection show "a very special episode of *Less Than Perfect*."

Apparently, the only way the Sooners weren't going to the Sugar Bowl is if they'd lost to Dartmouth.

I kept switching back and forth to LSU-Georgia. And I swear at one point I heard Verne Lundquist say, "Remember, this is best of seven."

Army became the first Division I team to go 0–13. However, Donald Rumsfeld is still insisting they have enough manpower.

MAGIC GOES 1–19 If the team continues at this pace, it will be mathematically eliminated from the Eastern Conference playoffs by Memorial Day.

The Knicks are on a five-game Western road trip. They better be careful. The parts warranty on Antonio McDyess is void in Oregon and Utah.

Just got the latest version of Microsoft Word. Unbelievable. If you press CTRL + Z, it automatically prints "another Blazer arrested."

STILL 186 FREE AGENTS AVAILABLE The Yankees have offers out to everyone except Albert Belle, Tony Fossas and Sidd Finch. (And that's because Brian Cashman can't find a current phone number for Finch.)

The Reds' Great American Ballpark will have $20 million of construction during the off-season. Or $19.5 million more than Carl Lindner will spend on free agents.

PATS PLOW DOLPHINS FOR AFC EAST TITLE Actually, Foxboro Stadium was in good condition despite the blizzard. A quick-thinking ground crew had the field covered until just before game time with Ted Washington's road jersey.

Elsewhere, Indianapolis edged Tennessee in a battle for first place. The Colts are now 10–3

and in danger of not collapsing for the first time in three years.

More than 19 million viewers watched the Lawrence Taylor interview on *60 Minutes*, the show's biggest audience since 2000. CBS was so impressed, they're thinking of giving LT his own series, *Everybody Loves Rehab*.

Advertising experts say the Rush Limbaugh controversy has done wonders for Donovan McNabb's marketability. Forget that, what about what Limbaugh has done for the marketability of OxyContin?

Bill Callahan recently called the Raiders "the dumbest team in America" after their loss to Denver. Hey, wait a minute, I think the Buccaneers may have something to say about this.

And speaking of dumb teams, what about Paris Hilton and Nicole Richie?

What about Paris Hilton and anyone?

BUSH HOSTS WINSTON CUP DRIVERS Nine out of the top 10 finishers showed up at the White House. Jeff Gordon had to drop out at the last minute.... Gear box problems.

The President made a big NASCAR entrance. He arrived in the pocket of a tobacco industry executive.

One embarrassing moment. Bush asked Bill France why his country didn't support the war in Iraq.

INSTANT REPLAY CELEBRATES 40TH ANNIVERSARY Coincidentally, it's also the 40th anniversary of the first husband who said, "Honey, just let me see this one more time, I swear."

Did I say "husband"? I meant ex-husband.

MADDEN 2004 WINS TOP PRIZE AT FIRST-EVER VIDEO GAME AWARDS The awards were televised on Spike TV. I missed the ceremony. Is it true there was a huge protest out front from the anti-"Abort Game" people?

My time is up. You've been great. Enjoy Soft Cell.

THE **NOTES**

(Just got the latest version of Microsoft Word…) Blazers owner Paul Allen is one of the original investors in Microsoft. And I picked CTRL + Z because it's the command for "undo typing," which is an insanely inside joke with myself.

(The President made a big NASCAR entrance…) Got this in just under the corporate sponsorship deadline.

(One embarrassing moment…) Between this and the Rumsfeld Army joke, I will never be a guest on Fox Sports Net's *Best Damn Shock and Awe, Period.*

THE **CUTS**

The Trail Blazers are desperately trying to change their image. From now on, the starters will not come onto the floor with jackets over their heads. After CTRL + Z, this fight is over.

USC overwhelmed Oregon State 52–28, and somehow dropped from No. 2 to No. 3. Help me out here. Was the BCS committee trying to send a message to O.J.? O.K., I know this doesn't make sense. Unlike the first verdict.…

THE **HIT(S)**

"Tainted Love"

Good to be here. I don't want to pile on, but are you wondering if Grady Little would have left Saddam in the mud hut just a little longer?

BCS PROMISES TO MAKE CHANGES FOR NEXT SEASON What, they're adding a swimsuit competition?

Are you like me? Are you thinking if the BCS were in charge of all big TV matchups, Trista would have married Ryan Leaf?

Elsewhere in Bowl Land, TCU declined an invitation to the GMAC Bowl because it conflicted with the school's exams schedule. Look, if you don't want to go to Mobile, you've got to come up with a more believable excuse than that.

George O'Leary was named head coach at Central Florida. Apparently the search committee was very impressed with his last three jobs: defensive coordinator for the Vikings, Supreme Court justice and CEO of Krispy Kreme Doughnuts.

COWBOYS BLANK SKINS 27–0 Washington QB Tim Hasselbeck was 6 for 26 with four interceptions for a 0.0 QB rating. Steve Spurrier is thinking of replacing him next week with Lisa Ling.

The Cowboys are now 9–5. But Bill Parcells still refuses to use the "p word." Peroxide?

Bruce Smith helped design a limited edition coin commemorating his NFL career sack record. I haven't seen it, but I assume former Jets quarterback Ken O'Brien is on tails.

RASHEED WALLACE APOLOGIZES FOR OBJECTIONABLE REMARKS During an interview with *The Oregonian*, Wallace accused the NBA of racism and exploiting its players. I'm going to give him the benefit of the doubt and assume this was his answer to the question, "What's the deal with Steve Nash's hair?"

Seattle center Jerome James was benched for a game after he fell asleep during a film session. Here's the sad part. The film was Ray Allen in *He Got Game*.

And for the next five games the front of his jersey will be changed to read SOMNICS.

The 76ers will try to break the record for the world's largest gathering of Santas at their Dec. 22 game against Orlando. Remember, this is Philly, so at the very least they'll set the record for most Santas booed.

You know the best part of getting a lot of Santas together in one place? Elf hookers.

BASEBALL EXECS MEET AT A NEW ORLEANS MARRIOT Although the Expos' brass had to spend a couple of days at the El San Juan.

The Yankees acquired Kevin Brown from the Dodgers for Jeff Weaver and a minor leaguer. I was shocked. The Yankees still have someone left in the minors?

Come on. The Joads had a more promising farm system.

Brown is thrilled. He's excited about finally getting the opportunity to be on an American League disabled list.

Red Sox shortstop Nomar Garciaparra is still the subject of trade rumors. So far only two teams are interested: Los Angeles and a Japanese expansion franchise, the Mia Hamm Fighters.

PROFESSIONAL LACROSSE PLAYERS ASSOCIATION STRIKE NOW IN WEEK 2 Unfortunately you can't read the picket signs because they keep cradling them.

MIKE TYSON FIRES MANAGER SHELLY FINKEL He now gets all his advice from a yam that looks like Cus D'Amato.

My time is up. You've been great. Enjoy Nick Gilder.

THE **NOTES**

(Good to be here. I don't want to pile on...) Yeah, still bitter.

(Cowboys blank Skins 27–0...) Hasselbeck's wife, Elizabeth, a former *Survivor* contestant, replaced Lisa Ling on *The View*. Unfortunately, for ridicule's sake, Tim was not wearing the immunity necklace here.

(Bruce Smith helped design a limited edition coin...) Smith recorded more sacks against O'Brien than he did against any other NFL QB. Big deal. Who didn't?

(Come on. The Joads had a more promising farm system...) TEN WORDS!!!!! Check from God....

THE **CUTS**

Good to be here. Big score at the Mickey Mantle memorabilia auction. I bought Thomas Jane's SAG card for $10, then sold it back to him for $50. Thomas Jane was the actor who played the Mick in *61**. This line is not nearly as funny as one I read in Linda Stasi's review of the same movie, where a friend of hers walked in midway and thought the guys playing Mantle and Maris were "gay cops."

Florida will play Iowa in the Outback Steakhouse Bowl. Wait a minute. I thought at Outback, it was your choice of sides. Every night, before I go to bed, I get down on my knees and pray there's an Outback Steakhouse Bowl this year so I can revive this joke.

Pretty inflammatory stuff. Rasheed used the n-word so many times, Mark Fuhrman was awarded two shots and the ball on the side. See last week's cut BCS joke.

Speaking of getting things on the side, is Kobe still leading the All-Star voting? Tragically, this got lost as well.

THE **HIT(S)**

"Hot Child in the City"

Good to be back. Tried to TiVo the Humanitarian Bowl. Ended up with two hours of the Dalai Lama getting tips from Pete Weber.

USC ROSES UP, OVERWHELMS MICHIGAN O.K., anyone still think there's no pro-level football in the L.A. area?

I don't want to say the BCS is embarrassed, but its next meeting is in Saddam's spider hole.

The USC defense had nine sacks. One more and John Navarre would have had to legally change his last name to Bledsoe.

LSU won the Sugar Bowl 21–14. Are you like me? At the last minute were you worried Oklahoma would still finish No. 1, based on "quality losses"?

Nobody went away empty-handed from the Superdome. The Tigers took home the AT&T National Championship trophy, and the Sooners got 1,000 anytime minutes on Joe Horn's end zone cellphone.

COLTS BUCK BRONCOS 41–10 You know that playoff monkey on Peyton Manning's back? It had five catches for 110 yards and a touchdown.

Green Bay edged Seattle in OT. The Seahawks were trying to win their first post-season game in nearly 20 years. To give you an idea how long ago that was, in 1984, Steve Largent was still allowed to go to his left.

The Titans beat the Ravens on a last-minute field goal by 44-year-old Gary Anderson that just cleared the crossbar. Fortunately, just before the kick Baltimore cops stopped Art Modell when he tried to move the goalpost back...to Cleveland.

Ravens offensive tackle Orlando Brown was called for two costly personal fouls. But this was nice. Each time the refs let him throw the flag.

Carolina routed Dallas 29–10. John Fox anticipated Bill Parcells's offensive and defensive tendencies so well that ABC offered him a spot on *Celebrity Mole*.

You know it's that time of year in the NFL. We go from 12 to eight to just four. I'm talking about head coaches who still have jobs.

Steve Spurrier resigned after just two years with the Redskins. Does that now make it the Fund 'n' Gone offense?

No names have been mentioned as a successor in Washington, although Howard Dean insists he is the front-runner.

STARBUCKS NOW THE OFFICIAL COFFEE OF MADISON SQUARE GARDEN You can get anything to go...except Charles Dolan.

Try their new menu item: salary cappuccino.

COYOTES' NEW LAIR OPENS Glendale Arena is a gorgeous, state-of-the-art NHL facility. Which means there'll be no obstructed views of next year's lockout.

So far the new rink has been getting rave reviews in every department—except for the ice surface. So, just to be on the safe side, Wayne Gretzky hired a couple of lifeguards from the pool at the BOB.

GATORADE TO INTRODUCE ESPN-FLAVORED DRINK I believe they're calling it Outside the Limes.

ESPN-flavored Gatorade. Odd combination. It tastes like lemon, but smells like cross-promotion.

STEINBRENNER GIVEN CLEAN BILL OF HEALTH Doctors are still wondering what caused the Yankees' owner's fainting spell. They've narrowed it down to low blood sugar, poor circulation or the phrase *$48.8 million in revenue sharing*.

BEN AFFLECK TO PORTRAY FAMED TEXAS WESTERN COACH DON HASKINS And how's this for a coincidence? Big Daddy Lattin is his nickname for J. Lo's butt.

My time is up. You've been great. Enjoy The Honeydrippers.

THE **NOTES**

(Green Bay edged Seattle in OT…) Steve Largent, the greatest possession receiver of his era, became a Republican congressman from Oklahoma. Okay, fine, that's his choice. But J.C. Watts, former OU quarterback, black Republican congressman? I need this explained to me very slowly. Talk about a misdirection play.

(ESPN-flavored Gatorade. Odd combination…) I know they're laughing about this in Bristol…if the Propaganda Minister didn't cut this out of all compound copies of *SI*.

(Ben Affleck to portray famed Texas Western coach Don Haskins…) David Lattin was the star of the all-black Texas Western team that defeated all-white Kentucky to win the 1966 NCAA basketball title. Affleck has since been replaced in the film by Josh Lucas, not, as you may have thought, by Marc Anthony.

THE **CUTS**

Good to be back. I don't know if this will help, but for all future New York Jets functions, Joe Namath has to wear a throwback jersey with "Boozer" on the back. Legal would not let this run because at the time of this incident we couldn't say Joe had a drinking problem. The only thing that made less sense was my desperate justification that he was a big fan of his former halfback, Emerson Boozer.

LeBron has 22 points, 10 rebounds on 19th birthday. *After the game, James wanted to celebrate with a bottle of champagne, but he couldn't convince Paul Silas to go into the liquor store for him.* Sad. All LeBron could legally do was wear a throwback jersey with "Boozer" on it.

THE **HIT(S)**

None. (That week's "Q+A" opposite the column was with former Led Zeppelin lead singer Robert Plant. Kostya, a serious bass player, chose the '80s all-star band Plant fronted as a vague tribute. The fact that Paul Shaffer played keyboards in a later revival of the group only clinched it for me.)

Good to be here. Is it me, or does the Mars Rover look like the cart that used to bring Joe Sambito in from the Astros' bullpen?

PANTHERS EXTRA-FRAME RAMS You know, I thought I had a great joke about the end of this game, but I couldn't get it off in time.

Jeff Wilkins helped send the game into overtime when he recovered his own onside kick. I haven't witnessed spin like that since the ESPN broadcasters referred to Joe Namath as "happy."

SEVENTEEN-BELOW WINDCHILL IN FOX-BORO New England edged the Titans 17–14 in the extreme cold. At one point Tom Brady kept his hands in his pants for so long, he almost got flagged for violating the tuck rule.

The Colts outpaced Kansas City 38–31. The Chiefs' D was so nonexistent against Peyton Manning, after the game, they changed the name of their home field to "Arrowhea Staium."

Indy is confident. For the last two weeks, punter Hunter Smith has been on the sidelines wearing clogs.

Donovan McNabb passed for 248 yards and ran for 107 in the overtime win over Green Bay to send Philadelphia to its third straight NFC title game. And you thought Rush Limbaugh was in pain before....

Elsewhere, the Redskins lured Joe Gibbs back. Gibbs has been out of coaching for 12 years. To give you an idea of how long that is, in 1992 Daniel Snyder was firing his homeroom teacher.

I think Joe may have been in NASCAR too long. He said his first priority is taking the restrictor plate off the offense.

IN NEW BOOK PETE ROSE ADMITS HE BET ON BASEBALL WHILE MANAGING THE REDS Finally, after 14 years, somebody mixed some sodium pentathol with his hair dye.

The book is called *My Prison Without Bars*. I prefer the original title, *The Big Book of Vig*.

I think Pete may have needed the money. Every chapter in the book is Chapter 11.

Rose says he's still gambling. It's sad. He's 2–6 betting against the Cougars on *Playmakers*. And three of those were repeat episodes.

ISIAH THOMAS SHAKES UP MSG And he's not done making changes. Tomorrow he's replacing all the strings on Don Chaney.

Thomas is desperate to class up the entire Knicks organization. Starting Feb. 1, Marv Albert's trademark expression will be "Oui!"

PHOENIX GOALIE BREAKS NHL RECORD The Coyotes' Brian Boucher went 332:01 without allowing a score. Long time. Hell, when the streak started, he was wearing a Winnipeg Jets jersey.

Boucher broke the 55-year-old mark set by the Canadiens' Bill Durnan. But to be fair, back then, NHL goalies played without masks—and without Finns.

Boucher became the first goalie to get five consecutive shutouts since they put in the red line in 1944. And if you know your hockey, you know the red line was the brainchild of Ottawa Senator Joe McCarthy.

LEGENDARY HORSE RACING COLUMNIST ANDY BEYER ACCEPTS VOLUNTARY RETIREMENT PACKAGE FROM *WASHINGTON POST* This gives new meaning to the expression "early money."

You know what's strange? My speed figures had him leaving at the end of the month.

JUDGE SCHEDULES PRETRIAL HEARINGS FOR KOBE BRYANT FEB. 2–3 It was supposed to be three days, but because of the prosecution's case they canceled the slam dunk competition.

My time is up. You've been great. Enjoy Spirit.

THE **NOTES**

(The book is called My Prison Without Bars…*)* "Vig" is short for "vigorish," the cut a bookie takes on all losing bets.

Confession time. I stopped gambling nine and a half years ago. The closest thing I do now is make jokes about gamblers. The more jokes I make, the more it is on my mind. This week, as you can see, it was much on my mind.

(Rose says he's still gambling…) I knew I was in denial about my problem when I found myself watching a football game and saying, "Hey, maybe they'll score on *this* replay…."

(Legendary horse racing columnist Andy Beyer…) Andy Beyer is arguably the most influential writer on thoroughbred wagering in the last half-century. And for all his brilliance and wit, after a loss, he can be as bitterly disbelieving as the degenerate ripping tickets next to you at OTB. Did I say next to you? I meant next to me.

(You know what's strange? My speed figures had him leaving…) Beyer's betting philosophy relies on his formula for determining the relative speed of each horse in each race. In fact, the term "Beyer Speed Figures" was eventually included in the *Daily Racing Form*. Sadly, year after year, he is snubbed by the petty geeks who vote on the Nobel Prize for Mathematics.

THE **CUTS**

Pete says his reinstatement is up to the commissioner and "the big umpire in the sky." Hey, let's leave Eric Gregg out of this. Eric Gregg was a longtime NL umpire with a, uh, weight problem. You know Charles Barkley? Imagine if Barkley ate himself. O.K., now double it. That's Eric Gregg.

Many people thought the Eagles were up against destiny. But at halftime, a quick-thinking Duce Staley was able to motivate his teammates by telling them his father was in the hospital with nonspecific urethritis. The week before, Brett Favre's father had passed away. The joke was strictly for "the room." Moments later, the door to "the room" was locked.

THE **HIT(S)**

"I Got a Line on You"

Good to be here. I know I'm early, but I already put down my first Super Bowl bet. I took CBS, minus 2½ men.

PATS REIN IN COLTS 24–14 Are you like me? Are you wondering if Peyton Manning has called an audible on his vacation plans?

Manning tossed four interceptions and completed only three passes to Marvin Harrison for 19 yards. Hell, Greg Gumbel had more success throwing it to Bonnie Bernstein.

In the NFC final, the Panthers beat the Eagles 14–3. Carolina is going to the big dance. Here's what I don't get. Matt Doherty is taking credit for recruiting both starting guards and the center.

See the game? Let me tell you something: Ricky Manning Jr. is making everyone forget about Ricky Manning Sr. I don't mean that. What I mean is, he's making everybody say, "Who the hell is Ricky Manning Sr.?"

For the third straight year the Eagles fell one game short. But this is nice. They'll still be given a ticker-tape parade downtown. Downtown Buffalo.

In other football news, NBC will air three episodes of *Queer Eye for the Straight Guy* opposite the Super Bowl. You know, if NBC were really smart, the Fab Five would show up unannounced at Matt Millen's pad.

New Redskins coach Joe Gibbs is already getting his staff together. Gregg Williams will be his defensive coordinator, Joe Bugel the offensive line coach, and Tony Stewart will start fights in practice.

ASTROS FANS OVER THE MOON FOR ROCKET Roger Clemens signed a guaranteed one-season deal for $5 million. He wanted to stay at home, but his wife offered only $4 million, and that's with performance clauses.

Clemens was retired for 78 days. And it's that kind of serious commitment to leisure that's earned him the respect of Sugar Ray Leonard.

Last week in San Francisco workers took down the 10-foot-high letters that spell out PACIFIC BELL PARK. What do you want to bet some idiot was in a raft with a butterfly net waiting to catch them?

WIZARDS FORWARD CHRISTIAN LAETTNER SUSPENDED FIVE GAMES FOR VIOLATING LEAGUE DRUG POLICY The suspension was actually for 15 games, but because it's his first offense, the other 10 will be served by Roy Tarpley.

Meanwhile, LeBron James filmed a guest appearance on the sitcom *My Wife and Kids*. And ABC was so impressed, they're now developing a comedy series for LeBron, *According to Gym*.

MICHELLE WIE MISSES PGA CUT BY ONE STROKE She's 14 years old. Fourteen! Bernhard Langer has stood over putts longer.

In the end, it worked out for the native Hawaiian. Had she made the cut at the Sony Open, it would have interfered with her Saturday plans: returning punts at the Hula Bowl.

JOHN McENROE ADMITS HE UNWITTINGLY TOOK STEROIDS FOR SIX YEARS DURING PLAYING CAREER What a shame. I hate to think he achieved his violent mood swings artificially.

McEnroe is getting his own talk show on CNBC. Pretty shrewd move by the network. They're hoping the yelling will drown out Bill O'Reilly.

Busy week for Mac. He also signed with Kellogg's. He will promote its soy-based cereal, Smart Start, and his own brand, Rice Krankies.

HOCKEY NEWS RELEASES ANNUAL 100 MOST POWERFUL PEOPLE IN HOCKEY Big surprise at No. 4: Barry Melrose's mousse importer.

JORDANS, D.C.-AREA RESTAURANT OWNED BY MJ, CLOSES AFTER TWO YEARS It was either that, or change the name to Jerry Steakhouse.

My time is up. You've been great. Enjoy Lipps, Inc.

THE **NOTES**

(Clemens was retired for 78 days. And it's that kind of serious commitment...) Yeah, still cranky.

*(**Wizards forward Christian Laettner suspended...**)* Roy Tarpley received so many lifetime drug suspensions, Steve Howe makes fun of him.

(Busy week for Mac. He also signed with Kellogg's...) Unlike Rice Krankies, I stay crispy in milk.

*(**Jordan's, D.C.-area restaurant owned by MJ, closes...**)* This is a play on Jerry Stackhouse. As opposed to a play with Jerry Stackhouse, neither of which Jordan would be thrilled with.

THE **CUTS**

The Rocket's deal includes provisions for him to miss road trips if he's not scheduled to pitch so he can stay home and watch his kids play baseball. Or if there's something really good on TV. Do I sound a little bitchy here? Well, what if someone told you he would never go to a team in the AL East and would only go where he was closer to his kids in Katy, Texas, and then spends six years in Toronto and New York? Would you be a little bitchy?

At the time, the steroids McEnroe took were not illegal, were not performance-enhancing and were given mostly to horses. Be honest. How many of you are now thinking of a joke involving the words "Tatum O'Neal" and "mount"? You know that thing I said about how well the formula, "How many of you are thinking of a joke..." works? Well, it doesn't if you are the only one thinking of the joke.

THE **HIT(S)**

"Funkytown"

Good to be here. Just back from Pete Rose's book signing at Foxwoods. Next week he's heading to Vegas to see if he can get his apology annulled.

AVERAGE PRICE FOR SUPER BOWL SPOT UP TO $2.25 MILLION CBS still has time available. Which makes this a buy week.

By the way, get your bets down. The over-under on Super Bowl ads with Snoop Dogg is 3½. And the money line is 50 Cent.

Gillette is running its first Super Bowl ads in 10 years. It's taken them that long to get over the ill-conceived 1994 campaign promoting Bennie Blades.

Reliant Stadium's retractable roof will be rolled back for the game, weather permitting. The roof takes 10 minutes to open. As compared to Panthers tight end Jermaine Wiggins, who takes 10 minutes to get open.

PRESIDENT BUSH CALLS ON ATHLETES TO END USE OF PERFORMANCE ENHANCING DRUGS Except, of course, those supplements manufactured by Halliburton.

Bush is serious. Starting this spring, he's instituting mandatory testing at the White House T-ball field.

During the State of the Union, the President said there are no shortcuts to accomplishment. Although a couple thousand defective voting machines don't hurt.

Are you like me? Were you disappointed Bush didn't refer to steroids as "weapons of muscle mass destruction?"

NASCAR CHANGES SCORING SYSTEM Starting this year you can only win the overall championship in the last 2½ months of the season. In other words, it's the exact opposite of the BCS.

The old method had flaws. Last year, Winston Cup champ Matt Kenseth won only one race, while Ryan Newman won eight races and finished sixth. I think we've found another serious side effect of long-term dependence on tobacco.

Internet fan polls were running 70% to 80% against the new system. However, half of those people said they'd change their minds for a Skoal Bandit windbreaker.

The fan polls may have been a little biased. The results were based on the question, "Do you hate the new scoring system and/or Jeff Gordon?"

NETS SOLD TO BROOKLYN DEVELOPER The team could be playing in a new arena in Brooklyn by the end of 2006. Right around the time jury selection is completed in the Jayson Williams trial.

You have to feel bad for New Jersey fans. Twenty-seven years of indifference, and this is the thanks they get.

You can tell Brooklyn is excited about getting a team. The number of Trans Ams in the parking lot of Continental Airlines Arena has quadrupled.

CHESTER BREWER, BULLS MASCOT, ARRESTED FOR ALLEGEDLY SELLING POT OUT OF HIS CAR Police found six ounces of marijuana and a scale. And this is a little lame: Brewer told them the scale was for Weight Watchers, and his goal was to one day fit into the Phoenix Suns' Gorilla costume.

This is cute. He dealt pot under the name Spliff Levingston.

Brewer's biggest seller was the "M-Jay." Two hits, and you think about playing minor league baseball.

RANGERS OPEN CZECH BOOK FOR JAGR And I guess this isn't surprising. Pending league approval, Washington's team will now be known as the Hard Caps.

McDONALD'S CUTS TIES WITH KOBE The decision came after a focus group rejected a proposed menu item: the Egg McMistrial.

My time is up. You've been great. Enjoy The Jaggerz.

THE **NOTES**

(Gillette is running its first Super Bowl ads in 10 years…) Bennie Blades was a Lions DB who retired after the 1997 season. He later was arrested for failing to pay child support and desertion. Which, compared with the fake ad campaign, is really ill-conceived.

(During the State of the Union the President…) A really good monologuist never lets his audience know how he feels politically. That's why this joke was written by my, uh, cousin.…

(Chester Brewer, Bulls mascot, arrested for allegedly…) These are the dream items. Any combination of "mascot," "pot" and "car." First, you get to test your creativity coming up with an excuse for the cops.…

*(This is cute. He dealt pot under the name Spliff Levingston…)*Then, you run through past Bulls players looking for a good dealer alias.…

(Brewer's biggest seller was the "M-Jay"…) Then, without a call to Jerry Stackhouse, you nail Jordan two weeks in a row.

THE **CUTS**

The day after the State of the Union, Bush had dinner with several baseball executives at a Mexican restaurant in Phoenix. And what are the odds of this? The special that night was "Chili Re-andros." For you fans scoring at home, this joke is a "force play."

Dean supporters to sponsor a "Howard Dean for President" Chevrolet in NASCAR's Busch series. You can tell it's a Dean Chevrolet. The wheels come off in Iowa. I told my editors, look, if we put my cousin's joke in, we also need to put in this one from my, uh, barber.

THE **HIT(S)**

"The Rapper"

(As I have mentioned, people never give me jokes, just bands. This was suggested by a man in Jackson, Tennessee, one of four people to show up at a reading of my novel I gave at a bookstore there. Why alienate 25% of your audience?)

Don't you love Justin Timberlake calling the Janet Jackson incident a "wardrobe malfunction"? I believe that, and I also believe that was really Neil Armstrong on the fake moon set.

RE-UP AND ADAM. PATS SUPER AGAIN The two defenses combined to give up 61 points and 867 total yards. You know who made the most adjustments at halftime? That guy who ran on the field naked before the third-quarter kickoff.

Pass coverage on both sides was a little soft. Midway through the third quarter Ricky Manning Jr. changed his name to Ricky Zoning Jr.

So, is Stephen Davis with MoveOn.org? He wasn't allowed to run during the Super Bowl either.

See that H&R Block spot? What, did the IRS put a lien on Willie Nelson's self-esteem?

Houston went all out. The half-dollar they used for the coin toss was the last piece of cash belonging to Andrew Fastow.

ROGER AND OUT IN OZ Australian Open champ Roger Federer became the 23rd player to get the No. 1 ranking since the advent on the ATP computer in 1973. Are you kidding? We've had that many No. 1's in college basketball since Thursday.

Disappointing tourney for the Americans. The only good news was when Andy Roddick finally hit 160 mph. Unfortunately, it happened driving to Melbourne Airport.

INDIANS PITCHER ASKS FOR FORGIVENESS FOR PART IN JAPANESE GAY PORN VIDEO Kaz Tadano made only one film while in college, where he appeared under the name Joel Foreskinner.

Last year the 23-year-old reliever confessed to performing a graphic act in the video but didn't say whether he was the setup man or the closer.

Tadano told his teammates he was not a homosexual; he just needed the money. This is painful, but I can relate. When I was 13, my dad gave me two bucks to eat my Brussels sprouts.

JAZZ PUNISHED FOR DELIVERING JUNK MAILMAN The NBA fined the team $15,000 for airing a comedy bit of a man impersonating Karl Malone in the middle of a Utah-Lakers game. Uncanny impression. The guy sounded so much like Malone, Greg Ostertag immediately started complaining about his minutes.

Meanwhile, and I don't think this is necessary, Jason Kidd has been claiming he has nothing to do with Donald Trump's firing people on *The Apprentice*.

CAPS OWNER TED LEONSIS SETTLES WITH FAN Leonsis apologized profusely for an incident in which he grabbed a season-ticket holder and threw him down during a game with the Flyers. I believe his exact words were, "I'm sorry I wasn't wearing my old Chris Simon jersey."

OLYMPIC FIGURE SKATER VIKTOR PETRENKO CHARGED WITH DRUNKEN DRIVING Petrenko failed several field sobriety tests, including walking a straight Salchow and touching his nose with a camel toe.

My time is up. You've been great. Enjoy Steam.

THE **NOTES**

(Don't you love Justin Timberlake calling the Janet Jackson incident...) By the time this issue came out, four days after the Super Bowl, every joke had been written. So I had to refer to something else at halftime.

(Houston went all out. The half-dollar they used for the coin toss...) Fastow was the former CEO of Houston-based Enron. I think he now goes by his prison bitch nickname, End Ron.

(Tadano told his teammates he was not a homosexual; he just needed the money...) Maybe now that I've shared some of my pain, you'll understand my confusion about the way I feel about everything except Rick Pitino, Grady Little and Roger Clemens.

THE **CUTS**

Jake Delhomme started 1-for-9 passing, then turned things around after he watched some film...of Mike Ditka throwing it through the Levitra tire. For the life of me, I don't get the connection between erectile dysfunction and passing accuracy. Now, if Ditka was shown inflating a football...

Jazz punished for delivering junk Mailman. *The NBA fined the team $15,000 for airing a tape of a man impersonating Karl Malone during the middle of a Utah-Lakers game. Not only that, but the check has to be handed in to the league office by a guy who looks like John Stockton.* When the choice is between John Stockton and Greg Ostertag, you go with quickness.

THE **HIT(S)**

"Nah Nah Hey Hey (Kiss Him Goodbye)"

If I seem a little peeved, bear with me. They cut me out of *Miracle*. I played the sportswriter who asked Herb Brooks, "Hey, how about giving Steve Janaszak a shot in goal?"

REPRIMAND FOR A HEAVYWEIGHT Bob Knight escaped suspension after getting into a public dispute with Texas Tech chancellor David Smith. The argument erupted at a local supermarket salad bar. Pretty heated exchange. They had to replace the sneeze guards three times.

But thanks to anger management, the only time Knight raised his hands during the incident was when he waved to the manager for more imitation crabmeat.

At one point there was an ultimatum: Either take a five-day suspension or be fired. Can a coach say that to a chancellor?

Elsewhere in college basketball, good seats are still available for St. John's–Georgetown. Yeah, there's at least six on the Red Storm bench.

SUPER BOWL HALFTIME BACKLASH CONTINUES That's right, backlash. I wanted to use the word *fallout*, but this is a family column.

Meanwhile, you know what brother you're hearing a lot about all of a sudden? TiVo Jackson.

More than a million fans showed up for the Patriots' second Super Bowl victory party in three years. In a related story, Buffalo Bills safety Lawyer Milloy got $20 off on a Toro snowblower.

Dan Marino resigned as senior V.P. of the Dolphins after less than three weeks on the job. Wow. He worked longer on *Ace Ventura*.

Buccaneers defensive end Simeon Rice was dropped from the NFC Pro Bowl squad for disciplinary reasons. And how better to make an example of a player than a free week in Hawaii without pads?

DREW HENSON RUNS OPTION His decision to quit baseball and pursue a football career came the day after the Yankees invited only his left ACL to big league camp.

Meanwhile, Aaron Boone may forfeit his $5.75 million salary because he tore knee ligaments playing basketball, which is forbidden in his contract. So, he's thinking about telling Steinbrenner he hurt himself tripping over Jeff Kent's motorcycle.

ESPN CANCELS *PLAYMAKERS* So now if you want to see a bunch of guys who are prone to infidelity, racism and homophobia, you'll have to start watching C-SPAN.

The controversial drama will be replaced by a new show, *Pardon the NFL Interruption*.

Despite strong ratings and critical acclaim, ESPN decided against a second season after considering the objections of the NFL. Man, I haven't seen a cave-in like that since Charles Bronson's in *The Great Escape*.

LENNOX LEWIS RETIRES And, in accordance with WBC rules, he will be stripped of his title and given 60 days to come up with a design for a grill.

Lewis made his announcement during a live press conference from the space above Vitali Klitschko's eye.

Lewis had fought only two times in the last 20 months. And one of those fights was with a telemarketer.

JEREMY ROENICK WINS SHOOTING-ACCURACY TITLE AT ALL-STAR SKILLS COMPETITION The Flyers forward nailed a perfect 4 for 4. Four refs, four water bottles.

Elsewhere in the NHL, there was a rumor that Avalanche general manager Pierre Lacroix tried to arrange a private Celine Dion concert for the G.M. meetings in Las Vegas. Hey, speaking of the theme from the *Titanic*, how are those labor talks going?

JUDGE CLEARS MAURICE CLARETT TO ENTER NFL DRAFT This really sets a dangerous precedent. Now my nephew wants to have his bar mitzvah at the scouting combine.

NBA EXPECTED TO OFFICIALLY CLASSIFY THG AS A BANNED SUBSTANCE NEXT SEASON Until then, it's still listed as a side dish.

My time is up. You've been great. Enjoy the DeFranco Family.

THE **NOTES**

(Reprimand for a heavyweight...) Once I found out the fight had occurred at a salad bar, I knew I'd have unlimited choices, and I could keep going back.

(Super Bowl halftime backlash continues...) That's right. The family column that has given you *"He's got about an 18-footer..."* and *Joel Foreskinner.*

(Judge clears Maurice Clarett to enter NFL Draft...) This is preposterous. Everybody knows the turf inside the Hoosier Dome is *traif.*

THE **CUTS**

Garth Brooks to attend spring training with Royals. *It's all to raise money for his pet charity, the "Make a Shamelessly Self-Indulgent Wish" Foundation. I'm sorry, I know he raised millions of dollars, but on the cynical side, what about the five grand he saved not going to fantasy camp?*

Garth is 1 for 43 against big league pitching. Go ahead and laugh, but that's one more hit than Chris Gaines had. Chris Gaines was the name of Garth's alter ego who cut an album in 2000. And remember, all these jokes are for charity.

You know, every time Michael Jordan hears about Garth Brooks, he must think, "Hmm. Just suck at big league camp. Why didn't I think of that?" Unwritten *SI* rule: Only one crack every six months about MJ and minor league ball.

THE **HIT(S)**

"Heartbeat (It's a Love Beat)"

Good to be here. Are you like me? Are you waiting for Rush Limbaugh to say the dog who won best-in-show at Westminster is overrated because he's black?

FATHER'S DAY-TONA FOR DALE JR. Earnhardt won the 500 for the first time, finishing just ahead of Tony Stewart from Joe Gibbs Racing. But to be fair, Stewart had to run the last 20 laps with Mark Brunell in the backseat.

The race drew its fewest entrants in 10 years, only 45 cars. And here's the really sad part: 18 of those were in President Bush's motorcade.

Bush attended the Great American Race, and next month, he's going to stand at the front gate of Talladega for two hours to complete his National Guard commitment.

Bobby Labonte's number 18 Chevy featured an ad for *The Passion of the Christ*. Honestly, didn't you think the car would drop out, then come back and finish three days later?

This is fascinating. Labonte's crew couldn't put the signage on the hood until Barabbas agreed to get off the intake manifold.

MIAMI'S TOP FOOTBALL RECRUIT WILLIE WILLIAMS CHARGED WITH MISDEMEANOR BATTERY The *Parade* All-America linebacker allegedly committed a felony and two misdemeanors just two days before his 18-month-probation term for burglary was due to end. Is it me, or could this guy be easily fooled by the snap count?

School officials said they were unaware Williams had been arrested 10 times between 1999 and 2002. Although they suspected that something might be amiss when his letter of intent was co-signed by a bail bondsman.

Williams has already accepted a scholarship, so this raises a serious ethical question for Miami: Is a trainer allowed to tape over an electronic ankle bracelet?

NBA ALL-STARS COLLATE AT STAPLES CENTER The young stars put on a streetball show during the Rookie Challenge game. My favorite LeBron James dunk was the 360 with a marketing guy from Sprite on his back.

For the first time, the NBA All-Star Game was broadcast in high definition. What a difference. You could actually hear Mike Fratello sniffing around for a job.

The Sixers fired coach Randy Ayers. Forget the Pearl Islands, how about *Survivor: Allen Iverson*?

Rasheed Wallace is now an Atlanta Hawk. Wow. Is that the best plea agreement his lawyer could come up with?

ALL PITCHERS AND CATCHERS REPORT Help me out here. Was that to spring training, or to the BALCO steroid indictments?

Barry Bonds's trainer pleaded not guilty to charges he provided steroids to athletes. He has a pretty good defense: "If his rookie hat fits, you must acquit."

ROTO FINISH? YANKS GRAB A-ROD The All-Star shortstop will move to third base. And Derek Jeter will move from Elite Models to the Ford Agency.

Elsewhere, an auction of items from Veterans Stadium raised $700,000. I paid $75 for what I thought was a Steve Carlton rosin bag. Turned out to be the Phillie Phanatic's spleen.

PATRIOTS TACKLE MATT LIGHT TO APPEAR ON *QUEER EYE FOR THE STRAIGHT GUY* I guess he wants to work on his pass blocking.

GEORGE FOREMAN, 55, CONSIDERS COMEBACK Insiders say he's furious about the new Klitschko Brothers Hibachi.

My time is up. You've been great. Enjoy Every Mother's Son.

THE **NOTES**

(Good to be here. Are you like me?) Kostya Kennedy and Ed Markey came up with this independently. Comedy Kismet, or Kismedy.

(Bush attended the Great American Race, and next month…) Talladega is in Alabama. Otherwise, I become part of the liberal media elite agenda.

(This is fascinating. Labonte's crew couldn't put the signage…) Bob Roe, another senior editor at *SI*, switched this joke from *"…couldn't put the signage on the hood until they got Barabbas off the intake manifold."* He thought it was more accurate. I had no idea the crucifixion was optional.

(Barry Bonds's trainer pleaded not guilty to charges…) Look, I'm not saying Barry's on anything…right now. I'm just saying his head looks like a carrying case for his head.

THE **CUTS**

Jeff Burton ran in the "TNT NBA All-Star" car. He finished last. Well, sure. With Ernie Johnson's face on the back, it couldn't get in edgewise. Ernie Johnson serves two purposes on the TNT NBA shows. He's the guy who says, "We'll be right back," and "O.K., Charles, get up on the scale."

For the first time in the history of the race, smoking was not allowed in the press box. However, a section was set aside for all members of the media with wet, hacking coughs. Maybe it's me, but I think if I eliminate the word "wet," this gets in.

THE **HIT(S)**

"Come on Down to My Boat"

I need to check with City Hall, but I believe right now that the only two men in San Francisco trying to break up are Barry Bonds and his personal trainer.

GARY BARNETT GOES TO THE FAR SIDELINE The Colorado football coach was placed on administrative leave. Yeah, in the same way Elvis is on administrative leave.

Memo to the university's Board of Regents: While you're at it, you may want to think of a new nickname to replace "Buffs."

Maybe I dreamed this, but the other day, at the end of *The Price Is Right*, I could have sworn I heard Bob Barker urge people to spay or neuter their returning lettermen.

SCOUTING COMBINE TELEVISED ON NFL NETWORK Just to jazz things up, they added three lifelines to the Wonderlic test.

Maurice Clarett announced he would skip the combine workouts. However, next month he'll conduct a private session in Columbus, where he'll vertical-leap three federal judges.

RANGERS TO ASSUME MORE THAN A THIRD OF A-ROD'S SALARY You know the only good thing about eating $67 million? No carbs.

But don't kid yourself. This trade has all kinds of financial windfalls for the Rangers. Just yesterday, demand at The Ballpark souvenir shop forced them to order three more Hank Blalock jerseys.

Red Sox fans are still distraught over the deal. I heard Ben Affleck was furious. I missed it because his reaction went straight to video.

CHRIS WEBBER SERVES EIGHT-GAME SUSPENSION He had been on the injured list since last year's playoffs. First, he underwent surgery to repair torn cartilage in his left knee; then, just as he recovered from that, his meniscus was found in contempt.

Elsewhere, Rasheed Wallace was pulled in his debut for the Pistons because the NBA hadn't received documentation of the trade. On the bright side, it's a nice change to have the league looking for papers, instead of Rasheed.

Speaking of which, technically, shouldn't Rasheed's Hawks jersey be considered a throwback?

A man who attacked the Magic's mascot last Friday was charged with battery and resisting arrest. It took police three stun gun shots before they were able to drag him out of the O-rena. And he still wasn't as tough to move as Juwan Howard.

PENGUINS SET NHL RECORD WITH 14 STRAIGHT HOME LOSSES Mario Lemieux is so desperate, he's now looking for available rinks in San Juan.

Elsewhere, Brett Hull tied the career record for power-play goals. Savvy fans at Joe Louis Arena gave him a standing ovation that lasted just under two minutes.

In his State of the NHL address, commissioner Gary Bettman said revenue sharing would be a necessity. I'm no Sam Waksal, but before you have have revenue sharing, wouldn't it be nice to have a, uh, profit?

GEORGE FOREMAN AGREES TO $20 MILLION COMEBACK BOUT DEAL It's a tentative, verbal agreement with Don King. A tentative, verbal agreement with Don King? Milk of magnesia is more binding.

NBA STORE REMOVES SWEATSHIRTS MADE IN MYANMAR You can always tell the items from Burma. The NBA logo is a silhouette of Jerry West at a sewing machine.

AUGUSTA NATIONAL RAISES PRICES FOR TUESDAY MASTERS PRACTICE ROUNDS FROM $21 TO $31 But ladies drink free.

My time is up. You've been great. Enjoy Uriah Heep.

THE **NOTES**

(Maybe I dreamed this, but the other day…) Ugly, ugly story of allegations of rape. That week, Rick Reilly wrote a groundbreaking column on one of the victims, former Colorado placekicker Katie Hnida. I did a Bob Barker joke.

(Elsewhere, Rasheed Wallace was pulled in his debut for the Pistons…) Pot joke. And I know it's a good pot joke, because I've got the munchies.

(NBA Store removes sweatshirts made in Myanmar…) I begged for this slightly vague sweatshop reference. Although somehow, making sweatshirts in a sweatshop seems appropriate.

(Augusta National raises prices for Tuesday Masters practice rounds…) The key to this joke is Tuesday. Sure, ladies can drink free any night, but Tuesday is traditional. And what's the Masters without tradition?

THE **CUTS**

Clarett limited his combine participation to team interviews and all physical examinations…except the one where you sprint 40 yards, turn and cough. Maybe if I'd added "hacking," this would have made it funnier, I think, because you stay on point.

Thirty-three-year-old Nets coach Lawrence Frank set an NBA record by winning his first 11 games. Sadly, he is still stopped by Meadowlands security and asked if he's looking for his parents. Kostya does not like jokes that just make fun of someone for being too young or too old. I agree. But the deeper humor I was going for here was that security at the Meadowlands has nothing to do. You ain't buying it either, are you?

George Foreman agrees to a $20 million comeback bout deal. *Foreman says he will not get back into the ring until he weighs 225 pounds. Which explains why Don King is only negotiating with arenas on the moon.* This was cut because, unbeknownst to me, Don King had his license to do business on the moon revoked in 1982.

THE **HIT(S)**

None. (Suggested by my drummer friend J.P. Patterson. Heavy metal standard-bearers of early '70s British rock. No influence on me personally, but I like the name and the Dickens reference.)

Well, I guess this isn't surprising: Steinbrenner just signed Peter Jackson.

SELIG LIMITS CLUBHOUSE ACCESS TO AUTHORIZED PERSONNEL ONLY Sounds like somebody didn't get his Oscar comps from Billy Crystal.

Wait a minute. You mean all of a sudden Dr. Phil can't pop by and help Jeff Weaver with his control?

Meanwhile, have you seen photos of Jason Giambi lately? If he goes down another size, he's going to have to change his name to Jason Giambi-Hilton.

Giambi's teammate Bernie Williams will miss at least three weeks recovering from an emergency appendectomy. Grady Little wanted to leave it in.

Former MLB umpire Al Clark pleads guilty to conspiracy to commit mail fraud. And what are the odds of this? He was busted by an undercover QuesTec machine.

One buyer became suspicious when he received a ball allegedly used in Cal Ripken's 2,131st consecutive game, signed by Ripken, Lou Gehrig and Teresa Wright.

So please, if you feel you have been victimized by this scam, contact Clark through his new business manager, Denny McLain.

MARK CUBAN TO HOST REALITY SHOW ABC is calling the show *The Benefactor*. I guess *My Big Fat Obnoxious Fine Recipient* was taken.

I hear that each week Cuban will eliminate one contestant. Or a guy in the NBA office.

Elsewhere, the league suspended referee Michael Henderson for three games after he blew a crucial call in Denver that helped the Lakers. Hmmm.... Is that enough for a mistrial?

The Magic signed Desmond Penigar to another 10-day contract. He'll be tried at small forward, and at long snapper for Tracy McGrady.

WOODS HAS NO MATCH AT WORLD MATCH PLAY CHAMPIONSHIP The only disappointment for Tiger came at the award ceremony, when Accenture refused to make the giant $1.2 million check out to Carl Spackler.

Davis Love III played 114 holes over the five days. Or, as it's known in golf vernacular, an O.J. Getaway Weekend.

The whole tournament setup was kind of bogus. Come on. Sixty-four seeds, and no St. Joe's?

MIKE TYSON DECLARES BANKRUPTCY He claims that in the month of November 2003, his entire income was $5.68. And that included a mail-in rebate from Purina Tiger Chow.

It's not all bad news. Thanks to the Bush tax cut, he only owes 71 cents.

CAPITALS TRADE SCORING LEADER ROBERT LANG TO RED WINGS The Caps' marketing department is already in full damage control. On March 18, all fans 15 and under will receive a coupon good for a free swing at Ted Leonsis.

ESPN GREENLIGHTS ORIGINAL MOVIE ABOUT PETE ROSE Preproduction gets underway as soon as the 10-gallon drum of red hair dye arrives at Brian Dennehy's house.

BRITISH SPRINTER BANNED FROM OLYMPICS FOR LIFE AFTER TESTING POSITIVE FOR STEROIDS European 100-meter champion Dwain Chambers was linked to now infamous BALCO. Of course when he did business with them, they were known by their original name, THG Fridays.

My time is up. You've been great. Enjoy the Thompson Twins.

THE **NOTES**

(Meanwhile, have you seen photos of Jason Giambi lately?) I had a big week for props from colleagues. Mike Lupica, the fine columnist from the *New York Daily News,* quoted this in his Sunday column....

(Giambi's teammate Bernie Williams will miss at least three weeks...) ...and then Ken Singleton did this line on the air during a Yankees spring training game. I was so full of myself, Barry Bonds's hat didn't fit me.

(One buyer became suspicious when he received a ball...) Teresa Wright played Lou Gehrig's wife in *The Pride of the Yankees,* was nominated for a Best Supporting Actress Oscar, then denied clubhouse access by Bud Selig.

(So please, if you feel you have been victimized...) Former 31-game winner McLain did two separate prison bits for fraud. For a while, he would tell anyone who listened he was railroaded, then try to sell them a railroad.

THE **CUTS**

Last week in Detroit, vandals were arrested after painting the famed bronze Joe Louis Fist white. And this is a little lame. They insist they were just getting it ready for the Olympic boxing trials. This is a reference to the small white scoring area on Olympic gloves. As opposed to the white scoring area in the NBA, which is even smaller.

Elsewhere, Gary Payton is now seeing major minutes after complaining about his playing time. He had a point. During the month of February, he was told to approach the bench more often than Kobe's lawyer. Apparently, there was a brief moratorium on the Kobe trial jokes in this issue (How about how I didn't use "adjournment" or "recess" here?)

THE **HIT(S)**

"Hold Me Now"

(Kostya said he was at the first Live Aid and the Thompson Twins got the biggest ovation. And he worries about my judgment?)

Before we begin, program reminder: Don't miss ESPN's *Dream Job*. This week they vote off Michael Eisner.

WASHINGTON RUINS STANFORD'S PERFECT SEASON That erasing sound you hear is Rick Neuheisel reworking his brackets.

Elsewhere in college basketball Georgia Tech ended Duke's 41-game home winning streak. As if that weren't bad enough, after the game 15 Cameron Crazies tested positive for Ritalin.

Ten more and they have to legally change their name to the Cameron Chemically Imbalanced.

CAVS GIVE AWAY 10,000 LEBRON JAMES BOBBLEHEADS The LeBron doll is a little different. The head bobbles as he counts his money.

LeBron's teammate, center Ruben Boumtje Boumtje, is still on the injured list. He's been experiencing tightness in his left boumtje.

The Hawks' Terry Stotts is now the longest tenured coach in the East. But who knows? Yesterday G.M. Billy Knight had the phone company install Dick Motta Waiting.

REPORT ALLEGES BONDS, SHEFFIELD AND JASON GIAMBI RECEIVED STEROIDS FROM BALCO They were delivered by a 7-foot, 400-pound FedEx guy.

Players' union executive Gene Orza claims steroids are no worse than cigarettes. Except that with steroids, the only thing you light up is the Tigers' bullpen.

John Smoltz is demanding tougher testing for steroids. Like what, an essay question?

You know what's sad? Even if all the allegations are false, no one is going to look at a Marvin Benard ground rule double the same way again.

Are you like me? You want to put on muscle while lowering your body fat, but you can't stand that human growth hormone aftertaste?

I once saw a vial of human growth hormone. On the side there was a warning: "Keep out of reach of Muggsy Bogues."

In other baseball news, at The Ballpark in Arlington gift shop, a life-sized cutout of Alex Rodriguez has been marked down from $25 to $15. Actually, it's still $25, but Tom Hicks pays the other $10.

RANGERS BEAT CAPITALS 3–2 Big win. It means the Rangers move on to the first round of the AHL playoffs.

I don't want to say the Blueshirts have shut it down, but starting next week the part of Jaromir Jagr will be played by John Stamos.

49ERS MAKE ALL KINDS OF CHANGES They dealt Terrell Owens, released Jeff Garcia and now they're thinking about allowing the field judge at 3Com Park to perform gay weddings.

Bad week for TO. First he threatened to file a grievance over his trade to Baltimore, then he found out his agent missed the deadline to text-message his vote for *American Idol*.

Meanwhile the Bengals named Carson Palmer their starting QB even though the former Heisman winner did not take a snap last year. Apparently Marvin Lewis is impressed with how he's hitting his long irons.

The Raiders parted ways with linebacker Bill Romanowski. Let me guess. Pharmaceutical differences?

NFL EXTENDS SPONSORSHIP DEAL WITH GATORADE However, Gatorade must discontinue its new flavor, Andro Blast.

TRANSSEXUAL PLAYS IN WOMEN'S GOLF TOURNAMENT Here's what I don't get. Martha Burk is demanding the gal be allowed to play the front nine at Augusta.

My time is up. You've been great. Enjoy the Del Fuegos.

THE **NOTES**

(LeBron's teammate, center Ruben Boumtje Boumtje, is still on…) I wish this guy was more well-known. Then, I could rewrite all my old Boutros Boutros-Ghali jokes from Letterman.

(Are you like me? You want to put on muscle while lowering your body fat…) One of my Top Five favorites. And I say that not even knowing if you actually drink human growth hormone.

(49ers make all kinds of changes…) Five months later, in an interview, T.O. implied that his former teammate Jeff Garcia was gay. Does this make me a homopsychic?

THE **CUTS**

In the last few years, Gatorade has added five new product flavor lines, such as Ice, Fierce, Frost, Xtremo and X-Factor. (By the way, the last time all those names were used in one sentence, Mike Adamle was doing an opening teaser for American Gladiators.*)* I like this better than Andro Blast. For those of you who remember *American Gladiators*, it was like the WWF, but with less steroids and more integrity. So it failed. Mike Adamle was a former small white NFL running back, and the first player Howard Cosell ever called a "little monkey" on the air. The second, the black wide receiver Alvin Garrett, led to his resignation from *Monday Night Football*.

According to a recent Hockey News poll, 39% support the league's position in the labor talks, 11% support the players and the other 50% support Dominik Hasek's groin. This was a rewrite of a joke I'd written the week before about his groin siding with management and walking out. Unfortunately, 100% of the editors did not support either line.

THE **HIT(S)**

None. (A wildly popular garage band from Boston in the early '80s whose career was ruined when they sold out and did a national beer ad.)

Just came from *NASCAR 3D: The IMAX Experience*. Talk about realistic! You're only allowed to go to the men's room when they're running under yellow.

"BIG DANCE" CARD FILLED Did you see the NCAA selection show? Or, as CBS calls it, *CSI: RPI*.

Despite an 18–10 record, Colorado did not make the tournament. That may be a blessing. These days the school might want to stay away from the term "at large."

PLAYERS UNION OFFERS DONALD FEHR NEW CONTRACT It's $2.5 million a year for three more years. Or three more witch hunts, whichever comes first.

I believe for his new deal to be approved, Fehr needs a majority. Well, we know he's got at least 5–7% of the vote.

Last week Fehr and Bud Selig appeared on Capitol Hill during a hearing on performance enhancement drugs in sports. Fehr was attacked so strongly by Senator John McCain, you would have thought one of the side effects of steroids was soft money.

Meanwhile, the FDA banned the sale of androstenedione. Now the only way you can buy it over the counter is in a new breakfast cereal, "McGwire Jacks."

The 23 companies that make andro must stop selling it by the second week of April. Good move. The last thing you want to see is the Easter Bunny with huge pecs.

In other baseball news Garth Brooks singled in a spring training game for the Royals. Pretty impressive: His hit came two pitches after he'd been knocked down by LeAnn Rimes.

The Marlins' championship rings were unveiled last week. Each ring contains 229 diamonds, one for each fan who still remembers Jeff Torborg.

The Marlins received requests for rings from 12 former Expos limited partners who are suing majority owner Jeffrey Loria. He told

them to be patient. They're on the sizing list, just after Wayne Huizenga and the late Carl Barger.

TAGLIABUE CANCELS NEXT YEAR'S NFL KICKOFF CONCERT Too bad. Steven Tyler of Aerosmith was planning a scarf malfunction.

Ty Law is anxious to get out of New England. Today he showed up in Baltimore and offered to take Terrell Owens's physical.

TRACY MCGRADY GOES OFF FOR 62 POINTS Amazingly, the Orlando scoring machine missed 10 of his last 11 shots. And that was after Darrell Imhoff had fouled out.

Portland guard Damon Stoudamire passed a random drug test at the request of a local sports columnist. What a relief. The last thing you'd want to hear is that his sample was taken out of context.

Several teams are reportedly interested in Dennis Rodman after his Long Beach Jam won the ABA league championship. Rodman is serious about an NBA comeback. He's already changed his name to Paul Pierced.

THIRTY-TWO PLAYERS CHANGE TEAMS BEFORE NHL TRADE DEADLINE Ron Francis waived his no-trade clause and was dealt from Carolina to Toronto. He wanted to finish his career in a place with less snow.

Elsewhere, the Rangers obtained Sandy McCarthy off waivers from the Bruins. Nice to see this salary dump has a recycling bin.

TONYA HARDING APPEARS AT MINOR LEAGUE HOCKEY GAME The former Olympic skater put on a boxing exhibition. Fans were disappointed. They thought she'd be between the pipes.

NEW YORK CITY CONDUCTS DISASTER DRILL AT SHEA STADIUM Remember, the drill does not start until you hear the P.A. announcer say, "Now pitching, number 49, Armando Benitez...."

My time is up. You've been great. Enjoy Musical Youth.

THE **NOTES**

(Last week, Fehr and Bud Selig appeared on Capitol Hill…) One of McCain's passions is campaign finance reform. And is it me, or does "soft money" sound like something you use to buy Viagra?

(Tracy McGrady goes off for 62 points…) Imhoff was the opposing center the night Wilt Chamberlain scored 100 points. And to his credit, not once the entire game did he yell, "Hey, little help over here!"

(Portland guard Damon Stoudamire passed a random drug test…) Rick Reilly once tried to take Sammy Sosa up on his offer to be tested. Sammy went nuts. He later claimed his offer was just used for batting practice.

THE **CUTS**

Speaking of the Ravens, I'm no Mel Kiper Jr., but I think I know their draft strategy: Take the best player available not named "Lewis." Four years after Ray Lewis was implicated in a murder case, Jamal Lewis was indicted for drug trafficking. Wouldn't it have been great if he'd been trafficking drugs to Jerry Lewis?

O.J. Simpson sued $20,000 for allegedly pirating DirecTV signal. *Suddenly, this explains why Fred Goldman has been getting the NFL Network and the Spice Channel for free.* Let me stress something here. I'm not saying Fred Goldman watches the Spice Channel, I'm just saying he gets it as part of the civil settlement. Maybe there's something less ugly, like, *"Actually, he was getting the Spice Channel, then had it blocked out by Reggie McKenzie."*

THE **HIT(S)**

"Pass the Dutchie"

Before we begin, by applause, how many of you remember when March Madness referred to spring break at the Kennedy compound?

MLB AND THE PLAYERS' UNION AGREE TO BAN DESIGNER STEROID THG In a related story Clearasil is six weeks from perfecting a cream for hamstring acne.

The Phillies have acknowledged that Citizens Bank Park may not be completely finished by April 3. They're going to need at least another week to put up the rubber walls in Larry Bowa's office.

The new ballpark may have some temporary portable concession stands. Does this mean we'll get to see Roberto Hernandez come in from the bullpen on a hot dog cart?

ALABAMA UPENDS NO. 1 STANFORD Speaking of the Crimson Tide, anyone seen Billy Packer's face lately?

Packer's favorite dis, Saint Joseph's, advanced to the Sweet 16 with a victory over Texas Tech. After the defeat, Bobby Knight was gracious, he was respectful, he was courteous to the media ....Wait a minute. Does that doctor from *Eternal Sunshine of the Spotless Mind* have an office in Buffalo?

Elsewhere in Round 2, Wake Forest edged upstart Manhattan. Close game. During the last timeout, Manhattan coach Bobby Gonzalez tried to get Sebastian Telfair to sign a letter of intent.

Cincinnati's Tony Bobbitt hit a three-pointer with 16 seconds left to help the Bearcats avoid elimination in the opener. That was six days after he was punched in the groin by DePaul's LeVar Seals. What is it about guys named Bobbitt and that, uh, region?

Meanwhile, former Iowa State basketball coach Larry Eustachy has been talked about for the job at Texas A&M. Eustachy's a changed man. He plans to show up for interviews with a photo of himself and three nuns tapping a keg of Snapple.

T.O. GETS W-A-Y New Eagles wide receiver Terrell Owens has promised to tone down some of his antics. Which raises the question: Do Sharpies come in muted colors?

Warren Sapp signed a seven-year deal with the Raiders the day after it looked as if he was headed to the Bengals. Someone must have told him black was even more slimming than stripes.

Jeff Garcia was sentenced to seven days in a work-release program after pleading guilty to DUI. And I don't get this. Butch Davis says he wants Kelly Holcomb to do the last 3½ days.

ALLEN IVERSON BENCHES HIMSELF AFTER NONSTART Not only that, he told himself he wouldn't play again until he made a commitment to not show up for practice.

Iverson sat out last week's Sixers loss against the Pistons. Detroit fans were so angry they tried to recall Chris Ford.

During the game Iverson paid a ball boy to bring him nachos on the bench. What is he, nuts? Everyone knows to get the pizza at the Palace.

Rick Adelman became the winningest coach in Kings history, surpassing Les Harrison. Be honest. How many of you thought Les Harrison was the guy in *My Fair Lady*?

ESPN AND NHL IN NEGOTIATIONS OVER NEW TV CONTRACT And this is a little lame. Gary Bettman is claiming that with a lockout it'll be much easier for viewers to follow the puck.

RAPTORS FIRE DANCE-TEAM MEMBER AFTER DISCOVERING SHE POSED ON AN ADULTS-ONLY INTERNET SITE I haven't seen the site, but I understand she stays with her man better than Vince Carter.

My time is up. You've been great. Enjoy Rockwell.

THE **NOTES**

(Cincinnati's Tony Bobbitt hit a three-pointer with 16 seconds…) Ten years later, and you can still dine out on a John Wayne Bobbitt reference. Meanwhile, I heard he wanted to get back together with his ex-wife. No, I'm sorry. He wanted to get back together with himself.

(Meanwhile, former Iowa State basketball coach Larry Eustachy…) Eustachy lost his job when photographs surfaced of him hugging some coeds at a U. Missouri kegger. Apparently, you can only do this with nonconference opponents.

(T.O. gets w-a-y…) Two years before, Terrell had pulled a Sharpie out of his sock after scoring, signed a ball and handed it to a fan. No, I'm sorry. I was thinking about John Wayne Bobbitt.…

THE **CUTS**

Expos 3B Tony Batista is sidelined with chicken pox. Fortunately, his stance is so wide, he only has it on his left leg. Three years before, when a couple was seen having sex in one of the hotel rooms at Skydome, I wrote, *"Everybody was distracted by the display. You thought Tony Batista had a wide stance before.…"*

The Dolphins acquired WR David Boston from the Chargers. The deal was contingent on Boston passing a physical. Or a mirror. David Boston is big-time vain. Bodybuilding vain. In fact, when I first heard about the trade, I thought, "What, did they run out of posing oil in San Diego?"

THE **HIT(S)**

"Somebody's Watching Me"

Before we begin, did you read where the pope wants people to stop watching sports on Sunday? Sounds like somebody had Xavier only going one round....

FIELD SET FOR SAN ANTONIO Well, we've gone from 16 down to four. Of course, I'm talking about players who'll end up graduating.

CBS is keeping the self-promotion to a minimum. Although I did think it was a bit much when Jeff Probst showed up and put out Phil Martelli's torch.

JETS HOPE TO PLAY IN $1.4 BILLION RETRACTABLE ROOF STADIUM IN NEW YORK CITY Less than 60% of the cost for the 75,000-seat facility will be privately financed. Hey, I hope I'm not too early with a name: The Fleeced Center.

About $600 million will come from the city and state, $800 million from the Jets and the rest from proceeds off the pay-per-view fight between Omarosa and Heidi of *The Apprentice*.

The city claims it can raise half a billion on a new $1.50 a night hotel key tax. A buck-fifty a night? There goes your hooker's tip.

The Mayor's office has everything figured out. During construction West Side traffic will be rerouted through Nova Scotia.

TIGER WOODS TO TRAIN WITH ARMY AT FORT BRAGG FOR FOUR DAYS Well, he's tried everything else, maybe military discipline will straighten out his driver.

Seriously, it'll be a nice change to see Tiger taking marching orders from someone other than Phil Knight.

Tiger kept his streak alive at the Players Championship: Twenty-eight straight tournaments at which some idiot at the tee has yelled, "You da nanny!!!"

Adam Scott's win at the Players Championships helped ensure John Daly would remain in the top 10 on the money list and qualify for the Masters. And this is nice. In Daly's honor, they're renaming holes 11 through 13 "M&M Corner."

NEW ENGLAND DEVELOPER SAYS HE HAS FINANCING TO BUY EXPOS AND MOVE THEM TO CONNECTICUT Jon Alevizos would rename the team the Colonials. Come on. How about something more indigenous to Connecticut: the NoSox.

Alevizos says if the sale goes through, he would hire former president George Bush as chairman of the board. Why? So he can trade Sammy Sosa's father?

Curt Schilling demanded MLB drug testing be conducted by a third party—which is how it's already done. From now on, he'll only make ill-informed remarks on four days' rest.

Toronto has a new logo this year. It's J.P. Ricciardi dismantling a blue jay's nest by the All-Star break.

GRIZZLIES CLINCH PLAYOFF SPOT Memphis is going wild. Next week the mayor will present Hubie Brown and Jerry West with the key ... to the main refrigerator at Graceland.

Elsewhere, Charles Barkley became the 10th person inducted into the Phoenix Suns' Ring of Honor. The ceremony was supposed to take place at the start of the season, but it took five months to let the ring out a couple of sizes.

MATTHEW MODINE STARS AS HONUS WAGNER IN TV MOVIE *THE WINNING SEASON* Talk about dedicated. To prepare for the role, Modine spent six months in Wayne Gretzky's safe deposit box.

MICHELLE KWAN'S REIGN ENDS AT WORLDS The five-time champion never recovered from her fall on Day One. I know what you're thinking, but Todd Bertuzzi was home the whole time.

My time is up. You've been great. Enjoy Van McCoy.

THE **NOTES**

(Before we begin, did you read where the pope wants…) This raises an interesting question of spirituality: Does the pope do his own brackets, or is it one of the Louisville Cardinals?

(Adam Scott's win at the Players Championship…) John Daly has admitted addictions to the following: alcohol, gambling, diet Coke and M&M's. Not only that, he's been married so many times, he refers to his present wife as "the leader in the clubhouse."

(New England developer says he has financing…) Normally, I wouldn't mention an unknown's name if it wasn't germane to the joke, but Jon Alevizos was once the G.M. of the Braves and his son was a fine pitcher at Harvard. Even more important, he saw me play in college and told me years later I was screwed by the coaching staff. So he gets a giant shout-out.

(Matthew Modine stars as Honus Wagner in TV movie…) Wayne Gretzky is the owner of one of those rare Honus Wagner baseball cards. It's worth like $10 million—$11 million if you still have the gum.…

THE **CUTS**

The Red Sox are trying to get permission to serve alcohol in the field box seats. They've already developed a new cocktail: the Grady Little. It's a martini that puts a bad taste in your mouth after the olive is left in too long. Six months later, the word came down from above: O.K., that's enough.

Jays pitcher Justin Miller was ordered to wear a long-sleeved jersey to cover up tattoos on his arm. Which is a shame, because the snake with the lightning bolt through its head has yet to let an inherited runner score. I guess the image was too bizarre. Maybe something more accessible, like Elvis with a lightning bolt through his head.

THE **HIT(S)**

"The Hustle"

THE **SHOW** |

Are you excited about *The Bachelor* with Giants quarterback Jesse Palmer? I can't wait for this exchange: "Do you have protection?" "Not unless we draft Robert Gallery."

NCAA PRESIDENT MILES BRAND DOES NOT THINK FINAL FOUR HAS BECOME TOO COMMERCIALIZED Here's my question: Did he say that before Cingular at the Half or just after the Dasani Sideline Report?

Not too commercialized? Come on. My finals bracket had Papa John's versus DiGiorno.

Georgia Tech reached the final despite disappointing contributions from its stars. In fact, I thought all the CBS promos for *Without a Trace* were referring to B.J. Elder's offense.

MAJOR LEAGUE UMPIRES MAY JOIN UP WITH TEAMSTERS So get ready for five-man crews: home plate, three bases and one guy holding a flashlight for no reason.

Teamster umps. And you thought Steve Trachsel slowed up games.

Are you like me? Do you figure six months from now, they'll find a QuesTec machine buried in the south end zone at Giants Stadium?

DEVIL RAYS AND YANKEES SPLIT IN TOKYO The Yankees made an estimated $20 million for the two games. Great. That covers A-Rod until Memorial Day.

It wasn't all good news. The day after the teams returned, Jason Giambi tested positive for wasabi.

Did you see that Ricoh patch the Yankees were wearing in Japan? The Ricoh patch. What's that for, when you need to cut back to two rolls of film a day?

Meanwhile, President Bush threw out the first pitch at the Cardinals' opener. I heard it was a preemptive strike.

You know what's sad? Richard Clarke is claiming Bush was supposed to be there three years ago.

Elsewhere, Dick Cheney threw out the first pitch at the Reds' opener. Cincinnati catcher Jason LaRue said he had nice movement but undisclosed location.

NFL VOTES TO EXTEND INSTANT REPLAY FIVE MORE YEARS The (slow) motion passed almost unanimously. The only votes against were from Kansas City, Indianapolis and Justin Timberlake.

Also during the owners' meetings, commissioner Paul Tagliabue was offered a three-year contract extension, which would raise his yearly salary from $5 million to $8 million. Unfortunately, his celebration lasted too long, and he now has to walk an additional 15 yards to the bank.

LAKERS WIN 11 STRAIGHT, SURGE INTO FIRST IN WEST Kobe Bryant was named Western Conference Player of the Month. See what happens when all those little distractions are out of the way?

Three life-sized bobblehead dolls of Shaquille O'Neal are selling at the Staples Center gift shop for $25,000 apiece. Sure, it sounds like a bargain, but it balloons up to 400 pounds in the off-season.

The doll is incredibly lifelike. If you put it behind the free throw line, the head bobbles from side to side.

Allen Iverson will miss the rest of the season with pain in his right knee. But doctors are confident he'll be 100% in time to skip the first Dream Team practice.

RUMORS FLY THAT U.S. POSTAL SERVICE MAY DROP SPONSORSHIP OF U.S. PRO CYCLING TEAM It won't be official until you see the sign on the back of Lance Armstrong's bike: NEXT WINDOW, PLEASE.

NEW LOGO UNVEILED FOR IRAQ'S OLYMPIC TEAM Pretty clever. It's the five Olympic rings, joined together by two welders from Halliburton.

My time is up. You've been great. Enjoy the Floaters.

THE **NOTES**

(Major league umpires may join up with Teamsters…) To any member of the Teamsters who may read these next three jokes: I took some very strong cough medicine before I wrote this. Very strong.

(Elsewhere, Dick Cheney threw out the first pitch at the Reds' opener…) How come I feel even less safe making fun of the Vice President than the Teamsters?

(Rumors fly that U.S. Postal Service may drop…) Never give up. Don't ever give up.

(New logo unveiled for Iraq's Olympic team…) This is just in case you weren't sure how I felt about Cheney.

THE **CUTS**

Wake up the egos calling her name…. Hornung didn't help himself. First, he insisted he didn't say anything wrong, then he apologized, then he claimed he was forced to make his comments after losing a bet with Alex Karras. In 1964, Hornung and Karras were suspended for an entire season for gambling. We've come a long way. Today, to get suspended for a year, you have to kill a pharmacist.

The Boston archdiocese has ordered all Catholics to not consume meat during the Red Sox' home opener on Good Friday. I'm confused. Since when did they start putting meat in Fenway Franks? To give you an idea how old this joke is, they used to say the same thing about the hot dogs at the Last Supper.

On the bright side, isn't it nice to hear from the Boston archdiocese without the phrase "hush money"? Or the phrase "Grady Little"?

THE **HIT(S)**

"Float On"

THE SHOW | April 19, 2004

I don't know if this has anything to do with Title IX, but just as many cars were turned over and set on fire after the UConn women won their NCAA title.

MAJOR BREAKTHROUGH FOR PHIL Here's the story they won't tell you. When Mickelson lost his lead and fell three shots back with seven holes to go, a local hospital began fitting him for a green straitjacket.

Wild Sunday. There was so much movement during the final round, the two guys posting numbers on the leader board had to go in for rotator-cuff surgery.

Playing in his final Masters, Arnold Palmer had to sidestep a snake at the 13th hole. Course marshals immediately returned the snake to its natural habitat, Hootie Johnson's legal team.

Martha Burk was not in Augusta this year. She's too busy with her latest crusade, trying to get a woman admitted into the first five rows of a Bette Midler concert.

Once again the Masters was commercial-free … if you don't count John Daly's shirt.

Speaking of which, isn't it time for somebody to stitch in COULD USE just above TRIM SPA?

Three days before the opening round, Daly's wife pleaded guilty to money laundering. She got a good deal. Five years' probation, six months' mobile-home arrest.

BARRY BONDS TRIES TO CHANGE PUBLIC PERCEPTION WITH NEW WEBSITE It's www.barrybonds.com. I guess that www.getouttamyface.com was taken.

Pretty sophisticated website. You can actually download a urine sample.

Pedro Martinez has readjusted his goals since his opening-night loss. He now wants to complete at least 30 games—in his own dugout.

Ben & Jerry's signed a five-year sponsorship deal with the Mariners. Which means they

got Freddy Garcia to legally change his first name to Cherry.

GIANTS THINKING OF TRADING UP FOR ELI MANNING The Giants are concerned about their quarterback situation. During the next three episodes of *The Bachelor*, Jesse Palmer has been ordered to wear the red jersey so he can't be sacked.

Last week, at a private workout for NFL scouts, Maurice Clarett ran a so-so 4.6 40. And now he's thinking of suing the company who made the stopwatch.

FLYERS GO UP 2–0 ON DEFENDING CHAMP DEVILS Jeremy Roenick is not shaving his jaw wire until Philly is eliminated.

The Devils are without captain Scott Stevens, who is suffering from postconcussion syndrome or, as it's known in the NHL, Acute Lindrosia.

Andrew Raycroft was the first Bruins goalie to get a shutout in his playoff debut since Tiny Thompson in 1929. Look, I know everyone suffered during the Depression, but if you're a guy and your nickname was Tiny, you win.

SERENA WILLIAMS MAY BECOME NEWEST BOND GIRL She'll appear in the upcoming film *From Russia with Love, Love.*

Martina Navratilova played her first singles match in the U.S. in 10 years. To give you an idea of how long her layoff was, in 1994 the most dangerous person in women's tennis was Mary Pierce's dad.

REPUBLICAN NATIONAL COMMITTEE USING DON KING IN ANTI-KERRY ADS Good move. He'll charge much less to fix this election than whomever they used last time.

CLEAR CHANNEL COMMUNICATIONS FINED $495,000 FOR HOWARD STERN TRANSGRESSION What did he do, criticize the officiating on "Lesbian Dial-A-Date"?

My time is up. You've been great. Enjoy Wishbone Ash.

THE **NOTES**

(Martha Burk was not in Augusta this year…) Judy is dead, Liza wasn't touring. You have to be adaptable.

(Andrew Raycroft was the first Bruins goalie to get a shutout…) If I was still doing stand-up, this is the kind of thing I would have loved to have in my act. What Jerry Seinfeld used to call "bulls——t logic." Of course, back then he used to curse.

(Clear Channel Communications fined $495,000…) When I saw the amount of the fine, I immediately thought of Mark Cuban. Then I needed to think of a bit Howard did 10 years ago, the last time I listened to him.

THE **CUTS**

Last month, Cleveland outfielder Matt Lawton had more than $100,000 of jewelry stolen from his hotel room in Philadelphia. Poor Lawton: $100,000 in stolen jewelry, and he no longer has Torii Hunter to get it back at the fence. Good line, contingent upon knowing the term "fence." Which raises the question: Can you get a subscription to *SI* in the joint?

Bruins star Joe Thornton has been hampered by a sore wrist or rib, which the team is still describing as an "upper body injury." I was shocked. I had no idea Mike Shanahan had another job. Do you remember the controversy over Shanahan's falsely reporting injuries? If your answer is "Mike Shanahan who?" we have a big problem.

THE **HIT(S)**

None. (Another '70s hard-rock British band suggested by a friend. Again, to recap, other than my wife, Ed Markey and Mark Patrick, people never give me jokes, just bands.)

Did you see the photo of Tiger Woods in the Army Humvee? Butch Harmon thinks his hands are four degrees too far apart on the mounted machine gun.

NBA PLAYOFFS: BEGIN STRETCHING The Rockets had a desperate strategy for the first round against the Lakers: Get Shaq's mouth into foul trouble.

Miami put on a furious stretch run to grab the fourth seed in the East. The Heat is the NBA's best-kept secret. Seriously, I still look at the end of their bench and think, Jeez, Pat Riley really let himself go.

Mark Cuban made an offer to Kwame, the runner-up from *The Apprentice*. I have no idea what that offer was, but I'm sure it's going to end up costing Antawn Jamison minutes.

Before the playoffs there were some strange events near the end of the regular season. The Hawks apologized to fans at Philips Arena after playing a hip-hop song by DMX with obscene lyrics. Not only that, Bob Sura grabbed the tape out of the sound booth and wanted credit for a rebound.

The Magic had 4,000 no-shows for Fan Appreciation Night. Can't blame them. The biggest attraction was getting your X-ray taken with Grant Hill.

BARRY BONDS HITS 660, 661 Is it me, or did Willie Mays look as comfortable passing the torch as he did digging in against Drysdale?

The Rangers and Dr Pepper have announced a joint can-redemption program. Speaking of saving cans, how's Buck Showalter's job security these days?

Meanwhile, gas prices are headed through the roof, everyone in the Middle East hates us, Toronto and Seattle are in last place—happy 1978, everybody!

NFL 2004 SCHEDULE RELEASED For the first time in the show's 35-year history, neither Oakland nor San Francisco will appear on *Monday Night Football*. Thanks a lot, BALCO.

The Bengals will play their first Monday-night game in 12 years and their first one at home since 1989. It's the longest ban in Cincinnati that wasn't caused by allegations from Tommy Gioiosa.

NO DEFENSE OF STANLEY CUP Be honest. Did you ever think the Devils would have their season finale before *Friends* did?

Elsewhere, the Canucks won Game 6 in triple OT after blowing a 4–0 lead to Calgary. You know what would be great? If Vancouver police dropped the Todd Bertuzzi case and started investigating whether the way the Flames came from behind was premeditated.

The Canucks seemed confused. They thought it was best-of-seven goalies.

MASTERS RATINGS LOWEST SINCE 1993 CBS attributes the drop to three factors: Easter weekend, the 1:30 final-round start and Kirk Triplett's dorky hat.

Sunday's round started early due to the threat of bad weather. I feel so foolish. I thought it was due to the threat of Bernhard Langer not finishing in time to get his taxes in.

This may explain things. *Langer* is German for "Trachsel."

Two days after his victory, Phil Mickelson wore his green jacket on *The Tonight Show*. I have to check, but I believe it's the first piece of original material they've had on that show since Johnny left.

ACTOR WHO PLAYED JESUS IN MEL GIBSON MOVIE PORTRAYS GOLF LEGEND BOBBY JONES I can't wait for the scene when he walks on Rae's Creek.

JAYSON WILLIAMS BECOMES FATHER AGAIN Quite a moment. The doctor came out of the delivery room and said, "Congratulations. It's a character witness!"

My time is up. You've been great. Enjoy Rick Astley.

THE **NOTES**

(Miami put on a furious stretch run to grab…) This was a slightly unfair poke at Heat head coach Stan Van Gundy, but placed a distant second to a future issue of *SI*, when they ran side-by-side lookalike shots of him and Ron Jeremy.

(Elsewhere, the Canucks won Game 6 in triple OT…) Kostya did a rewrite of this joke. So clean and concise, he should be hired by Bertuzzi's defense.

(This may explain things. Langer is German for "Trachsel.") Nine words! Check from God. And the Teamsters.

(Two days after his victory, Phil Mickelson wore his green jacket on The Tonight Show…*)* I had left Letterman after 13 years the month before, so I felt free to take this swipe. I don't want to say I had thought of this joke long before that, but the Vancouver police may investigate me for acting premeditated.

THE **CUTS**

Good to be here. You think you have a bad job? How'd you like to be the guy who explains the photo of Tiger Woods in an Army hummer to Donald Rumsfeld? The Butch Harmon line is smarter, but I love the Dukakis-ness of this image.

Barry celebrated in his customary fashion on the historic dinger. He crossed home plate, then pointed skyward…to the luxury box where his licensing director was sitting. Bonds had taken over his own licensing, away from MLB. You know, if he doesn't watch it, people are going to begin to think he's a little self-involved.

THE **HIT(S)**

"Never Gonna Give You Up"

Good to be here. Just wondering: If David Beckham gets a red card, does he have to sit out his next two women on the side?

NFL DRAFT: SAN DIEGO TAKES DICTATION WELL Shrewd move by the Chargers. In exchange for top draft pick Eli Manning, San Diego received Philip Rivers and three Giants picks and got Archie Manning to assume custody of Ryan Leaf.

Archie may be getting a little drunk with power. Sunday he flew to Florida and ordered Anna Kournikova out of her parents' house.

Promising weekend at Madison Square Garden for New York teams. The Giants bagged Manning, the Jets upgraded with Jonathan Vilma and Isiah Thomas didn't file a protest about the clock.

Once again, Mel Kiper Jr. was a little over-prepared. Come on. Did we really need his list of Best Available Supreme Court Justices?

The Patriots came in looking for help at cornerback. Makes sense. Ty Law allegedly did only a 4.75 running from the Miami police.

The University of Miami set a record when six Hurricanes went in the first round. Nice to have that many Miami football players picked out of something other than a lineup.

Maybe I dozed off late in round 1 and dreamed this, but I could have sworn I heard Kenechi Udeze pick up the phone and say, "No, what are you wearing?"

RED SOX SWEEP YANKEES New York scored four runs in three games. Sad. The only one at Yankee Stadium hitting after the seventh inning was Ronan Tynan, the Irish tenor.

The Blue Jays are off to their worst start in history. Experts believe the only way Toronto will win a seventh game in April is if it's played against Ottawa.

Elsewhere, business at the Orioles shop at Camden Yards is up 20% from last year. The biggest-selling item is the Peter Angelos Radar Detector, which starts screaming any time the Expos come within 50 miles of Washington, D.C.

New York City is raising money by selling old seats from Yankee Stadium. Three seats together went for $1,500, plus whatever Joe Pepitone charges for delivery.

PACERS SPREADING NO. 1 SEED Before getting swept, the Celtics suffered their worst home playoff loss in history in Game 3. They were so overmatched, midway through the second half Danny Ainge tried to break into the NBA office and sneak 10 Ping-Pong balls into the lottery machine.

I must have missed a memo from David Stern's office. Is Nets-Knicks best-of-seven digs?

Knicks forward Tim Thomas called the Nets' Kenyon Martin "a fugazy guy," a slang term for fake used in the movie *Donnie Brasco*. Speaking of going undercover for years, has anybody seen Dikembe Mutombo?

Jamal Mashburn was sent home by the Hornets after he complained that the team had mishandled his medical care in New Orleans. Apparently he had his knee scoped twice by Emeril.

SHARKS GO UP 2–0 ON AVALANCHE They're confident in San Jose. The HP Pavilion ordered enough toner to laser-print tickets for the Cup finals.

JOCKEYS FILE SUIT TO WEAR ADS AT KENTUCKY DERBY This is wrong. You can't deprive Jose Santos of the chance to be the AOL Messenger guy.

VITALI KLITSCHKO TKO'S SANDERS TO WIN VACANT WBC TITLE And how's this for handy? The championship belt folds up and fits in the hole Lennox Lewis opened over his eye.

My time is up. You've been great. Enjoy Ace.

THE **NOTES**

(Archie may be getting a little drunk with power…) Earlier in the week, a story had surfaced that Anna couldn't get her parents out of a house she had bought them. Or something like that. Other than downloading photos, do we really pay attention to her?

(Once again, Mel Kiper Jr. was a little overprepared…) Jeff Wong did a tremendous illustration with this column of Tagliabue handing a custom-made jersey to Ruth Bader Ginsburg. So good, Ginsburg's people called and asked for the original. Does it bother you the Supreme Court is reading my column, or do you think *Roe v. Wade* was the undercard in Gatti-Ward III?

(Maybe I dozed off late in round 1 and dreamed this…) Another gift from my wife, who walked by the living room as they showed a first-rounder on the phone and said, "Wouldn't it be great if he said, 'No, what are *you* wearing?'" Uh, yeah, it would.

THE **CUTS**

Good to be here. Just saw a sneak preview of Troy. *Give me a break. Over two hours, not one mention of RPI hockey.* RPI is a fine engineering school in Troy, New York, which won the NCAA hockey title in 1983. The only reason I know that is because I covered the team during the 1979–80 season. I was so so pleased with this opener until Kostya gently reminded me, "Uh, we're trying to welcome people into the tent with the opening line."

Hubie Brown named NBA Coach of the Year. *Incredibly, he's using the same defense that worked against Chamberlain. Neville Chamberlain.* An Ed Markey special. Of course, the difference between Wilt and Neville is about 40,000 points and 19,999 women.

THE **HIT(S)**

"How Long Has This Been Going On?"

Before we begin, I'm a little confused about the NBA playoffs. This is a bye week, right?

SMARTY LEAVES DERBY FIELD PANTING

Thirty-nine-year-old jockey Stewart Elliot won in his first Kentucky Derby. To give you an idea how unknown this guy is, the only advertising on his silks was a KFC discount coupon sticking out of his back pocket.

A thunderstorm just before the race made bad conditions worse. I haven't seen that much mud fly since Richard Clarke testified before the 9/11 commission.

On the other hand it was nice to hear the phrase "sloppy track" and not have it refer to Marion Jones's joint checking account.

Different feel at this year's Derby. No Jerry Bailey, no D. Wayne Lukas, no Bob Baffert, no kids asking, "Daddy, what's a gelding?"

MLB ATTENDANCE UP 15%

And if it gets to 17%, you know what that means: Mandatory testing of mascots.

According to reports, BALCO president Victor Conte volunteered the names of 27 athletes who received steroids. And he can expand that list to 40 after Sept. 1.

Oakland's stadium is now known as McAfee Coliseum. But I'm not sure if this tradition is going to catch on: the seventh-inning virus scan.

LIGHTNING BOLT HABS IN FOUR STRAIGHT

The series was over so fast the Canadiens' Mike Ribeiro had to fake an injury in the handshake line.

The Red Wings went down three games to two in their conference semifinal against the Flames. Detroit is desperate for offense. They're thinking of putting Chauncey Billups on the point.

The difference in those games was Flames goaltender Miikka Kiprusoff. He's got it all:

the glove hand of a young Patrick Roy and the groin of a young Dominik Hasek.

Commissioner Gary Bettman and NHLPA chief Bob Goodenow sat together at Game 3 of the Flyers-Leafs series. And this doesn't bode well. They couldn't agree on nacho toppings.

TIMBERWOLVES BEAT THE NUGGETS TO ADVANCE

Carmelo Anthony sat out the deciding game with a sprained knee. Jon Barry took the Denver rookie's place, scoring seven points and dishing out eight denials that he and Christina Aguilera were an item.

Shaquille O'Neal stands to make millions on the proposed IPO of Google. Shaq has always been a shrewd investor. Ten years ago he was the first guy to cash out of *Blue Chips*.

In other NBA news the Celtics hired Doc Rivers. He fulfilled three key criteria: He has experience, he's good with young players and he doesn't mind having his clothes laid out for him by Danny Ainge.

GIANTS RELEASE KERRY COLLINS

Kind of sad the way Collins found out. He walked into the Giants' locker room at the Meadowlands and saw Archie Manning measuring his stall for curtains.

Elsewhere Drew Bledsoe agreed to renegotiate his contract with the Bills. The team has agreed to defer 30 sacks.

IOC TAKES OUT $170 MILLION INSURANCE POLICY ON OLYMPICS

Pretty comprehensive. It pays off if any Olympic official is severely injured by a kickback.

JAYSON WILLIAMS ACQUITTED OF MANSLAUGHTER

And I don't think this was called for, but after four days of deliberations the jury ruled Benoit Benjamin's NBA career was also an accident.

My time is up. You've been great. Enjoy Sugarloaf.

THE **NOTES**

(On the other hand, it was nice to hear the phrase "sloppy track"…) Marion Jones's ex-husband, shot-putter C.J. Hunter, had tested positive for steroids and later admitted to authorities to writing a check for over $7,000 to BALCO owner Victor Conte from their account. Of course, he claimed it was for a specimen cup holder for the car.

(Different feel at this year's Derby. No Jerry Bailer, no D. Wayne Lukas…) Had to. I absolutely had to. (Kids, go ask your dad.)

*(**Lightning bolt Habs in four straight**…)* Ribeiro had taken so many dives during the first-round series with Boston, Peter McNeeley sued him for identity theft.

*(**Jayson Williams acquitted of manslaughter**…)* Benjamin, Williams's former teammate, provided some devastating testimony. But, once again, failed to convert in crunch time.

THE **CUTS**

Red Sox 2B Mark Bellhorn continues to lead AL in walks. *I'm not going to take this seriously until he gets a package from BALCO.* This punch line originally was, *See what happens when the CIA and FBI don't talk to each other?* But I figured that was a payoff I could use for just about anything. Never did.

Meanwhile, Derek Jeter's slump continues. Last night, he was caught looking on three straight belt-high models. At the time, Jeter was hitting .179. He finished at .292. This joke is that rare combination of pity and envy.

Speaking of things deferred, anyone seen Dick Cheney's military record? And this is the even rarer combination of arrogance and arrogance.

THE **HIT(S)**

"Green-Eyed Lady"

Good to be here. I'll be honest, I've been in better spirits. Two days ago my psychotherapist presented me with the Crybaby Award.

NO CHANCE FOR A WEB GEM Major League Baseball suddenly canceled plans to have promotional symbols for the film *Spider-Man 2* adorn bases next month. What happened? Did they find a bottle of andro in Peter Parker's locker?

MLB claimed the promotion was an attempt to attract kids to the ballpark. Oh, like all of a sudden, eating sugar, hearing fat guys curse and watching your dad get hammered isn't attractive enough?

It's not the first time baseball has had a marketing tie-in with the movies. Don Zimmer still makes promotional appearances as Shrek.

The logo was going to be everywhere. Bases, on-deck circles, Barry Bonds's left biceps....

No, I'm wrong. Barry's left biceps already has a separate marketing deal with the movie *Envy*.

The Rangers came from 10 runs down to beat the Tigers 16–15 last week. See what happens when Buck Showalter finally gets some decent pitching?

The Dodgers are off to their best start in years. Great team chemistry so far. The other day Adrian Beltre popped up to second, and Milton Bradley offered to run it out for him.

IT'S NOT THE HEAT, IT'S THE HUMILITY The Pacers jumped out to a 2–0 lead on Miami. They're very confident in Indiana. Ron Artest is carrying enough cash on him to pay technical foul fines for five weeks.

The Pacers had 11 days between the first round and the start of the Heat series. Hey, not even Rik Smits is that well-rested.

After dropping the first two games to the Spurs, the Lakers put Game 3 away early. Speaking of garbage time, what do you think the ratings will be for a San Antonio–Indiana final?

Kobe Bryant was scheduled to be arraigned this week in Eagle, Colo. And I don't know if this will help, but he plans to show up with Bruce Bowen defending him.

The Mavericks were fined $25,000 by the league for showing a pregame video that ridiculed the Sacramento Kings. Too bad. That wipes out Mark Cuban's advertising budget for the DVD.

Hoops phenom Sebastian Telfair declared himself eligible for the draft. In a related story, the Clippers will be represented at the lottery by a Hummer salesman.

WELL, IT'S DOWN TO PHILLY, TAMPA, SAN JOSE AND CALGARY Of course, I'm talking about the last four stops on the Guess Who reunion tour.

Calgary and San Jose share an interesting history. The Flames' Darryl Sutter coached the Sharks until 2002. Or was that his other brother, Daryl?

CBC commentator Don Cherry will reportedly be let go after the Stanley Cup playoffs. Cherry has been with Hockey Night in Canada for 23 years. You know what's sad? His pit bull's pension doesn't kick in until the dog turns 165.

Last week Alex Trebek appeared on *Live with Regis and Kelly* wearing a Maple Leafs jersey. Ladies and gentlemen, John Ferguson and Pat Quinn have got to stop signing guys way past their prime.

RAVENS LINEBACKER RAY LEWIS SETTLES OUT OF COURT TO AVOID A CIVIL TRIAL Too bad. Michele Tafoya was all set to work the sideline.

RAIDERS CONSIDER HIRING NICK FROM *THE APPRENTICE* TO SELL LUXURY SUITES What's next? Al Davis putting Omarosa on retainer in case he needs someone to lie under oath?

My time is up. You've been great. Enjoy the Brothers Johnson.

THE **NOTES**

(Good to be here. I'll be honest, I've been in better spirits…) Earlier that week, a junior high school basketball coach had presented one of his players with the "Crybaby Award" at a team dinner. He claims he did it partly as a joke and partly as motivation. Yeah, in the same way I try to motivate Grady Little and Rick Pitino.

(The Pacers had 11 days between the first round and the start…) The way David Stern stretches out the NBA playoffs is manipulative and sanctimonious. And Spider-Man will back me up on this.

(Calgary and San Jose share an interesting history…) Six Sutter brothers played in the NHL. Brian, Brent, Duane, Darryl, Ron and Rich. The tag is from the *Newhart* show. Newhart had a great line about people in L.A. telling time by their divorces: *"I haven't been to a Dodger game since…well, I know I was married to Janet back then…."*

THE **CUTS**

Before the plan was changed, the Yankees had announced they would not participate in the Spider-Man promotion. Of course not. They didn't want to piss off Batman. This was cut after careful consideration by myself and the editors. We didn't want to piss off Batman.

Tom Sizemore to portray Pete Rose in upcoming film. *This explains the new scene where Pete misses a few payments and his bookie beats up Heidi Fleiss.* Sizemore actually served time for assaulting the former Hollywood Madam. Kostya asked me, "Do you really want a joke that ends with the words, 'Beats up Heidi Fleiss'?" And I'll never forget my response: "Uh, you want me to say no, right?"

CBC commentator Don Cherry will reportedly be let go after the Stanley Cup playoffs. Times have really changed. Now, the only network that pays people to make fun of Europeans is Al Qaeda. Good idea, ruined by the fact that Al Qaeda doesn't exactly make fun of Europeans.

THE **HIT(S)**

"I'll Be Good to You"

"Strawberry Letter #22"

Try to keep it down. We don't want to wake up Roy Jones Jr.

SMARTY JONES ROMPS BY 11½ LENGTHS IN PREAKNESS In the 13 days between victories, Smarty did not have a workout. However, on Thursday afternoon in the paddock, he did 20 minutes of Strippercise.

Gary Stevens flew in from Paris to ride runner-up Rock Hard Ten. I guess Tobey Maguire couldn't make weight.

MLB MOVES OFFICIAL DRUG TESTING FACILITIES TO LAB IN MONTREAL Are you like me? Are you expecting Bud Selig to announce that 22 samples this season will be processed in San Juan?

Previously, much of the testing had been done at a laboratory in Southern California. I believe it was called Centrifuges 'n Things.

A document from 1791 was found in Pittsfield, Mass., which contains the first recorded mention of the word baseball. And what are the odds of this? Later in the same document is the first recorded mention of Spider-Man.

Congratulations to Red Sox outfielder Manny Ramirez who became a U.S. citizen. Manny had done very well on the citizenship test. A couple of questions were over his head and he didn't even drop his bat and charge the test monitor.

Roger Clemens is 7–0. And I'm not sure if this is part of his contract, but during his last start he got a visit on the mound from Astros pitching coach Burt Hooten and three visits from his sons.

LAKERS GET OVER THEMSELVES, GET OVER ON SPURS Kobe Bryant went for a double double in the deciding game: 26 points, 12 words spoken to Phil Jackson.

Not exactly offensive fireworks in the playoffs. TNT is thinking of changing its slogan to, "Shoot 32% from the floor, or go home."

FLYERS-LIGHTNING SERIES STARTS UGLY, GETS UGLIER Philadelphia coach Ken Hitchcock claimed fans in Tampa were throwing food at his players. Not only that, it was stuff Jeremy Roenick is still not allowed to chew.

During Game 1, the Lightning offered free beer to anyone who put down a deposit on season tickets for next year. By the third period they had to add an express lane to the men's room.

I don't get it. This is the one season in Tampa Bay you didn't have to be drunk to enjoy the team.

Free beer, but there was one catch. Before every refill you had to touch your finger to your nose and spell *Khabibulin*.

NFL TODAY WAIVES DEION SANDERS Sad the way it happened. CBS told Deion's tailor to let out his contract.

The Rams have given quarterback Kurt Warner permission to talk with other teams. It's working great. So far, 20 call-in radio stations are interested in signing his wife.

FORMER PRESIDENT BUSH TO LEAD U.S. DELEGATION INTO ATHENS His son George W. is thrilled. He asked his dad to get a picture taken with Uga VI.

Meanwhile, Iraq qualified for the Olympic soccer tournament. But that didn't stop Halliburton from requesting $50 million to rebuild the team.

BCS SIMPLIFICATIONS DISCUSSED If the proposed new system had been in place, this year's national championship would have been LSU versus Clay Aiken.

SYRACUSE CHANGES NICKNAME FROM ORANGEMEN TO ORANGE Great marketing strategy. Why be represented by some cute, innocuous mascot when you can be associated with a threat level on the terror alert chart?

My time is up. You've been great. Enjoy Katrina and the Waves.

THE **NOTES**

(Previously, much of the testing had been done at a laboratory…) I don't know whether they use that device to process a drug test, but I'm pretty sure most people in Southern California think "centrifuge" is a topping.

(Roger Clemens is 7–0. And I'm not sure…) Part of Roger's deal was that he didn't have to go on road trips if he wasn't pitching so he could watch his sons play. Why does this continue to bother only me?

(Former President Bush to lead U.S. delegation into Athens…) This is obviously a play on Athens, Ga., where the University of Georgia has its campus. Of course, George W. probably thinks Uga VI is a topping.

THE **CUTS**

The start of the Preakness was delayed 10 minutes. First, Imperialism threw a shoe, then stewards had trouble loading Bob Neumeier into his seat. Bob Neumeier is not heavy, just excited. And Imperialism? Where did that horse come from, Halliburton Stables?

Of course, if you know your history, you remember 1791 was also the year George Washington was accused of corking his teeth. The man had wooden teeth. I figured this was a slam dunk. Nothing. No love. Come on. The guy had his root canal work done by a beaver. Anything? Anyone? Bueller?

Several Giants players have filed complaints with the union about Tom Coughlin's off-season training program. And today, a confused Mara family said it was standing behind Donald Rumsfeld. A less than vague reference to Abu Ghraib, the Iraqi prison that was taken over by U.S. soldiers. Be honest, though. How many of you would like to see Kurt Warner on a leash? Put your hand down, Brenda.

THE **HIT(S)**

"Walking on Sunshine"

Great news. The Green Monster section at Fenway Park is now available for gay bachelor parties.

2012 OLYMPICS RINGS IN FINAL FIVE The IOC narrowed the list of potential host cities to Paris, London, New York, Moscow and a long shot, Troy.

Paris scored the highest among the finalists on the IOC's list of technical criteria. New York was fourth. Apparently, the IOC was less than impressed that the city hasn't quite cleared the traffic from people leaving the 1999 NBA All-Star Game.

Not only that, they'd like the organizers to find a better venue for boxing than Dick Ebersol's Connecticut guesthouse.

Surprisingly, Rio de Janeiro failed to make the finals. However, it's now considered the front-runner for the Expos.

BIG UNIT TOSSES PERFECT GAME Randy Johnson set down 27 Atlanta hitters in a row. It was such a dominant performance that by the fifth inning Skip Caray stopped referring to the Braves as "we."

Elsewhere, the Cubs' Sammy Sosa is out with a sprained ligament in his lower back. The injury was discovered after two violent sneezes brought on back spasms. The treatment is rest, ultrasound and corking his nose.

The Angels still have the best record in baseball despite playing with five regulars on the DL. That doesn't include the Rally Monkey, who is out indefinitely after some botched collagen injections.

First-year Angels owner Arturo Moreno is doing a great job attracting new fans. He lowered ticket prices and beer prices and just added an SAP button to the Jumbotron.

LAKERS AND T-WOLVES TIED 1–1 IN WESTERN FINALS Tough start for Kevin Garnett. He lost home arsenal advantage.

Shaquille O'Neal made 9 of 11 from the line in Game 1 after Phil Jackson gave him an article about an 80-year-old man who made more than 3,000 consecutive free throws. An 80-year-old free-throw-shooting expert? What was his name, Rick Barium?

CHARLES BARKLEY TURNS DOWN OVERTURES FROM *MONDAY NIGHT FOOTBALL* What a relief. With him and John Madden yakking in the same booth, ABC would have had to change Hank Williams Jr.'s lyrics to "Are you ready for Al Michaels to recap the last six plays?"

Barkley has an exclusive contract with TNT. What does that mean? He can only be weighed by Ernie Johnson?

NBC SIGNS TWO-YEAR DEAL TO BROADCAST NHL Pretty interesting premise. Every week Donald Trump locks out another team.

The Peacock will air regular-season NHL games for the first time in 29 years. (They've hushed this up, but NBC lost the rights in 1975 after its animated mascot, Peter Puck, appeared in the low-budget porno film *Third Man In*.)

The Flames are the first Canadian team to reach the finals in 10 years. Or right around the time when Dave Andreychuk started getting *Modern Maturity* in the mail.

The Flames and the Lightning had the NHL's 19th- and 21st-highest payrolls. What do you say, for this year we rename it the Stanley Cap?

PLAYBOY PLANS UPCOMING PICTORIAL, *GIRLS OF NASCAR* Actually, it's one photo: Four babes in heat suits changing the plugs on Mark Martin's Viagra car.

FREDDY ADU FINISHES HIGH SCHOOL AT 14 I believe he graduated Magna Cum Nike.

My time is up. You've been great. Enjoy Poco.

THE **NOTES**

(Great news. The Green Monster section at Fenway Park is now available…) Massachusetts had legalized gay marriage that week. You know who pops out of a cake at a gay bachelor party? A stripper covered in decorator swatches.

(Shaquille O'Neal made 9 of 11 from the line in Game 1…) Rick Barry was, of course, the Hall of Fame foul-shooting wizard. Barium is the stuff they shoot up your…Daddy, what's a gelding?

(The Peacock will air regular-season NHL games for the first time…) I'm gonna guess legal let this through because the statute of limitations for animation to sue is 17 years.

(Playboy *plans upcoming pictorial,* **Girls of NASCAR)** On the other hand, I have no idea how this got through.

THE **CUTS**

In another Game 7, the Pistons routed the Nets, 90–69. Darko Milicic even got in the game. It took a while. When he tried to check in at the scorer's table, Darko was asked, "Are you on the list?" This would have been a great scene in a movie. Then there would have been the little matter of the other 89½ minutes. Well, that didn't stop *King Ralph.*

NBC Sports has really learned its lesson over the last few years. Thanks to the success of the XFL, all hockey fights will be fixed. I'm delighted this joke didn't make it. As I reread it, it seems way too supportive of Vince McMahon.

THE **HIT(S)**

"Crazy Love"

Good to be here. Is it just me, or does it seem that the only place from which the United States has an effective exit strategy is Roland Garros?

REDS WIN SEVEN STRAIGHT, MOVE INTO FIRST PLACE Veteran pitcher Paul Wilson is 7–0. He's so confident, he's already rented out his summer place on the disabled list.

In fact, the Great American Ballpark has become a pitchers' haven since the Ken Griffey Jr. trade winds died down.

The Giants have hired Harvey Shields, Barry Bonds's personal stretch man. He'll continue to work with Barry, but he can see other groins on the side.

Traveling home after a recent start, Red Sox pitcher Curt Schilling used his cellphone to call police and get a drunk driver off the road. Be honest. How many of you are waiting for me to say Grady Little would have left him out there?

The A's finally retired Reggie Jackson's number 9. What took them so long? Did they have to get written permission from Mike Gallego?

BUDDY SYSTEM PREVAILS OVER ELEMENTS, FIELD AT INDY Buddy Rice, the first pole sitter to take the 500 since 1997, won the rain-shortened race under a yellow caution flag. Tense finish. During the last lap he was going so slowly, he was almost passed by two guys from Kenya.

Twice the race was delayed for two hours because of passing storms. At one point a desperate IRL president, Tony George, was out trying to dry the track using Jessica Simpson's hair blower.

Financial concerns plagued the field. Two entries were without primary sponsors, and gas is so expensive, Roger Penske came very close to having Helio Castroneves and Sam Hornish Jr. carpool.

MAGIC WINS NBA DRAFT LOTTERY Big night for the troubled franchise. Pat Williams held up a back brace inscribed with OKAFOR 1.

In the playoffs Pacers forward Ron Artest was fined $10,000 for making an obscene gesture at the end of Game 2. Wait a minute. I thought it was O.K. to make an obscene gesture on cable after 10 p.m.

For the first time all games in the conference finals will be on cable. Do you think David Stern would mind if, just until June 3, we referred to the league as NBA&E?

Not that there isn't any pro basketball on ABC. I think I saw former All-Star Shawn Kemp's name on the closing credits as "technical adviser" for *My Wife and Kids*.

This is getting a little out of hand. On the way back from Minneapolis for Game 6, Shaq was fouled 12 times at baggage claim.

Quick impression. Flip Saunders's wife: "You're not leaving this house until you put in the back screens...."

LOW TV RATINGS FOR STANLEY CUP The NHL wants young viewers. They're thinking about adding Simon Cowell as a goal judge.

The exact numbers aren't in, but I'm pretty sure that by the end of Game 2, there were more people in the penalty box than watching at home.

Hockey fever has gripped Tampa. The other night, Lou Piniella used a Lightning thunderstick to signal for a righthander.

PAUL TAGLIABUE SAYS HE'D LIKE AN NFL TEAM IN LOS ANGELES BY 2008 That's nice, but right now the only one in L.A. who could come up with the franchise fee and stadium funding is Shrek.

DON KING BANNED FROM DOING BUSINESS IN ATLANTIC CITY This is serious. For the next year the only thing he's allowed to fix in that town is Donald Trump's hair.

My time is up. You've been great. Enjoy the Neon Philharmonic.

THE **NOTES**

(Reds win seven straight, move into first place...) Too bad. By August, he was on the disabled list and forfeited his security deposit.

(Traveling home after a recent start, Red Sox pitcher Curt Schilling used his cellphone...) See what I did here? I pretended like I was the guy forced to make the remark. Little trick I picked up from Mark Fuhrman.

(The A's finally retired Reggie Jackson's number 9...) They unretired Jackson's number 9 when he came back to the A's for his final season in 1987 and wore 44. Gallego was the first player to wear 9. You know what's frightening? I didn't have to look this up.

(Twice the race was delayed for two hours because of passing storms...) Jessica sang the national anthem, and probably still thinks "Carburetion Day" has something to do with bread and pasta.

THE **CUTS**

After two two-hour rain delays and numerous cautions, Buddy Rice took home the checkered flag for the team owned by Bobby Rahal and Dave Letterman. Of course, Leno is claiming more 18- to 34-year-olds were watching the other drivers. Ladies and gentlemen of the jury, I spent 13 years working for Dave. How can I not make this crack? I have a moral obligation. Actually, I have amoral obligation.

Artest made the gesture with 3:30 left in the game. Too bad. If he had waited another 91 seconds, it only would have cost him two shots and the ball on the side. With less than two minutes, a flagrant foul carries this punishment. You're right. Too much math.

NASCAR's Sterling Marlin appears at Academy of Country Music Awards. *He presented a new award, "Best Use of Throttle on Pedal-Steel Guitar."* You're right. Too much throttle.

THE **HIT(S)**

"Morning Girl"

Good to be here. How about a hand for my opening act, Junior "Dice" Seau?

BIRDSTONE LEAVES HORSE FANS JONESING The New York–bred went off at a distant 36–1. In fact, the only person in his inner circle to put a win bet down was Marylou Whitney's chauffeur's valet's assistant.

So, once again, no Triple Crown. And today, a confused Visa CEO Carl Pascarella presented a $5 million check to Carl Yastrzemski.

Here's some interesting trivia. The idea for the Visa Triple Crown was inspired a few years back by a little-known 3-year-old—APR Indy.

NBC really dragged out the prerace coverage. Come on. Did we really need to see a feature on the *Queer Eye* guys redecorating the two-dollar window?

I don't want to say anything, but maybe the horse would have performed better commuting the day of the race from Eagle, Colorado?

If he'd won the Belmont, Smarty might have received $40 million in stud fees. Sure, it sounds like a lot, but 75% of that goes to his pimp horse.

GAUDIO BEATS CORIA IN FRENCH OPEN Or, as it's also known, *Argentinean Idol.*

Coria advanced to the final by defeating Tim Henman of Great Britain 3–6, 6–4, 6–0, 7–5. Too bad. If they'd gone to a fifth set, the match would have lasted longer than the Falkland Islands war.

The Williams sisters didn't even reach the semifinals. Serena had 45 unforced errors against Jennifer Capriati. Forty-six, if you count her outfit.

DODGERS OWNER FRANK MCCOURT NAMES HIMSELF TEAM PRESIDENT Apparently he really impressed himself during the interview.

A man awaiting trial for murder in L.A. was released after his lawyers showed tapes from *Curb Your Enthusiasm* that proved he was at Dodger Stadium at the time of the crime. Didn't I see this on an episode of *Seinfeld*?

The lawyer had previously gone through Fox footage from the game and couldn't find his client. Although he did spot some lady shoplifting Vin Scully's hand makeup.

FINALLY, THE FINALS The Pistons could be tough. Richard Hamilton is playing well enough to turn down a spot on the Olympic team.

The Lakers' resiliency during the playoffs has been amazing. Were you like me? Were you thinking they wouldn't last as long as *The Magic Hour*?

BOB PROBERT ARRESTED IN FLORIDA The former NHL enforcer fought with police and had to be shocked several times with a Taser gun. Of course, Darryl Sutter is claiming he did this to take attention away from the Flames.

Sutter made statements implying the league was rooting for the Lightning to win the Cup. Come on. That's like saying David Stern is rooting for the Lakers to…O.K., bad example.

Darryl is serious about the conspiracy. For Game 7 he replaced Ville Nieminen on the point with Oliver Stone.

No, I'm sorry. That's Oliwa Stone.

MIKE POWELL TO TRY OUT FOR U.S. OLYMPIC TEAM The 40-year-old long jumper is in great shape. Last week he cleared 27 feet. And that was just to distance himself from Kelli White.

ALLEN IVERSON'S CAR TICKETED AT PHILADELPHIA AIRPORT The Sixers All-Star received a $300 citation for illegally parking in a handicapped zone. I'd fight it. Not handicapped? What do you call playing in an offense where your second option is Derrick Coleman?

My time is up. You've been great. Enjoy the Greg Kihn Band.

THE **NOTES**

(Good to be here. How about a hand for my opening act, Junior "Dice" Seau?) In the span of eight months, Seau had made less-than-nonstereotypical cracks about his former teammate LaDainian Tomlinson and gays. The deeper inside joke here is that I spent a year in the late '80s opening for Dice at the height of his career. In places like the Meadowlands and the Spectrum. The irony of Dice: The supposed cretins that came to see him got that the whole thing was an act, the great literary intellects who compared him to Hitler did not.

(Here's some interesting trivia. The idea for the Visa Triple Crown...) AP Indy won the 1992 Belmont. Add an "R" and the joke gets 17.9% more interest.

(Dodgers owner Frank McCourt names himself team president...) Uh, I think I owe Marv Albert some money....

(No, I'm sorry. That's Oliwa Stone...) Krzysztof Oliwa plays for the Flames. Forget that—SIX WORDS! Check from God... endorsed over to Marv Albert.

THE **CUTS**

Anastasia Myskina routed countrywoman Elena Dementieva in the all-Russian women's final, 6–1, 6–2. Dementieva went down so quickly she was almost mistaken for Marat Safin's shorts. Safin had pulled down his shorts in an early round match. You know what would have been great? If the chair umpire had looked at his underwear and yelled, "Ad out!"

Busy week for the Dodgers. Odalis Perez had to be escorted off the field after he was called for a balk. The rulebook is very clear on this. You have to have both feet on the rubber before you can throw a tantrum. I loved this, but I guess it was a bit obtuse. I almost managed to make this premise work four months later with Jose Guillen. You'll see.

THE **HIT(S)**

"Jeopardy"

Saw *The Chronicles of Riddick*. What a rip-off. Over two hours, not one mention of boot camp or the parachute guy.

PISTONS PUMPING DIESEL AND CO. Are you like me? Are you waiting for J.Lo to dump Marc Anthony and go after Bill Davidson?

Kid Rock sang "America the Beautiful" before Game 4. Speaking of Kid Rock, how about Shaq's new free throw technique?

Magic Johnson called the Lakers' effort in their Game 3 loss unacceptable. In fact, he's been so disappointed in the team, he's this close to changing the slogan at his 30 Burger King franchises to Have It Yao Way.

Detroit's run has been so inspiring, Larry Brown is actually thinking about unpacking.

Police in Detroit are investigating a Pistons fan's claim that Karl Malone poked him in the face before Game 3. If the allegation turns out to be true, the fan gets to guest-host *Jimmy Kimmel*.

Sales of Lakers merchandise are up 50% from last year's playoffs. In fact, the most common thing you hear at the NBA Store is, "Look, pal, all we have is Medvedenko...."

Meanwhile, somebody stop Larry Bird. Now he's claiming he'd like to see more white superstars on the Washington Generals.

In an interview on ESPN, Bird said he felt "personally insulted" when a white player was assigned to guard him. Psychiatrists have a name for this syndrome: paranoid Schintzius-ophrenia.

INTERLEAGUE PLAY RESUMES, WORLDS COLLIDE A lot of people bash interleague play, but seriously, is there anything more exciting than the chance to see Barry Bonds take four wide ones in an American League park?

I prefer when the National League hosts the games, and the AL managers have to hire guys from the Rand Corporation to explain how to work a double switch.

The Royals had a smart promotion for their series with the Mets: Carlos Beltran Bobblehead on the Trading Block Night.

Nomar Garciaparra returned to the Red Sox' lineup after missing the first 57 games. Despite that time off he is a close second in the All-Star voting for shortstop. Something's amiss. Guess who's running fourth among outfielders? Pat Buchanan.

The walls at Tropicana Field have been painted dark green. Apparently, they had a few extra buckets left over after putting a second coat on the outfield.

PARCELLS APOLOGIZES FOR INSENSITIVE REMARK ABOUT JAPANESE And I don't know if this will help. He's offering to change his nickname from Tuna to Maguro.

During a press conference, Parcells referred to surprise plays as "Jap plays." Sounds like somebody hired one of Junior Seau's writers.

Meanwhile, the Cowboys renewed their licensing agreement with Dr Pepper. There's a nice change: Jerry Jones getting a pound of flesh from a doctor.

SONY PICTURES BEGINS ADAPTATION OF BEST-SELLING BOOK *MONEYBALL* Hollywood insiders believe the picture will be in development for three years, then get rid of all the stars.

MICHAEL JORDAN AND DEREK JETER PAY $2 MILLION EACH FOR VILLAS AT TRUMP NATIONAL GOLF CLUB Of course, Jordan could have had his villa for $1 million—if he'd just been dealt a face card.

MIKE TYSON'S HOUSE IN VEGAS UP FOR SALE The asking price is $3.9 million, but this may take a while. Three real estate agents have already been mauled by tigers.

SCOTTY BOWMAN A SPOKESMAN FOR LEVITRA So now it's official. The only time Bowman failed to perform was with the Sabres.

My time is up. You've been great. Enjoy Argent.

THE **NOTES**

(Detroit's run has been so inspiring…) This is a switch on a joke I wrote for Bob Costas 10 years ago about Jamie Quirk (see Costas's foreword).

(In an interview on ESPN, Bird said he felt "personally insulted"…) You've already met Dwayne Schinztius on "Dwayne Schintzius Eve" (see January 20, 2003, column). Is it me, or does it seem like I'm phoning it in here?

(Meanwhile, the Cowboys renewed their licensing agreement…) Just taking care…

(Michael Jordan and Derek Jeter pay $2 million…) …of business.

THE **CUTS**

During their 17-inning win over the Angels last week, Brewer hitters set a major league mark with 26 strikeouts. And just to make sure they'd get the record, Jose Hernandez drove down from Los Angeles to play the final three innings. Jose Hernandez had played in Milwaukee the season before and was on pace to break the major league record of 188 strikeouts in a season (since broken by Cincinnati's Adam Dunn). His manager, Davey Lopes, sat him in the last week to avoid setting the record. Lopes was fired, Hernandez traded to the Dodgers. The drive from L.A. to Anaheim takes like 45 minutes with no traffic. He could have made it easy.

Nomar Garciaparra returned to the Red Sox lineup after missing the first 57 games. And here's great news. His Achilles has now healed enough to be in the sequel of Troy. I majored in Classics in college. Latin and Greek. Guess I thought the church was going to come back.

Sony Pictures gets screen rights to Moneyball. *A* Moneyball *movie. Well, you know Kevin Youkilis will get a walk-on role.* Billy Beane, the A's G.M. on whom *Moneyball* was based, dubbed then–Red Sox minor leaguer Youkilis "The Greek God of Walks" for his ability to get on base. This, and the Nomar/*Troy* line cut. Bad week for the Classics.

THE **HIT(S)**

"Hold Your Head Up"

Let's hurry this up. I have to visit my six-year-old niece in the hospital. Freak accident. She got between me and a foul ball. But, in my defense, I did call for it.

MICKELSON CAN'T DUCK, DUCK GOOSEN AT U.S. OPEN Poor Phil. First he double-bogeyed 17, then Lizzie Grubman backed over his caddie in the parking lot.

NBC used 50 cameras. Forty-seven on the course and three shooting continuous promos for *Joey*.

By the way, does anyone have the number of the Shinnecock course superintendent? I'd love to know how they were able to change the pin placements on the cart path.

You didn't need spin for your ball to stay on the 7th green, you needed a Sherpa.

Please. The only person consistently on the green during the final round was the guy with the hose.

Meanwhile, Tiger's problems off the tee continued. Woods was so far right he was offered a job with Fox News.

OLYMPIC TORCH COMES TO LOS ANGELES Things got off to a bad start when 10,000 people showed up to protest the second-hand smoke.

Meanwhile, USADA intends to lower the burden of proof for athletes suspected of steroid use. The antidoping agency wants to relax the criterion from "beyond a reasonable doubt" to "comfortable satisfaction." Which, of course, is just above "pure chewing satisfaction."

Attorneys for Marion Jones claim she recently passed a lie detector test in which she was asked if she'd ever taken performance-enhancing drugs. Unfortunately, the results of the polygraph may not count because they were wind-aided.

DEVIL RAYS POST MLB'S SECOND-BEST RECORD OVER LAST MONTH Yeah, right. Next thing you're going to tell me, the majors' winningest pitcher is Kenny Rogers.

Indians pitcher Cliff Lee was suspended six games for throwing behind the head of Ken Griffey Jr. Here's what I don't get. Before Griffey hit number 500, the Reds wanted to appeal the suspension and have him sit out the next two series on the road.

JAGS SUBJECT OF TRAINING CAMP DOCUMENTARY Pretty catchy title: *Fahrenheit 4th and 11*.

The Patriots handed out Super Bowl rings, which cost the team more than $20,000 apiece. And thanks to some tinkering by Scott Pioli, only $9.95 will count against the cap.

Tests on Jeremy Shockey's injured right foot have uncovered a "hot spot." What does that mean? At the base of his arch there's a VIP room?

Giants QB Jesse Palmer and the woman he chose on *The Bachelor* have broken up. Apparently, she's getting more reps with Eli Manning.

PISTONS RUN RINGS AROUND LAKERS The Lakers are in complete disarray. Phil Jackson's gone, and the only people under contract for next year are Shaq, Luke Walton and Vanessa Williams.

Game 5 was such a blowout, at one point ABC cut away to prerecorded footage of Regis selecting a tie for work.

Sad. By the second quarter, after Shaq was called for his third foul, management had already rented out the Staples Center that weekend for a BriteSmile convention.

NASHVILLE SOUNDS GIVE AWAY 10,000 MOSES BOBBLEHEADS Yes, I believe it was Moses who said, "Let my people promote."

MARV ALBERT'S CONTRACT NOT RENEWED The MSG Network reportedly was not thrilled by the negative tone of some of Marv's Knicks broadcasts. It's true. He was only saying "Yessss!" 34% from the floor.

My time is up. You've been great. Enjoy Stealers Wheel.

THE **NOTES**

(You didn't need spin for your ball to stay on the 7th green…) Hey, by the third round, the Stimp Meter had vertigo! Am I right, duffers? Come on! Where are my Pro V1 people?

(Meanwhile, Tiger's problems off the tee continued…) A couple of weeks later, Gary McCord described a Tiger tee shot as "so far right, Michael Moore's going to do a documentary on it." *(me swallowing hard)* Advantage, McCord.

(Jags subject of training camp documentary…) Game, Scheft.

THE **CUTS**

Danny Almonte leads Monroe to New York City high school championship. *The former Little League star threw a one-hit shutout and fanned 11 in the title game. This is something he'll be able to tell his grandchildren about…when he sees them next weekend.* This beauty was set to type Sunday evening, ready to go as the closer. Monday morning, a story breaks in the New York tabloids: "Danny Almonte: 'My Mother is Dying and Needs Medicine!'" Fortunately, his mom turned out not to be seriously ill. The only thing killed was this joke.

The USADA has lowered the burden of proof to suspend athletes suspected of steroid abuse. Now, all you need is a photo of Lou Ferrigno. This line makes absolutely no sense, but still to this day makes me giggle. Lou Ferrigno was a former Mr. Universe who went on to become The Incredible Hulk. Yeah, you're right. Better not get him angry.

The Mets fired hitting coach Denny Walling. Turned out to be a clerical error. They thought they had hired Denny Hocking. I read this joke to my friend Ben Walker, the longtime, well-respected baseball writer for the AP in New York. Usually, he loves everything I come up with. Usually. On this occasion, he just said, "Bill, ah Bill…they're not going to let you run that, are they?" Goddamn psychic.

THE **HIT(S)**

"Stuck in the Middle with You"

Good to be here. This just in: David Stern has announced that only 3% of NBA players have records by the Police.

EIGHT HIGH SCHOOLERS SELECTED IN FIRST ROUND OF BASKETBALL DRAFT You know what the NBA needs? A child-proof salary cap.

Top draft pick Dwight Howard is very religious. He won't sign with Orlando unless the team changes its nickname to the Magi.

New York City high school star Sebastian Telfair, who was selected 13th by the Blazers, did not attend the draft. He was holed up in the pocket of a rep from Adidas.

Twelve players from Europe were chosen. Shocking. By the end of the night, there were no Ukrainians left for the NHL draft.

More than 20 of the NBA's 30 teams have called the Lakers about Shaquille O'Neal. It's going to be a tough deal to swing. The Lakers are looking for at least two starters whom Kobe Bryant is comfortable not getting the ball to.

RAIN RULES WIMBLEDON Weather postponements forced matches to be played on the middle Sunday for only the third time in the tournament's 127-year history. Or, if you're chair umpire Ted Watts, the 127th time in the tournament's three-year history.

Watts was fired after he incorrectly awarded Karolina Sprem a point during the second-set tiebreaker of her upset win over Venus Williams. This guy has no business making calls at Centre Court. He should be refereeing at Euro 2004.

Wimbledon organizers plan to install a retractable roof by 2008. The roof would be required to close within 10 minutes. Hmm. Maybe they could apply the same technology to Marat Safin's mouth.

CARLOS BELTRAN MINUTE MADE FOR ASTROS OUTFIELD Houston acquired the five-tool cen-terfielder in a three-way trade with the Royals and the A's. I don't want to call it a summer rental, but he comes with a cleaning deposit.

After two years Yankees pitcher Jose Contreras was reunited with his family from Cuba. They weren't due to arrive in South Florida until next month, but at the last minute, Billy Connors discovered a flaw in their delivery.

The Padres suspended their top draft choice, shortstop Matt Bush, after he was arrested for allegedly biting a bouncer at a bar in Arizona. Technically, does this make him one of those Bonus Rabies?

The surging Devil Rays became the first team in modern history to go from 18 games under .500 to a winning record in the same season. Lou Piniella was seen kicking a party hat.

FLORIDA STATE'S TWO NATIONAL CHAMPI-ONSHIP TROPHIES STOLEN The school is offering a $2,500 reward and a full scholarship to Miami.

It's the first time a school has been robbed of a championship trophy since, well, January.

NBC TO USE 99 ON-AIR ANNOUNCERS AT SUMMER OLYMPICS Or, one for every minute of live coverage.

Ninety-nine on-air personalities. They'll march in the opening ceremonies under the flag of a new nation, Egomania.

ESPN BROADCASTS FOURTH OF JULY HOT DOG EATING CONTEST FROM CONEY ISLAND The format is a little different this year. Woody Paige gets 45 seconds for rebuttal.

BEN AFFLECK WINS CALIFORNIA STATE POKER CHAMPIONSHIP Big week for Ben. The next day he flew to Vegas and was married for 55 hours to Sam Farha.

My time is up. You've been great. Enjoy Carl Carlton.

THE **NOTES**

(Good to be here. This just in: David Stern has announced...) A book had come out which claimed 40% of NBA players had police records. Of course, that figure jumped to 45% after that Fulbright Scholar threw the cup at Ron Artest. (By the way, I wonder if any guys on the Hornets have albums by Sting.)

(It's the first time a school has been robbed of a championship...) The BCS ruled that USC was not allowed to play for the national title and Oklahoma, which lost its Big 12 title to K-State, was. Oh yeah, one other thing: NO MIAMI PLAYER HAS EVER BEEN CONVICTED OF A FELONY....

*(**Ben Affleck wins California State Poker Championship...**)* Sam Farha is a final table fixture at the World Series of Poker. And he went the entire 55 hours without lighting his cigarette.

THE **CUTS**

Plenty of unwanted feedback at NBA Draft. *ESPN had trouble with the live audio all night. At one point, I could have sworn I heard fans at Madison Square Garden booing the selection of Kyle Brady.* Jet fans went ballistic in 1994 when the team drafted the Penn State tight end over...well, anyone.

Burglars make off with Florida State's two national championship trophies. *Police are on the lookout for two men of above-average height, with a weak strength of schedule and no common opponents.* This is a subtle reference to BCS criteria. The formula after a burglary of "Police are on the lookout..." usually works well. Usually. Remember *"Police describe the suspects as armed and extremely fly?"* Like that.

Speaking of common opponents, wouldn't you love to see a couple of BCS guys have to stand in a lineup? This is a not-so-subtle reference to the BCS. And by "not-so-subtle," I mean "not funny." And I mean it not so subtly.

THE **HIT(S)**

"Everlasting Love"

"She's a Bad Mama Jama"

Before we begin, did you hear about the seven-year-old skateboarder who signed an endorsement deal with Mattel? A seven-year-old pro skateboarder. What's his name, Freddy A-dude?

NOT SO FAST, SISTER. SHARAPOVA SCORES WIMBLEDON UPSET Blonde, Russian and beautiful. During her straight-set triumph over Serena Williams, Maria Sharapova had 17 winners, and two million unforced hits on the Internet.

Last Thursday, a young lady ran naked across Court 19 before a linesman covered her with a towel. I believe that's the farthest a British woman has advanced during the second week since Virginia Wade.

In the men's final Roger Federer defended his title over Andy Roddick. The crowd was not exactly rooting for the American. At one point his only allies were Brad Gilbert and Tony Blair.

I don't want to say Federer is a machine on the court, but this summer he's playing for the Davis Cup team from Stepford.

STAPLES CENTER WON'T BECOME COACH K'S CORNER The Lakers' attempt to hire away the Duke coaching legend got off to a rocky start. Mitch Kupchak had such trouble spelling his last name, he wound up offering $40 million to Mike Krushelnyski.

Shaquille O'Neal has put his Beverly Hills home on the market for $7.5 million, $6.5 million if you agree to take Travis Knight.

The place has its own movie theater. The bad news is the projector has been programmed to show only *Kazaam*.

Elsewhere, the Rockets got Tracy McGrady in a blockbuster trade with the Magic. The Rockets presented T-Mac with a customized away jersey. It says HOUSTON on the front and HOISTIN' on the back.

MLB SERVES UP "NATURAL RIVALS WEEKEND" IN INTERLEAGUE PLAY And seriously, is there anything more natural than Toronto-Montreal in San Juan?

Among the "natural rivals" matchups: Detroit at Colorado. Help me out here. Did Kris Draper get hit hard?

Earlier in the week the Yankees swept the Red Sox at the Stadium. Dick Cheney was at the opener. He spent the entire game deciding whether to invade Miguel Cairo.

I'm starting to worry about Cheney. He insists there's a connection between Saddam Hussein and Al Nipper.

Jason Giambi and Kevin Brown have been sidelined with intestinal parasites. These parasites are very aggressive. Doctors believe they're distant cousins of Scott Boras.

Barry Bonds was given a surprise party for his 40th birthday. Twenty close friends and relatives hid under his hat.

Congratulations to Randy Johnson, who got his 4,000th career strikeout. The Diamondbacks want Johnson to go into the Hall of Fame wearing an Arizona cap ... but with his Mariners mullet.

STEPHEN AMES TOP PERFORMER IN CIALIS WESTERN OPEN Remember, at the Cialis Western Open, if you play a round that lasts more than four hours, please consult your doctor.

Earlier in the week Tiger Woods and his former coach Butch Harmon ended their feud. It was an amicable patch-up. They agreed to swing with other people.

SIX WNBA PLAYERS APPEAR ON WHEATIES BOX If you want to make it an official WNBA breakfast, use a slightly smaller bowl and add 2,000 to the attendance in your kitchen.

ATHENS OLYMPIC STADIUM FLOOR TO BE FLOODED DURING OPENING CEREMONIES Organizers are still not sure whether this is a salute to Odysseus or insolvency.

My time is up. You've been great. Enjoy Dexy's Midnight Runners.

THE **NOTES**

(Staples Center won't become Coach K's corner...) Much, much better version of Denny Walling/Dennis Hocking. Always keep the jokes that aren't ready in R&D.

(I'm starting to worry about Cheney...) Al Nipper was a middle reliever for the Sox in the mid-'80s. And far and away the closest I could get to Al Qaeda. Which is closer than Cheney ever got.

(Six WNBA players appear on Wheaties box...) The WNBA ball is 10% smaller than the NBA. The paying audience is 75% smaller.

THE **CUTS**

Blond, Russian, beautiful and a champion. Or, as she'll now be known, Ann-not Kournikova. I just wanted to show that I was fully capable of writing like a spoiled 14-year-old girl.

Tigers manager Alan Trammell has been experiencing dizziness for the last month. Well, sure. He's never been this high in the standings for this long. ...Or a smug 48-year-old man.

THE **HIT(S)**

"Come on Eileen"

Good to be here. I missed the ESPYs. Help me out. Who won the award for Best BALCO Chemist?

ERNIE TAKES AN "EL" AT BRITISH OPEN
The world's No. 2 golfer lost in a four-hole playoff to unknown American Todd Hamilton. Wait. Wasn't Todd Hamilton the name of the guy who won the U.S. Figure Skating Championships?

Tiger Woods climbed back into contention with a strong 68 in the third round. I'm no Butch Harmon, but maybe he had to go to Great Britain to start driving on the other side.

Troon looked a little strange. You call this a British Open? What's with the green greens?

SHAQ ERA ENDS IN LOS ANGELES So, this explains all the black armbands at In-N-Out Burger.

The Heat acquired O'Neal in exchange for three players and a draft pick. Shaq is all set for South Beach. He's already changed his free throw from brick to stucco.

Kobe Bryant decided to remain with the Lakers after the team gave him about $30 million more than what the Clippers were offering. It wasn't easy to come up with the money. At the last minute they had to raid the Buss family's emergency plastic surgery fund.

IN CASE YOU WEREN'T WATCHING (AND YOU WEREN'T), AL WINS ALL-STAR GAME
Once again Major League Baseball tinkered with the All-Star Game format. This year the leagues were playing for Randy Johnson's home field in the World Series.

Home Run Derby winner Miguel Tejada set a record with 15 dingers in the second round. And it might have been 30 if Roger Clemens had been pitching.

Clemens got shelled for six runs in the first inning. Most of the hits came off his slider. I think it was his slider. The sign was Mike Piazza's middle finger.

The game was such a rout early on, I found myself looking past the batter to watch Barbara Bush scarf some nachos.

Fox went nuts with cross-promotion during the game. At one point I could have sworn I heard Tim McCarver say July 31 was the deadline for *Trading Spouses*.

ATHENS SUFFERS TEMPORARY BLACKOUT
City officials blamed the 104° heat and the fact that they haven't finished the roof on the main power plant.

Spectators at the Olympics could be removed from venues if they wear clothing bearing logos of companies that are competitors of the Games' sponsors. So, to recap: You can wear a sneaker bomb, just make sure it's not K-Swiss.

World 100-meter champion Torri Edwards tested positive for the banned stimulant nikethamide. Are you like me? Are you wondering how they fit that little swoosh on the pill?

Track and field insiders believe there may be a new, undetectable designer steroid that has replaced THG among sprinters. Not only that, it has zero carbs.

ILLINOIS REPUBLICANS ATTEMPT TO DRAFT MIKE DITKA FOR SENATE RUN Ditka a Republican? Is that one of those fine-print side effects of Levitra?

NHL RELEASES 2004–05 SCHEDULE It's a schedule all right … of daily nonstop flights to Switzerland.

U.S. HIGH JUMPER AMY ACUFF TO APPEAR IN AUGUST ISSUE OF *PLAYBOY* Let me guess. She's lying nude on a mattress, 6' 7¼" below a wobbling coatrack.

RAPPER PERCY MILLER, A.K.A. MASTER P, CUT FROM NUGGETS SUMMER LEAGUE TEAM Technically, doesn't this make him Master DNP?

My time is up. You've been great. Enjoy Free.

THE **NOTES**

(Clemens got shelled for six runs in the first inning…) This was the first time Clemens and Piazza had played together since the incident during the 2000 World Series when the Rocket threw the jagged-edged shard of a broken bat at the Mets catcher. I'm going to give Clemens the benefit of the doubt and say he thought it was a submarine sandwich.

(Fox went nuts with cross-promotion during the game…) For the life of me, I don't understand why people criticize Tim McCarver. In the last 20 years, he has revolutionized the job of baseball analyst. In my memory, he was the first guy to do two things in the booth: 1) first guess strategy in an accessible, conversational style; 2) unapologetically laugh out of control when Ralph Kiner said something like, "Tonight after the game on *Vegas*, Dan Tana picnics after shooting an innocent bystander…."

(U.S. high jumper Amy Acuff to appear…) I was kidding, but in the Amy Acuff pictorial, *Playboy* went with the mattress, not the coatrack. I know this because my, uh, cousin saw it.

THE **CUTS**

"This Time It Counts." Isn't that the catch phrase of the Kobe Bryant trial? The choice came down to this or the Buss Family Emergency Plastic Surgery Fund. And you thought Bush made tough decisions….

The Heat acquired Shaquille O'Neal in exchange for three players. Shaq would not approve the deal until Miami could promise that every two weeks, he'll get his salary in cash-filled duffel bags, delivered by Tony Montana's crew. If you're one of the 800 people who have watched *Scarface* more than 50 times, you are holding your sides and gasping for air right about now.

THE **HIT(S)**

"All Right Now"

Good to be here. Do me a favor. Try not to walk out when Linda Ronstadt dedicates *When Will I Be Loved* to Terry Francona.

THE JOY OF SIX FOR LANCE The incomparable Texan won a record sixth consecutive Tour de France. At the halfway point Lance was 9:35 behind. But Sheryl Crow's engineer remixed it to a 3:40 lead.

For the last six years, Lance has entered the Alps either behind or with a slight lead and emerged with an insurmountable margin. I wannatellya, I haven't seen anyone do that consistently well in the mountain stages since Mal Z. Lawrence.

Avid cyclist Robin Williams joined Armstrong's entourage for the last few days. Comedians love Lance. Roseanne Barr showed up at stage 19 to spit back at the German fans.

CARLOS DELGADO SITS DURING "GOD BLESS AMERICA" TO PROTEST WAR IN IRAQ Protest? You think he would be sympathetic. The only person who's left more guys stranded than Delgado is Bush.

Even though Delgado has been sitting out the seventh-inning stretch all season, Bud Selig found out about it last week. Don't be shocked. Two weeks ago he found out the Brewers were no longer in the AL East.

Meanwhile, in Chicago, Mayor Richard Daley ordered a structural inspection of Wrigley Field. Not only that, the Cubs were given seven days to post a sign in the clubhouse: EMPLOYEES MUST WASH HANDS AFTER HANDLING MOISES ALOU.

Three times in the last five weeks chunks of cement have fallen from the upper deck at Wrigley Field. But here's the good news. Each time, fans moved out of the way so players could catch them.

Elsewhere, the Rockies say they will only consider legitimate prospects for starter Shawn Estes. Legitimate prospect. What does that mean, the scout who signed him

has to be married?

KMART: MILE-HIGH SPECIAL In the week after signing Kenyon Martin, the Nuggets sold 180 season tickets. And six tattoo parlors opened in the Denver airport.

MARION JONES'S EX-HUSBAND CLAIMS SHE TOOK STEROIDS Why couldn't she have married someone quiet and noncontroversial, like Carl Lewis?

Meanwhile, U.S. 100-meter champion Torri Edwards, found guilty of using a banned stimulant, may avoid suspension from the Olympics because of "exceptional circumstances." Hmmm, exceptional circumstances. Like she's exceptionally fast?

SIDES MEET IN NHL LABOR DISPUTE It wasn't very productive. All they agreed on was a salary cap for 38-day *Jeopardy!* champ Ken Jennings.

More than half of the employees in the NHL offices were reportedly told they could be offered severance packages. Finally, some fiscal sense. It's not the players' union or the owners who have caused this mess, it's the guy who changes the toner on Gary Bettman's fax machine.

***THE NEW YORK TIMES* WILL NOT ALLOW ITS COLLEGE FOOTBALL POLL TO BE USED IN THE BCS RANKINGS** Good move. Why be part of a flawed, highly suspect, often ridiculed system, when you can take full credit for your own flawed, highly suspect, often ridiculed system?

LIBYA DICTATOR MU'AMMAR GADHAFI TRYING TO BUY ENGLISH PREMIER LEAGUE SOCCER TEAM I hope I'm not too late with a name: Dismantled Arsenal.

My time is up. You've been great. Enjoy Andrea True Connection.

THE **NOTES**

(The Joy of Six for Lance…) I was kind of hoping you would have forgotten the P. Diddy marathon remix joke by now.

(For the last six years, Lance has entered the Alps…) Mal Z. Lawrence was the star of the long-running 1990s revue *Catskills on Broadway*. He is the greatest comic nobody's ever heard of, and I get down on my knees every night and thank my Maker they let me keep this joke in.

(Meanwhile, in Chicago, Mayor Richard Daley…) In spring training, Alou had confided to reporters that instead of wearing batting gloves, he urinates on his hands to toughen them. I'll go with "Too Much Information" for $1,000, Alex.

(Libya dictator Mu'ammar Gadhafi…) You don't need Hans Blix to recognize a JMD—Joke of Mass Destruction.

THE **CUTS**

Elsewhere, Mike Piazza missed four games with a wrist injury. Not that there's anything wrong with that.… I have no proof, but I believe *SI* did not want to have to pay a huge rights fee to Jerry Seinfeld and Larry David for the use of this phrase. (Even though I like to believe I could've gotten Larry to waive his rights. From what I understand, he's been pretty good with his money.)

Post up, Post-Shaq. *Los Angeles signed free agent center Vlade Divac. Here's what I don't get. A Colorado judge ruled that Divac's past history with the Lakers was relevant.*

I'm worried about Vlade. At his first press conference, he said he was willing to split time with Mychal Thompson. I liked both of these, but I think this was one of those times where we were in the middle of an unannounced one-week Kobe hiatus. As well as an unannounced 12-year Mychal Thompson hiatus.

THE **HIT(S)**

"More More More"

Good to be here. Look, I'm no shill for Claritin, but I took one this morning and for the last 12 hours haven't even come close to saying Jonathan Cheechoo.

DEMS DA TICKET In Boston, John Kerry was making changes in his nomination speech up until the last minute. In fact, the slogan "Help is on the way" was originally "Orlando Cabrera is on the way."

Some delegates took batting practice at Fenway Park. And for an extra $500 donation to the DNC, they got their face shoved by Jason Varitek.

The convention went off without incident, although Bud Selig fined Al Gore $4,000 for covering his bald spot with pine tar.

While Madison Square Garden prepares for the Republican convention, the New York Liberty is playing its games at Radio City Music Hall. For those WNBA teams coming in, you've been warned: Don't even think of posting up Diana Ross.

Meanwhile, President Bush stopped by the Browns' training camp. He wanted to supervise the handoff of power to Jeff Garcia.

TRADE DEADLINE BECOMES SWAP MEET Steve Finley went to the Dodgers after saying he'd only accept a deal to a California team. Not only that, he'd like his position to be renamed center-dude.

Randy Johnson was forced to stay put in Arizona. The youngest prospect the Yankees could offer was Jumpin' Joe Dugan.

Meanwhile, the Yanks reportedly have plans to build a $700 million stadium without public funds. Shouldn't be a problem. Three parasites have already pledged $100 million.

Goldman Sachs has arranged a $225 million loan for the Yankees. Apparently, they were able to obtain a rate .5% below prime with A-Rod.

This raises a serious question of fiscal prudence: When the Yankees get okayed for a loan, does Mariano Rivera have to be at the closing?

Last week, a brawl broke out during batting practice before an Angels-Rangers game. Every player got five swings.

FISH OUT OF RUSHER Emotional last few days in Miami. The crying, the pleading, the begging... but enough about Leigh Steinberg.

Days before his announcement, Ricky Williams learned he had failed a third drug test. And he told the *Miami Herald* that marijuana played a role in his decision. Well, that should settle the issue of whether he was tired of taking hits.

You know, I'm not going to start worrying about Ricky until he buys a van from Nate Newton.

Meanwhile, tough start for the Cowboys. They have to decide whether to put Antonio Bryant on the "physically unable to kiss Parcells's ass" list.

UNHERALDED DANNY WILLIAMS KO'S MIKE TYSON Tyson is desperate. After the win he called his accountant and tried to get him to file and extend the referee's count from 10 seconds to 90 days.

During the fight Tyson suffered a serious knee injury. A guy showed up between rounds and repossessed his ACL.

After the win, Williams proposed to his girlfriend. He got down on one knee and gave her *The Ring*.

SPORTS BUSINESS DAILY NAMES MICHAEL PHELPS MOST MARKETABLE U.S. SUMMER OLYMPIAN The least marketable? Any team member who says, "Can you get a picture of me with Marion Jones?"

SUNS ACQUIRE FORMER CLIPPER QUENTIN RICHARDSON Now, the tough part: clearing cap space for Brandy.

My time is up. You've been great. Enjoy Nena.

THE **NOTES**

(Good to be here. Look, I'm no shill for Claritin...) Jonathan Cheecho plays for the San Jose Sharks. Which means I had written this joke two months before and had to wait for allergy season. Hey, at least there will be an allergy season this year.

(The convention went off without incident...) Selig had been busy fining players for covering up team and MLB logos on batting helmets with pine tar. (Should I have put quotes around "busy"?)

(Meanwhile, tough start for the Cowboys...) Bryant had thrown a jersey at the Dallas coach and walked off during a practice. Then he went into the locker room and replaced Parcells's peroxide with Tuna Helper.

THE **CUTS**

Seriously, I haven't heard this many empty promises in the Fleet Center since Rick Pitino left town. Two years, 99 columns, and finally, Kostya senses I may have a problem with Pitino.

The Cowboys are training in Oxnard, Calif., a city that fines or jails any member of the Colonia Chiques, a local gang, from wearing Cowboys para-phernalia. Luckily, the Chiques are away in August for their annual barn-storming chili cookoff series with the Bloods. This was too far to go for a cup of chili. Maybe I should have added ribs and biscuits.

THE **HIT(S)**

"99 Luftballons"

(In honor of the 99th column.)

Hey, good news. The boys at BALCO have turned their attention to a new project: developing a glue that actually seals evidence in the Kobe Bryant case.

CUBS CATCHER MICHAEL BARRETT GIVES HIS UNIFORM NUMBER 5 TO NOMAR GARCIAPARRA Not only that, he also offered to let Nomar use his Achilles any day game after a night game.

Boston fans are still dealing with the loss of Nomar. On the bright side Theo Epstein's doctor no longer spends five minutes adjusting his gloves.

Over the last two months the Cardinals have played nearly .750 ball. St. Louis fans are so thrilled, they're even giving Tony La Russa credit for keeping the humidity down.

DOLPHINS LOSE WIDE RECEIVER DAVID BOSTON FOR SEASON Are you like me? Are you thinking that Ricky Williams may have a little something to help Dave Wannstedt take his mind off all this?

Ricky says he may consider coming out of retirement next season, but only to play for the Raiders. Unless, of course, the NFL gets an expansion team in Jamaica.

Although Jim Fassel is working for the Ravens as a senior consultant, the Giants still have to pay him not to coach this season. Come on. That's like paying Tiki Barber not to hang on to the ball. Oh, wait. They're already doing that.

The NFLPA may file a grievance against the Cowboys for releasing Quincy Carter after he allegedly failed a drug test. The union would prefer he be cut the traditional way, when the team makes up an injury.

OLYMPIC VILLAGE OPENS IN ATHENS There are 2,292 apartments, and every one has those little bottles of shampoo, conditioner and Cipro.

Greek law enforcement officials have confiscated more than 100,000 illegal Olympic trinkets. Yeah, that's the No. 1 threat to security—bootleg Lenny Krayzelburg pins.

Meanwhile, the U.S. basketball team was routed by Italy in pre-Olympic tune-up. The Dream Team has only one natural point guard and no real jump shooters. I've seen more depth in a Jessica Simpson line reading.

SMARTY JONES PUT OUT TO STUD What a relief. He was tired of meeting fillies on the Internet.

The syndicators are very confident of Smarty's potential as a breeder. They're thinking of changing his name to Seedbiscuit.

Elsewhere in horse racing, Windsong's Legacy won the Hambletonian. The favorite, Tom Ridge, went off as a 5–2 favorite but finished eighth. So, I guess it was all a bunch of unsubstantiated chatter.

A trotter named after the head of Homeland Security. What's next? Dick Cheney in an undisclosed sulky?

POPE JOHN PAUL II STARTS SPORTS DEPARTMENT AT VATICAN And this fall he'll cohost a half-hour show with Keith Olbermann, *Pardon the Interdiction*.

The first project for the Vatican sports department: coming up with a college football ranking system that takes into account both major polls—and piety.

DENNIS RODMAN SELLS NEWPORT BEACH HOUSE FOR $3.8 MILLION CASH Rodman bought the house eight years ago for $825,000. This sale is the only thing he's done since 1998 that's involves the word *appreciation*.

BRETT HULL SIGNS TWO-YEAR DEAL WITH PHOENIX Shrewd negotiating. In case of a lockout the Coyotes have to pay all his greens fees.

My time is up. You've been great. Enjoy the Thamesmen.

THE **NOTES**

(Hey, good news. The boys at BALCO have turned their attention…) I wrote this the week before, but *SI* had broken a Bryant story based on leaked information in that issue. So it worked even better here. What a relief when you can get those pesky "ethics" out of the way.

(Boston fans are still dealing with the loss of Nomar…) The phrase "Theo Epstein's doctor" replaced "my brother's proctologist." Kostya wisely pointed out that readers did not know I had family in Boston, and my brother's proctologist might not want to advertise. The truth is I grew up in Boston and am a lifelong Red Sox fan. And I don't want to say Nomar was a cancer, but at the end, the Jimmy Fund was sending *him* checks.

(Olympic Village opens in Athens…) Cipro was the antibiotic people rushed out to buy during the anthrax scare. It is *not* a new sports drink from the makers of RC Cola.

THE **CUTS**

Elsewhere, Brock Lesnar, known to pro wrestling fans as "The Next Big Thing," is in camp with the Vikings. Big adjustment for the pro wrestler. The first day, he was in the trainer's room for a half hour, trying to get blood capsules. Lesnar, of course, was trying to make the 53-McMahon roster.

Roger Clemens received an apology from a youth league commissioner for being incorrectly tossed out of his 10-year-old son's game. However, he may still be investigated for throwing a Popsicle stick in the direction of some kid in a Mets hat. We're clear on this reference now, aren't we? Because the last thing we want is Mike Piazza calling a press conference to explain things.

THE **HIT(S)**

"Cups and Cakes"

(In honor of the 100th column, Kostya and I, both huge Spinal Tap fans, decided to pay tribute to the group's earlier incarnation and the scene in the movie where the band is sitting in the hotel, waiting to do a gig, and a local DJ plays this song and says, "That was the Thamesmen, who went on to become the group Spinal Tap. They are currently residing in our 'Where are they now?' file…." Again, just us.)

(Note to reader: For the next two weeks, if you miss any of the jokes, they will be replayed at 11 p.m. on Bravo and 4 a.m. on Telemundo.)

NBC DEEP INTO 1,210-HOUR OLYMPIC COVERAGE Here's how it breaks down: 30 hours of features, 45 hours of actual events, 1,135 hours of people going through the metal detector at the Athens airport.

See the opening ceremonies? I'm so embarrassed. I thought that fabric covering all the athletes was a Salute to Masking Agents.

Greece's top two sprinters suspended after missing a scheduled drug test. And yet whoever designed Björk's dress walks the streets a free man.

Konstantinos Kenteris, the defending 200-meter gold medalist, missed the test when he was involved in a suspicious motorcycle accident. I think I know his brother, Jeff Kenteris.

In soccer, the Iraqi team scored a big upset over Portugal and then beat Costa Rica. See? All that practice kicking around the head of the Saddam statue paid off.

You can really see the American influence. The best players on the Iraqi soccer team are the preemptive strikers.

IT'S ALL P.R.: DREAM TEAM SHOCKED IN OPENER O.K., that does it. Next Olympics we send the Globetrotters.

Puerto Rico was not even favored to win a medal. The team has only one NBA player, and the rest are guys from the Sharks.

Team USA has a lot of weaknesses. I'm no Antonin Scalia, but wouldn't any judge in the country consider two weeks of Kobe sticking jumpers in Athens a form of community service?

NFL PREPARES FOR KICKOFF CONCERT AT GILLETTE STADIUM To avoid a repeat of the Super Bowl halftime show, league officials will attend all rehearsals and monitor song selection, choreography and staging. Great. So now, we can be confident that Elton John will have both feet inbounds at all times.

Here's the lineup for the concert: Elton John, Destiny's Child, Toby Keith, Mary J. Blige and a new rap group, Run-FCC.

Meanwhile, the Browns signed their top draft choice, Kellen Winslow Jr., to the largest NFL contract ever for a tight end. They waited to announce the deal until all papers were filed with the league and Tony Gonzalez was properly sedated.

Forty million, and Winslow has yet to play a down in the NFL. Now there's a switch— a Miami player getting away with a holdup after he leaves school.

The Bucs-Bengals preseason game had to be postponed due to Hurricane Charley. In a related story Keenan McCardell is moving north of Tampa at 55 mph.

INDIANS SURGING IN AL CENTRAL The Tribe leads the majors in runs scored. What happened? Did Serrano finally learn to hit a curve?

Elsewhere Giants starter Kirk Rueter says he's been suffering from a sports hernia all season. Help me out here. Does a sports hernia occur when a pitcher keeps getting lifted?

The Royals demoted shortstop Angel Berroa to Wichita of the Texas League. I believe that makes him the first former Rookie of the Year sent to AA since Darryl Strawberry.

TERRELL OWENS MAKES LESS-THAN-VEILED REMARKS IN *PLAYBOY* ABOUT JEFF GARCIA'S SEXUALITY This coming from a guy who demanded a costume change.

My time is up. You've been great. Enjoy Bananarama.

THE **NOTES**

(Konstantinos Kenteris, the defending 200-meter gold medalist…) Jeff Kent, when he was with the Giants, once injured himself in a motorcycle accident, which he tried to cover up because it was not allowed in his contract. He told the Giants he fractured his wrist washing his truck. And I thought I was quick.

(Puerto Rico was not even favored to win a medal…) Ugh, I have to explain this. The Sharks were the Puerto Rican gang in *West Side Story*. Hey, I could have been more obscure and said Puerto Rico was playing without its shooting guard, George Chikaris.

(Indians surging in AL Central…) Serrano was the black-magic-obsessed DH in *Major League*, played by Dennis Haesbert. Funny, funny film—but enough about Corbin Bernsen swinging a bat.

THE **CUTS**

The U.S. team has a lot of weaknesses. In fact, the closest thing they have to a natural shooter are a couple of guys in Allen Iverson's posse. In order for this joke to work, one of Iverson's crew would have had to have killed a guy. Sometimes, you just can't catch a break.

Mets pitcher Tom Glavine will miss two starts with injuries suffered in a car accident on his way to Shea Stadium. Sad. It's the first time all season he's had a big hit behind him. Mets fan Kostya was quick to point out that Glavine's cab was hit on the door. Technically, does this count as a "side session"?

THE **HIT(S)**

"Venus"

Uh-oh, now it's serious. Philip Rivers's agent just cut off talks with all fantasy leagues.

NBC OLYMPIC RATINGS SLIGHTLY AHEAD OF SYDNEY'S Don't get excited. Those figures may not count because Bob Costas was seen doing an illegal dolphin kick under his desk.

The Peacock Network has gone a little nuts hyping the Games on all its outlets. Tomorrow night, John McEnroe interviews Rulon Gardner's amputated toe.

So far there have been no disruptions in Athens, although a hotel housing IOC sponsors was evacuated. I believe the sponsors were staying in the Bribal Suite.

The Dream Team is staying aboard the *Queen Mary 2*. After the loss to Lithuania the USOC switched the act in the lounge from Jay-Z to Billy Ray Cyrus.

Officials are letting spectators move to better sections at half-empty venues. But it's getting out of hand. A Long Island dentist slipped Larry Brown $20 and got to trade seats with Carmelo Anthony.

CARLY PATTERSON VAULTS TO GOLD MEDAL IN ALL-AROUND Don't worry about Svetlana Khorkina. Next month she'll be presented with a special Tony for Best Dramatic Revival.

Classy move by Michael Phelps. After he won his fifth gold medal, Phelps gave his spot on the relay to Ian Crocker. But that was only after he'd been turned down by Marion Jones and the Korean gymnast.

Just wondering. Would it besmirch the Olympic ideal if during the track and field medal ceremonies, instead of the national anthem they played the theme from *Jeopardy!* while we wait for test results?

MLB OWNERS GIVE BUD SELIG THREE-YEAR EXTENSION Help me out here. Is that a three-year extension on his contract, or to make a decision about the Expos?

White Sox manager Ozzie Guillen missed a game after being hospitalized with a kidney stone. Of course, he's claiming Hunter Wendelstedt told him the stone was out.

Elsewhere Phil Nevin was reprimanded by Padres management for criticizing new Petco Park. His biggest complaint about Petco: the way the fans start barking every time they hear an electric can opener.

"PRIME TIME" RERUN FOR RAVENS? Ray Lewis and Corey Fuller are trying to talk Deion Sanders into coming out of retirement and playing nickelback in Baltimore. Deion hasn't played in three years. Which means he hasn't made an open-field tackle in almost five.

Ravens RB Jamal Lewis's drug-conspiracy trial is scheduled to begin on Nov. 1, Week 8 of the season. However, he has to be down to his 26-man defense team by Week 4.

TIGER UN-CINKABLE AT WGC-NEC Despite finishing second at Firestone, Woods retained the No. 1 ranking. Vijay Singh needed to finish ahead of Tiger in the tourney. And stick his dismount.

JEREMY ROENICK ADMITS SHELLING OUT $100,000 FOR GAMBLING TIPS I don't know how good the tips were. One was to take the Jets plus 1½ goals.

One hundred thousand dollars in tips and no lap dances? Somebody call the Better Business Bureau.

ESPN AND ESPN2 AIRING 25 LITTLE LEAGUE WORLD SERIES GAMES This is smart. If a game is a blowout, they'll cut away to six guys playing no-limit hold 'em at the Williamsport Radisson.

IRAQI SOCCER FOOTAGE USED IN BUSH CAMPAIGN ADS The Iraqis aren't thrilled, especially when a referee hits John Kerry with a red card.

My time is up. You've been great. Enjoy the Rising Storm.

THE **NOTES**

(NBC Olympic ratings slightly ahead of Sydney's...) Costas told me he had his camera guy actually film him doing a dolphin kick under his desk, but the NBC fun police threw the tape into the steeplechase pond.

(Elsewhere, Phil Nevin was reprimanded by Padres management...) Quick, go ask someone who owns a dog to explain this joke. I'll wait....

(ESPN and ESPN2 airing 25 Little League...) The key to this joke was going to Yahoo!Travel and finding the Williamsport Radisson. The other key was having the discretion not to add that the guys playing hold 'em start barking every time they hear an electric can opener.

THE **CUTS**

Despite two defeats, the U.S. men's basketball team can still run the table and win the gold. I believe that, and I believe all those empty seats every-where are there to serve as a batter's eye. The batter's eye is the section of seats in centerfield blacked out during day games to help the hitter see the ball. Speaking of which, can you black out from one too many mixed metaphors?

Just wondering. Should I be worried that none of the U.S. women gymnasts has a voice higher than Rowdy Gaines? Gaines, the former gold medalist who was the analyst for all the Athens swimming events, has what's known in the business as a false start-setto.

THE **HIT(S)**

None. (Due to a clerical oversight on my part, Bananarama appeared two weeks in a row. So, for this anthology, I have decided to include my brother Tom's band at Andover. They recorded an album in 1967, *Calm Before*, that is now worth $5,000. John Kerry was in a band at St. Paul's six years before, the Electras. Their album is now worth $2,500. No further questions.)

THE **SHOW**

Well, the Republican convention is winding down. Are you like me? Are you waiting for John Kerry to hire Butch Harmon to work on the swing states?

COLIN POWELL CANCELS TRIP TO OLYMPICS He was too busy trying to build a coalition of support for Larry Brown's roster selections.

See the closing ceremonies? I thought this was nice. The Greek team chipped in and bought the pregnant woman with the glowing belly a car seat.

NBC kept the cross-promotion going to the very end. Twice, I could have sworn I saw Matt LeBlanc toweling off on the 10-meter platform.

GYMNASTICS SCORING CONTROVERSY CONTINUES Poor Paul Hamm. First he has to share a womb, now this.

The International Gymnastics Federation requested Hamm give up his gold medal in the all-around, but it was turned down flat by USOC chairman Peter Ueberroth. I hope the expression "Go take a flying FIG" was in there somewhere.

The request came from FIG president Bruno Grandi. I think I know his superior, Bruno Venti.

For those who don't remember Ueberroth, he rose to prominence when he turned a $225 million profit on the 1984 Games. Of course, the net profit was $24 million after they paid Carl Lewis's hair, makeup and wardrobe people.

Elsewhere, the U.S. had its lowest number of boxing medalists since 1948. Ladies and gentlemen, this is serious. Where is Don King supposed to find his future plaintiffs?

RICKY WILLIAMS CALLS DOLPHINS Don't get excited. He's not coming back, he just wanted to know if any linemen were holding.

Ricky was in Australia when he called the Dolphins. All I have is the punch line: "Oh, I thought you said Great Barrier Reefer!"

Paul Tagliabue issued a memo mandating that teams be more specific when reporting injuries. Which raises the question: Do you want to read anything more specific than "questionable (groin)"?

HOCKEY WORLD CUP BEGINS Everybody is getting ready for for the lockout. Starting Sept. 20, the Ice Capades will allow fighting.

FENWAY PARK BANS DEROGATORY T-SHIRTS Red Sox fans will be asked to turn the shirts inside out, or get a marker and write ALLEGEDLY in between YANKEES and SUCK.

JURY SELECTION BEGINS IN KOBE BRYANT TRIAL Prospective jurors have to fill out a questionnaire. The first question: "(Select one) William Kennedy Smith: Misunderstood or dreamy?"

My time is up. You've been great. Enjoy Shocking Blue.

THE **NOTES**

(The request came from FIG President Bruno Grandi...) Speaking of Starbucks, Paul Hamm's mouth is now available without foam.

(Ricky Williams calls Dolphins...) If you don't get this, ask a jazz musician, man.

(Jury selection begins in Kobe Bryant trial...) It looked more and more as if this thing would not go to trial. And only then could I invoke the name of William Kennedy Smith, whose 1991 acquittal was overshadowed by the twin images of the blue dot in front of his accuser, and Ted Kennedy running around without pants.

THE **CUTS**

Come on. The only thing ever held longer from the public during an Olympics was Richard Jewell. Richard Jewell was the guilty-until-proven-innocent bystander who was the chief suspect in the Olympic Village bombing at the 1996 Atlanta Games. As we all know, Jewell was cleared, then went on to bleach his hair, drop his first name and have a brilliant career as a singer/poet.

Last week, the NCAA denied Mike Williams his last year of eligibility at USC. Here's what I don't get. They said it was O.K. for him to ski.

The day before, the NCAA had turned down pro skier Jeremy Bloom's appeal to play football for Colorado. Let's be honest. On the depth chart for Colorado football p.r. nightmares, does this even make the traveling squad? Other than self-righteously protecting nothing but their own special interests, the NCAA can't get out of its own way. The fact that Mike Williams spent his last year doing nothing instead of winning the Heisman because of a ruling that was little more than vindictive is a clear indication....Whoa, who am I, Dan LeBatard?

THE **HIT(S)**

"Venus"

(I decided to make up for the Bananarama gaffe by including the other band who had one hit with the same song 17 years earlier.)

Good to be here. Look, I don't want to tell anyone his business, but if Kobe had a sense of humor, he'd pull into training camp behind the wheel of a white Ford Bronco.

RARE W AT MADISON SQUARE GARDEN After closing the RNC, President Bush told Donald Rumsfeld to leave 10,000 delegates in the Garden until the Rangers are capable of self-rule.

Former NFL defensive back Jason Sehorn addressed the convention, but it was not carried on network television. There's a switch. Somebody blowing coverage on him.

MARY PIERCE UPSETS MARIA SHARAPOVA AT U.S. OPEN Are you like me? Were you expecting to hear her father cheering from a court-ordered 500 feet away?

Sharapova is coming out with her own signature line of perfume. I have no idea what it smells like, but I guarantee the fragrance will last three rounds longer than the Anna Kournikova perfume.

I'm confused about this new U.S. Open bonus points series. What's Matt Kenseth doing in third place?

DEION SANDERS SIGNS WITH RAVENS I knew he was getting serious about returning when he had his tailor sew shoulder pads into all of his suits.

Deion is not a young man anymore. He's thinking of changing his nickname from Prime Time to Early Bird Special.

The Cowboys now have their own cable network. So far, all they have is a pregame show, a postgame show and the Jerry Jones reality series, *Trading Faces.*

ICHIRO BAGS 56 HITS IN AUGUST, MOST BY A MAJOR LEAGUER IN ONE MONTH IN 66 YEARS This hasn't happened since 1938, which, coincidentally, was the last time Edgar Martinez had to buy a glove.

Meanwhile, I think George Steinbrenner may be starting to crack. After the Yankees suf-

fered their worst loss ever, 22–0 to the Indians, he ordered Brian Cashman to spare no expense and make a deal for the scoreboard.

Yankees starter Kevin Brown broke two bones in his left hand when he punched a wall in the clubhouse during a loss to the Orioles. Damn. Why couldn't he have punched a wall en route to the clubhouse, then we could have renamed the passageway the metacarpal tunnel.

Wow, this was quick. The Red Sox voted the wall half a World Series share.

The Astros are back in the wild-card hunt. Phil Garner has shaken things up. He changed the "take" sign from touching his belt to holding up Carlos Beltran's contract.

CBS DEVELOPING SITCOM BASED ON LIFE OF BOB KNIGHT Good move. How much better would that video of him choking Neil Reed have been with a laugh track?

Which title do you like better: *Everybody Loves Raving*; *Bleep, Dear*; or *CSI: Lubbock*?

Wait a minute. Just cast Ted Danson in the lead and call it *Bicker.*

The next step is having a writer fly to Texas Tech and spend time with Knight at work and home. CBS just needs to find the right guy, with the right insurance.

OLYMPIC STARS PHELPS, PATTERSON AND GATLIN ON WHEATIES BOX Gymnast Paul Hamm was not selected, but he could be featured on a new cereal from Kellogg's, Sugar Frosted Asterisks.

COMPLAINT AGAINST CHARLES BARKLEY DROPPED The whole thing was a misunderstanding. Turns out an indecent assault charge cannot be filed by a buffet table.

CANADIAN DOLLAR RISES 10 CENTS AGAINST U.S. DOLLAR IN LAST YEAR Do you know what this means? Todd Bertuzzi's high-priced attorney is actually a high-priced attorney.

My time is up. You've been great. Enjoy Raydio.

THE **NOTES**

(Mary Pierce upsets Maria Sharapova…) If you never saw Mary Pierce's father in action, he made Richard Williams look like Dick Van Patten. Or his less-talented brother, Jerry Van Patten.

(I'm confused about this new U.S. Open bonus points series…) Matt Kenseth is a top NASCAR driver and a participant in the slightly more byzantine Nextel Cup point series.

(Wait a minute. Just cast Ted Danson in the lead…) You know, you may not believe I'm friends with Larry David. Fine. Here's a story. Three years ago, we're eating dinner. I say, "How about dessert?" He says, "Can't." I say, "Diet?" He says, "No. I can't because I have a bet with Ted Danson. No dessert for a year." Now, I'm thinking, it's Larry David, it's Ted Danson, the bet is no dessert for a year. Got to be a million-dollar wager, easy. I say, "What's the bet for?" He says, "$250." I say, "Have a piece of friggin' cake."

THE **CUTS**

Serious injury. The break goes all the way up to Brown's wrist. He may need Tommy Tune surgery. This is a switch on "Tommy John surgery." I'm not sure, but Tommy Tune surgery may involve a trip to Sweden.

THE **HIT(S)**

"Jack and Jill"

"You Can't Change That"

Still disappointed over the second-season premiere of *The Apprentice*. Be honest. How many of you were sure Trump was going to fire Gary Bettman?

JOE GIBBS IS HOMECOMING KING The Hall of Fame coach returned to Washington and stopped the Bucs 16–10. You can tell it's an emotional win when you see grown men blowing those giant hog noses.

The Lions won their first road game since 2000. It took a while, but Matt Millen was finally able to persuade the Ford family to remove the antilock brakes from the offense.

ABC used a 10-second delay during its opening kickoff show. Or 419 minutes, 50 seconds less than the delay NBC used from Athens.

The NFL may have been a little too cautious on opening night. For the first two quarters, Tom Brady was pixilated from the waist down.

NOTRE DAME STUNS MICHIGAN IN SOUTH BEND It's the first time in a year and a half that Touchdown Jesus has opened his eyes.

Elsewhere, Southern Miss defeated Nebraska. Don't worry about Bill Callahan. His grace period extends all the way to next week's coin flip.

Miami defeated Florida State as the Seminoles blew a 10–3 lead with 30 seconds remaining. Wide right, wide left and now Why'd Chris Rix throw on third down?

The Hurricanes and Seminoles were playing for bragging rights in the newly created conference, What's Left of the Atlantic Coast.

KUZNETSOVA SVETS IT OUT AT U.S. OPEN The Russian teenager defeated countrywoman Elena Dementieva for her first Grand Slam title. Immediately after the match, her orthodontist signed with IMG.

For the first time since 1986, no American man reached the semifinals at Flushing Meadow. O.K., what's Larry Brown's excuse this time?

The umpire who made several questionable calls in Serena Williams's quarterfinal loss to Jennifer Capriati was fired a day later. But she has a great shot at a gymnastics judging gig in Beijing.

The bad calls against Serena occurred the same night they were honoring Althea Gibson at Arthur Ashe Stadium. And I thought Jim McGreevey had bad timing....

Fans at Flushing Meadow were able to get their picture taken holding up a replica of the championship trophy in front of a photo of center court. And for an extra 50 bucks you got the photo and a small soda.

MLB MOVES FIRST TWO GAMES OF EXPOS-MARLINS SERIES FROM MIAMI TO CHICAGO It wasn't totally weather related. Bud Selig just wanted to give Frank Robinson the chance to cry on *Oprah*.

Meanwhile, George Steinbrenner was furious that the Yankees were not awarded a forfeit when the Devil Rays arrived late in New York due to Hurricane Frances. You know, if he doesn't watch it, people are going to start thinking he's petty.

Barry Bonds became the first player to draw 200 walks in a season. I don't want to say Barry isn't seeing any strikes, but the other night, during his third at bat, QuesTec started yawning.

DON KING HAS DONATED A REPORTED $40,000 TO THE REPUBLICAN NATIONAL COMMITTEE That's Step 1. Step 2: Try to get the Electoral College moved to the Mirage.

GARY PAYTON ARRESTED ON SUSPICION OF DUI The former All-Star was stopped after trying to back down an on-ramp on the San Diego Freeway. Sad. He's left the triangle offense, and he still can't operate in traffic.

My time is up. You've been great. Enjoy the Electric Prunes.

THE **NOTES**

(Kuznetsova Svets it out at U.S. Open…) By the time you read this, Kuznetsova's braces should be off. But her orthodontist will still be on retainer.

(Fans at Flushing Meadow were able to get their picture taken holding up…) I don't want to say the food at the Open is expensive, but at the end of your ham and cheese hero, there's an option to buy.

THE **CUTS**

Rick Ankiel pitched a scoreless inning in his first appearance in the big leagues since 2002. The former Cardinal phenom is recovering from Tommy John surgery, but his control was so erratic, it turned out to be Tommy Jo   hn surgery. The computerized typesetting *SI* uses could not create the space needed for this very visual joke. As I understand it, to get that kind of technology, you have to make a trip to Sweden.

Pittsburgh edged Oakland on a last-second field goal. Forget that, Jim Nantz made it through the entire game without calling Phil Simms "Lanny." Nantz had moved from *The NFL Today* into the booth with Simms. For the last few years, his only play-by-play had been on CBS's golf coverage. Hence the mild dementia in referring to his golf partner, Lanny Wadkins. Nothing, of course, when compared to the dementia of the guy writing the joke.

THE **HIT(S)**

"I Had Too Much to Dream Last Night"

(As I have said, people never give me jokes, just bands. One day, I'm picking up my mail. My mailman, who I've said maybe 10 words to in eight years, says, "Can I ask you a question? Have you ever heard of the Electric Prunes?" I say, "Sure. 'I Had Too Much to Dream Last Night.'" "Well," my mailman says, "when are you gonna use them?" I tell him next week. Then I puff my chest out and say, "So, you read my column?" And he says, "Nah. I just look for the bands every week.…")

Good to be here. Well, Maurice Clarett never gives up. Now, he's telling people he got his car from Oprah.

EUROS CASH IN AT RYDER CUP It was over so early on Sunday, NBC cut away for the last two hours to four babes playing beach volleyball in the bunker on 17.

The U.S. trailed 11–5 going into the final day. And a desperate John Kerry vowed to cut that deficit in half by 2006.

I don't want to question Hal Sutton's pairings, but what was Davis Love III doing with Dorf?

Far be it for me to pile on about Hal, but do you really want a guy who's been married four times trying to match up people?

Phil Mickelson had a tough first day. At one point he switched equipment three times ... during his backswing.

Before the matches began, Michael Jordan was a dinner guest of the U.S. team. He said a few inspirational words, posed for photos, then took Chris Riley for $50,000 by chipping three brussels sprouts onto the dessert cart.

CHAIR IN THE AIR Last week in Oakland, Rangers reliever Frank Francisco was arrested for aggravated battery after he threw a chair from the bullpen and hit two heckling fans in the head. Do you see what happens when the pitcher doesn't have to bat?

Francisco was released on a $15,000 bond, which was posted by his teammates. Quite a sacrifice. Twenty players had to give up two days of meal money.

MLB suspended Francisco for the remainder of the season for throwing the folding chair. Am I too cynical if I think his fine will be paid by Vince McMahon?

I'll tell you who's upset about all this. Oakland G.M. Billy Beane. He signed that chair for $5, developed it for three years,

and now it's gone.

Meanwhile, I don't know how seriously Art Howe is taking things as the lame-duck manager of the Mets. The other night he picked up the dugout phone and asked if Martha Stewart was in the pen.

And Barry Bonds finally hit 700. Help me out. Is that career homers or plate appearances in the last three seasons?

GIANTS TURN OVER SKINS 20–14 Despite the win, Tom Coughlin fined his offense $11,000 for not getting into the red zone early enough.

Giants team meetings begin five minutes earlier than their scheduled times. Which explains why Kurt Warner has been working on his seven-minute drill.

The Packers met the Bears at Lambeau Field. John Kerry was criticized last week for referring to it as "Lambert Field." That was only the start. Later on, he called defensive end Kabeer Gbaja-Biamila "Buddy Miles."

CANADA WINS WORLD CUP Pretty moving at the end, when the NHL players met at center ice to exchange handshakes and résumés.

I think I may have figured out a way to end the hockey work stoppage: replacement owners.

The owners rejected the players' last four-point proposal for a new CBA: 1) five percent salary rollbacks; 2) luxury tax; 3) revenue sharing; 4) backup goalies spending each game telemarketing.

***SPORTS ILLUSTRATED* CELEBRATES 50TH ANNIVERSARY** Many people don't know this, but it was the dream of Henry Luce that one day this magazine, his baby, would devote half a page every week to some wiseass making jokes.

My time is up. You've been great. Enjoy Undisputed Truth.

THE **NOTES**

(I don't want to question Hal Sutton's pairings…) Dorf is the hilarious midget golf character created by Tim Conway. I believe *Dorf on Golf* is the best-selling video in history, if you don't count the Rob Lowe tapes.

(Meanwhile, I don't know how seriously Art Howe is taking things…) This was the week before Martha went up the river. Seriously, though, how much worse could she have done against a righty than John Franco?

*(**Sports Illustrated** celebrates 50th anniversary…)* I felt the need to call attention to this incredible milestone, and the fact that there are subscribers out there who think my column is the worst thing to happen to *SI* since they retired Cheryl Tiegs's mesh bikini.

THE **CUTS**

Earlier in the week, Tiger vociferously denied reports that he and his fiancée have broken up. Turns out, he just sent her out to be regripped. This image is more than a little unseemly. Don't laugh, you'll just encourage me. Wait, I'll cover my ears. O.K., now laugh. What?

The European players had tremendous solidarity. In fact, by Sunday, if you wanted peroxide, you had to drive to Windsor, Ontario. The Europeans had all bleached their hair. Windsor is just across the border from Detroit. You'll find the peroxide right next to the Labatt Blue.

According to a recent phone survey among Canadians about the labor dispute, 27% said the players union should compromise, 21% said the owners, and the other 52% blamed the whole mess on Alan Thicke. Alan Thicke, despite being a nice guy, is the standard punch line when you need a Canadian celebrity. However, if you're in Windsor, Ontario, and under 18, Alan will be glad to buy peroxide for you. See? What did I tell you. Nice guy.

THE **HIT(S)**

"Smiling Faces (Sometimes)"

Finally saw *Wimbledon*. Unfortunately, I couldn't hear anything because Richard Williams was sitting behind me, whining about the line calls.

TWINS WIN THIRD STRAIGHT AL CENTRAL TITLE
And a giddy Carl Pohlad gave them 16 cases of champagne—at cost!

Ichiro Suzuki is a virtual lock to break George Sisler's 1920 major league record of 257 hits in a season. Of course, Sisler set the record in 154 games, which means the Maris family is busy bubble-wrapping the asterisk.

This is fascinating. According to scientists, if you were to lay all of Ichiro's hits end to end, it would short-hop the leftfield wall at Safeco.

The Giants have guaranteed Barry Bonds's contract through 2006. Although, whatever happens, this season will always be considered his walk year.

Shawn Green sat out Game 2 of the Dodgers-Giants series in observance of the Jewish high holy day Yom Kippur. On Friday night, he hit a key home run in L.A.'s opening win. Of course, that night, he was playing under the name Cole Needray.

Green got tremendous support for his gesture. Telegrams, e-mails and more than 500 Koufaxes.

NFL BEGINS CERTIFYING MANUFACTURERS WHOSE SUPPLEMENTS CONTAIN NO BANNED SUBSTANCES Now, you can tell a supplement is NFL-approved. Just look for the picture of Bill Romanowski with the red line through it.

And the child-proof cap by Reebok.

The Pittsburgh-Miami game was moved to Sunday night because of Hurricane Jeanne. Meterologists believe the mass of high pressure will continue until Ben Roethlisberger proves he can lead the Steelers' offense.

The Broncos were fined nearly $1 million for circumventing the salary cap. Jake Plummer aside, do you have a feeling there may be other guys in that organization nicknamed The Snake?

An arbitrator ruled in favor of the Dolphins' recovering an $8.6 million bonus from Ricky Williams. Ricky may not have helped himself. He was represented at the hearing by the Zig-Zag Man.

MICHAEL MICHAEL MICHAEL... MICHAEL?
Michael Jordan denied rumors he was coming out of retirement to play with Miami. He was thinking about it, but a last-minute slot opened up at the Birmingham Barons Fantasy Camp.

Jordan has been working out with Dennis Rodman. It's going well. Rodman has him concentrating on his outside Jell-O shot.

Rodman's tryout with the Nuggets was cut short because of an ingrown toenail. I believe that's the same excuse he used to get out of his marriage to Carmen Electra.

JOHN EDWARDS ON COVER OF *RUNNER'S WORLD* Not to be outdone, Dick Cheney will appear in two start-up monthlies, *ICU People* and *Undisclosed House & Garden*.

Edwards has run a marathon in 3:30. Although the Swift Boat Veterans claim he dropped out at mile 3 with a phantom heel spur.

TIGER DROPS OUT OF 84 LUMBER CLASSIC, CITES FATIGUE Tiger told reporters he was beat, and Phil Mickelson immediately piped up, "Well, what do you expect? We had to use the Nike ball."

CBS FINED $550,000 OVER SUPER BOWL HALF-TIME Half a million dollars for one boob. Wait. I'm sorry. I was thinking about Tom Arnold's salary.

My time is up. You've been great. Enjoy New Riders of the Purple Sage.

THE **NOTES**

(Shawn Green sat out Game 2 of the Dodgers-Giants series…)

(Green got tremendous support for his gesture. Telegrams, e-mails and more than 500 Koufaxes…) Kol Nidre is the prayer read on the first night of Yom Kippur. My sister called me and said people from her temple called the next week and told her how much they loved these jokes. I'm not sure, but I think for next year's high holy days, she'll get to move up three rows closer to the Torah.

(An arbitrator ruled in favor of the Dolphins' recovering an $8.6 million bonus…) I had been working with a version of a joke that Ricky Williams wouldn't return to Miami unless they replaced the offensive coordinator with the Zig Zag Man. But I scrapped that to get the chance to imply that the Zig Zag Man had some sort of law degree.

(CBS fined $550,000 over Super Bowl halftime…) This joke was all set up. All I had to do was think of a high-paid boob. Tom Arnold came to mind instantly. Then I thought, "Nah, too easy, There's somebody better." Two days later, there wasn't. Almost a year later, there isn't.

THE **CUTS**

Chiefs in Show Me State of Disarray. *Kansas City dropped to 0–3 after being upset by Houston at home, 24–21. After the game, Dick Vermeil was sobbing in Larry Johnson's diaper.*

Earlier in the week, Vermeil said if Priest Holmes was unavailable, Johnson would have to "take off his diaper" and play. This raises an interesting question of comedy etiquette: Should a 67-year-old man be making any jokes using the word "diaper"? These jokes were cut because the first one doesn't work without the explanation in the second. And the second doesn't work because 67-year-old men don't wear diapers. Unless they're in Vegas and they've paid a grand to a hooker.

Here's how the fines break down: Twenty CBS stations pay $27,000 each, and Dan Rather forges a check to cover the rest. Dan Rather received forged documents about President Bush's discharge from the National Guard. He didn't forge the documents. Once again, the integrity of an innocent joke is destroyed by petty accuracy.

THE **HIT(S)**

"Panama Red"

(This group, the poor man's Grateful Dead, had the nuts to trademark their name. And, like I have to tell you, nobody rocks like a trademark attorney.)

Bad dream last night. I was at the World Series of Poker, and I folded with A's and Cubs.

END OF AN ERROR: BASEBALL RETURNS TO NATION'S CAPITAL There may be trouble naming the new Washington team. The rights to *Senators* are owned by the Texas Rangers. And there's not enough room on a jersey for *Ineffectual Bureaucrats*.

Wait a minute. How about a name that captures the essence of the new franchise? The Angelos Dodgers?

Meanwhile, no disrespect to the Red Sox and the Astros, but weren't the wild-card slots already clinched by Jose Guillen and Milton Bradley?

The Angels suspended Guillen for the remainder of their season after he threw a tantrum late in a game. Not only that, the Rally Monkey is after Guillen for stealing his act.

Bradley was suspended after threatening a fan who threw a beer bottle in his direction. Turns out it was all a misunderstanding. The fan he was going after with that beer bottle was dressed as one of those blue recycling bins.

PRESIDENT BUSH SIGNS LAW ESTABLISHING TOUGHER PENALTIES FOR UNETHICAL SPORTS AGENTS Getting rid of sleazy agents? I don't think the economy can afford to lose another one million jobs.

The bill was promoted by Nebraska coach turned congressman Tom Osborne. It passed so overwhelmingly in the House that, at 42–0, Osborne put in his scout team.

PATRIOTS TIE NFL RECORD WITH 18TH STRAIGHT WIN Now that that's out of the way, throw a uniform on Bill Belichick and stick him in the Red Sox dugout for the next three weeks.

During the Packers' 14–7 loss to the Giants last Sunday, Brett Favre suffered a concussion then came back in for one play and threw a touchdown pass. Favre was hit so hard that for the next two series Troy Aikman didn't know what broadcast booth he was in.

3Com Park has been renamed Monster Park. I was shocked. Who knew the 49ers still had enough cap space for Charlize Theron?

In a *60 Minutes* interview, Bill Parcells claimed that over the years a few players have taken a swing at him. He didn't mention names, but I've got it narrowed down to 283.

The Dolphins lost running back Lamar Gordon for the season. Does anyone have Jim Kiick's phone number at the assisted living facility?

LET'S CONTINUE TO PLAY THE *FEUD*! This is getting ugly. Now Kobe is claiming Shaq paid women to keep quiet about his free-throw shooting.

Kobe claimed Shaq once paid up to $1 million in hush money. But to get that kind of dough, the woman had to keep quiet and also drain a half-court jumper.

FUNNY CIDE WINS JOCKEY CLUB GOLD CUP Of course, with a gelding, any cup is for display purposes only.

CHUCK WEPNER MOVING FORWARD WITH SUIT AGAINST SYLVESTER STALLONE Wepner feels he deserves a share of profits from the *Rocky* films. That's a switch. Wepner trying to bleed someone else.

PIGEON RELEASED AT OLYMPICS FOUND IN ROMANIA O.K., wake up the boys in the lab and get that bird's blood tested for Goose Growth Hormone.

My time is up. You've been great. Enjoy Cutting Crew.

THE **NOTES**

(Wait a minute. How about a name that captures the essence…) Orioles owner Peter Angelos had been trying to prevent the Expos from moving close to Baltimore and threatening his profit base. He ended up getting a nice settlement from MLB: A game-worn Camilio Pascual jersey and a day of beauty at a Georgetown spa.

(The Angels suspended Guillen for the remainder of their season…) I had a joke about them suspending Guillen because when he threw the tantrum he missed the cutoff man, but Kostya gave me the same look (over the phone) that he had for the line about Odalis Perez throwing a tantrum with both feet on the rubber.

(The bill was promoted by Nebraska coach turned congressman Tom Osborne…) Here's an editor's redemption. The original payoff on this joke was, *at 42–0 he took out his starters*, but Kostya pointed out it was too confusing because there are no starting congressmen. The "scout team," the fourth stringers who simulate an upcoming opponent's offense in practice, was cleaner, funnier and much much hipper.

(Chuck Wepner moving forward with suit against Sylvester Stallone…) Wepner, the unknown heavyweight who was turned into pudding by Ali in 1975, is the acknowledged inspiration for Rocky Balboa. His well-known nickname was the "Bayonne Bleeder." His lesser-known one was "Kid Plasma."

THE **CUTS**

There is speculation that the Orioles might move into the NL East and create a natural rivalry with the Expos. Tough adjustment. Boog Powell's barbecue would have to give up the DH. Boog Powell operates an outdoor barbecue behind the right-field fence. There's no DH in the National League. Would it help if I had said "designated hot sauce guy" instead? Didn't think so.

Meanwhile, did you see the debate? Wasn't that shocking when Kerry promised to send white go-go boots to the troops? Earlier in the week, a rookie pitcher for the Cleveland Indians had been hit in the leg with a stray bullet fired into the side of the team bus. Luckily, because of a rookie hazing prank, he was dressed in a cheerleader's outfit, complete with white go-go boots. Doctors said the boots prevented him from more serious injury. In the debate, Kerry had talked about soldiers in Iraq not having proper equipment. Bush blinked and smirked, which is his state-of-the-art defense system.

THE **HIT(S)**

"(I Just) Died in Your Arms"

Good to be here. Hey, great news. BALCO is six weeks away from developing a lactose-free steroid cream.

NEW SET OF WOODS Tiger Woods and Elin Nordegren were married last week in Barbados. Busy couple of days for Tiger. On Monday, he renewed his vows with Phil Knight.

The start of the wedding was delayed. Why? Was Bernhard Langer in the twosome ahead of them?

Michael Jordan also came. It was nice MJ could find time in his schedule between not coming out of retirement and not getting any offers of ownership.

Hootie and the Blowfish performed. Tiger loves their music and loves having someone around who's been in a slump longer than he has.

Of course, security on the island was tight. Butch Harmon was detained at the airport when he kept insisting he had to go to the reception and prevent Tiger from slicing the cake.

RED SOX–YANKEES: ALDS LANG SYNE In the first round, Twins manager Ron Gardenhire lost the lead in Game 2 when he left his closer in for a third inning. Or, as it's known among big league insiders, Grady Littleball.

I kept switching between Game 1 of the Yanks-Twins series and the vice presidential debate. At one point I swear I saw Dick Cheney get the green light on 3–0.

Yankees-Sox, Dodgers-Cards…everywhere you turn, this country is divided into reds and blues.

FOUR RANKED UNBEATEN TEAMS FALL Or, as the BCS calls it, Sigh of Relief Saturday.

Oklahoma blanked Texas 12–0. Freshman Adrian Peterson ran for 225 yards and was so dominant, Paul Tagliabue put five federal judges on speed dial.

By the end of the game the Longhorns were desperate. Twice Mack Brown asked for a measurement on Jason White's eligibility.

White is in his sixth year at OU. Even the guy on his Heisman Trophy is wearing a red shirt.

Elsewhere, Michigan edged Minnesota 27–24. There was even more at stake this year. The Little Brown Jug was filled with the flu shot vaccine.

STEELERS ROUT BROWNS 34–23 Pittsburgh is unbeaten with rookie QB Ben Roethlisberger starting. He's come on so strong in the last three weeks, the Steelers' home turf is now known as Heinz Kerry Field.

A woman filed a paternity suit against Ricky Williams. Well, Ricky really wasn't kidding when he said he felt as if he had no protection.

Williams is discussing a possible return to active status in the NFL. He'll either receive a one-year suspension or go on the IR with glaucoma.

NASCAR PENALIZES THE BLEEP OUT OF DALE EARNHARDT JR. Earnhardt was fined $10,000 and lost 25 Nextel points for cursing on-air. Believe me, the punishment could have been worse. NBC could have imposed a five-second delay on his pit crew.

Dale Jr. or, as he's known, Little E. Not to be confused with Jamal Lewis: Little Plea.

DON CHERRY ENDORSING A LINE OF MOUTH-GUARDS If you're European, they leave a bad taste.

JOHN MCENROE GUEST STARS ON *THE APPRENTICE* McEnroe met with the team that won the latest task. What a coincidence. His talk-show audience is also down to the final seven guys.

My time is up. You've been great. Enjoy Desmond Dekker and the Aces.

THE **NOTES**

(Good to be here. Hey, great news. BALCO is six weeks away...)
Apparently, after the Kobe trial was dismissed, they didn't have to work on the glue anymore.

(The start of the wedding was delayed...) I could have done an entire column on this wedding. Too many premises. This, however, was my favorite.

(White is in his sixth year at OU...) Redshirting is when a team holds a player back a season to preserve his full four years of NCAA eligibility. It gives a guy more time to learn the system, heal from an injury and not go to classes.

THE **CUTS**

Strange ceremony. Twice, they had to stop the procession for a ruling by David Fay. David Fay is the rules committee chairman of the USGA. To be fair, one of his rulings was on Langer for slow play in the two-some ahead.

Are you like me? Are you wondering if the bachelor party was alternate shots? I was trying to come up with someone to pop out of the cake at Tiger's bachelor party, but the best stripper names I could come up with were Tit Leist and B.J. Sing. And I got overruled by David Fay.

Oprah Winfrey was supposed to show up but had to cancel at the last minute. Too bad. She was hoping to get Tiger for a regular segment on her show, "Oprah's Hook Club." Had to choose between this and the Butch Harmon slicing joke, even though Tiger both hooks and slices. He's just that good.

THE **HIT(S)**

"The Israelites"

That's it. I'm suing Major League Baseball. They stole my idea for a T-shirt. Although mine said, WENDY SELIG-PRIEB, WHO'S YOUR DADDY?

YANKS REROUT SOX DREAMS New York won Game 3, 19–8. By the eighth inning the Red Sox were out of pitchers and had to bring in a nickelback.

The Yankees' offense was so relentless, it makes you wonder if Curt Schilling's ankle tendon split, or escaped.

The final debate easily outdrew Game 2 of the ALCS. Did I get this wrong? Did President Bush say he believed home field advantage was a choice?

Red Sox chairman Tom Werner and Katie Couric have reportedly broken up. You know how it is. She wanted to go all the way, and he hasn't since 1918.

Tony La Russa says he'll work for free next season if the Cards win the World Series. What that means is he won't accept any money personally, he'll just send Dave Duncan out to get it.

Just wondering. Is Dodge the official sponsor of Steve Lyons's nonapology to Shawn Green?

NFL SELECTS DON MISCHER PRODUCTIONS TO CREATE SUPER BOWL HALFTIME SHOW Mischer has produced eight Emmy Awards. Great. That's just what we need at halftime: a dead actor montage.

Mischer produced the 1993 Super Bowl half-time show, which starred Michael Jackson. Of course, 11 years ago it was legal to grab your crotch inside the five-yard chuck zone.

Meanwhile, I love this time of year. You get to see Norv Turner's face change colors.

The Eagle avenged last season's NFC Championship Game loss by trouncing the Panthers 30–8. Brutal day for Jake Delhomme. He threw four interceptions, was sacked twice and hurried six times by Donovan McNabb's mom.

Phil Simms does not want to broadcast any games involving the Buccaneers and his son Chris. Not to be outdone, John Madden has refused to ride Jerome Bettis.

Vikings running back Onterrio Smith was suspended four games for violating the league's substance abuse policy. However, Smith can cut the suspension in half if he makes his appeal to the league using Jamal Lewis's cell-phone.

IN RECENT INTERVIEW KOBE SAYS HE MISSES PHIL JACKSON This is not my field, but I'm pretty sure the feeling isn't consensual.

In an upcoming book the former Lakers coach said he had to consult a therapist to deal with Bryant. Tough. After three sessions the shrink said, "Can't you give me something easier, like bed-wetting?"

The therapist was an expert in narcissism. In fact, his technique is known as the "I-angle offense."

The NBA played its first preseason games in China. Speaking of the Great Wall, any progress in the NHL labor talks?

David Stern claims that the league didn't make any money going to China. But that's only because they couldn't fit a Gatorade billboard on the side of Yao Ming.

BCS RELEASES FIRST RANKINGS Are you like me? Are you waiting for the Swift Boat Veterans to attack USC's record?

DREAM JOB DOWN TO FINAL FIVE CONTESTANTS They've changed the format this year. The winner gets a high-paying on-air job with ESPN, then is fired three weeks later for a racially insensitive remark.

My time is up. You've been great. Enjoy Mel & Tim.

THE **NOTES**

(Just wondering. Is Dodge the official sponsor of Steve Lyons's nonapology…)
Steve Lyons had gone on-air with some less-than-enlightened comments about Green's decision to sit out on Yom Kippur: "He's not a practicing Jew," Lyons said. "He didn't marry a Jewish girl, and from what I understand, he never had a bar mitzvah, which is unfortunate because he didn't get the money." This deeply, deeply offended me—until I was able to come up with this line.

(Phil Simms does not want to broadcast any games involving the Buccaneers…) John Madden is notoriously afraid of flying and travels to games in the Madden Cruiser, a customized bus. Jerome Bettis's nickname is "the Bus." That's it. That's all. There's nothing sexual here. Everyone go back to your homes.

(The therapist was an expert in narcissism…) I am very proud of this switch on "triangle offense." Now, tell me. Does pointing this out make me a narcissist? Does the fact that I don't care how you answer that make me a solipsist? Or am I a solipsist wrapped in a narcissist? I don't know, but I am enjoying thinking about it.

THE **CUTS**

In an interview with Esquire, *Ricky said he'd lost 20 pounds on a vegetarian diet. How come I think the correct expression should be "went through 20 pounds on a vegetarian diet"?* This was a little unclear, even for a pot joke, which by its very nature should be unclear.

Jackson's book is based on a diary he kept last season. Here's what's odd: Every entry begins, "Dear Kitty…" "Dear Kitty" is the beginning of every entry in Anne Frank's diary. See what happens when you let Steve Lyons fax in jokes?

Mischer also produced the Democratic convention and was heard cursing on-air when balloons didn't fall on schedule. Technically, is that considered a word-drop malfunction? See what happens when you let William Safire fax in jokes?

THE **HIT(S)**

"Backfield in Motion"

Good to be here. Sorry, but this is getting out of hand. Now Barry Bonds's trainer is claiming he put something in Tiger's yacht that would make it undetected by the Coast Guard.

SO FAR, SO BLOODY GOOD The Sox are putting it all together. After two games they were hitting over .300 and fielding over .500.

Cold in Boston. The first pitch was thrown out by Ted Williams.

Curt Schilling tested his ankle before Game 2 by throwing on the side and spending a few minutes stomping on the Fox Diamond Cam.

Before suturing Schilling's injured tendon so he could pitch Game 6 of the ALCS, Red Sox team doctor Bill Morgan performed the procedure on a cadaver. Boy, I'm telling you, Teddy Ballgame is finding all kinds of ways to contribute.

As always, Fox heavily promoted its other shows. It took three games for me to realize *Arrested Development* was not a documentary on the Yankees' farm system.

I don't know about the Fox Right Now! box. Do we really need the pitcher, the batter, the runners on base *and* the status of lawsuits against Bill O'Reilly?

AUBURN STARTS 8–0 FOR THE FIRST TIME IN 10 YEARS School officials are so excited, they've stopped secretly interviewing replacements for Tommy Tuberville until next Friday.

Elsewhere, Sylvester Croom led Mississippi State over Florida for its first conference win in more than a year. Which means the longest SEC losing streak now belongs to Martha Stewart.

Boston College upset heavily favored Notre Dame in South Bend. I know what you're thinking, but they didn't come back from being down 0–3.

VIKINGS ROLL PAST TITANS Randy Moss did not catch a pass. Minnesota's staff is having trouble getting his hamstring to behave.

Drew Bledsoe has been sacked 23 times in the Bills' last five games. All his pants now come with a collapsing pocket.

The Raiders traded Jerry Rice to the Seahawks for a seventh-round draft choice. Other than that, the best offer was from Budweiser to have Rice back up "Leon."

Rice received approval from legendary Hall of Fame receiver Steve Largent to wear his retired number 80. And for the Seahawks game on Halloween, Jerry is planning to go as Brian Bosworth.

Ricky Williams now claims he retired because of a disputed drug test. And this is a little lame. He says the sample the NFL used was left by a friend of Carmelo Anthony's.

NASCAR CONSIDERS LIFTING BAN ON HARD-LIQUOR SPONSORSHIP So, figure a couple of years, and drivers will be competing for the Nextel Tumbler.

What's the difference between hard-liquor and beer sponsorship? Fewer pit stops?

Meanwhile, driver Kirk Shelmerdine has dedicated the space on his back fenders to read BUSH-CHENEY '04. And he's renamed his back suspension the Axle of Evil.

IN THE LAST MONTH 30 PEOPLE HAVE PURCHASED SEASON TICKETS FOR THE ATLANTA THRASHERS O.K., who wants to call the Better Business Bureau?

CAVALIERS GIVE TRYOUT TO JAYSON WILLIAMS It didn't go well. He kept trying to wipe his fingerprints off the ball.

My time is up. You've been great. Enjoy Bo Donaldson and the Heywoods.

THE **NOTES**

(Before suturing Schilling's injured tendon so he could pitch...) Originally, the part of the cadaver was played by Grady Little. Would you expect anything less from me? But because, a) Grady was actually being considered for managing jobs at the time, and b) Ted Williams was actually dead, Kostya and I decided to suit up the Splinter again.

(Boston College upset heavily favored Notre Dame...) This is astrologically rare. A shot at Notre Dame and the Yankees in the same joke.

(Ricky Williams now claims he retired because of a disputed drug test...) Earlier that week, Carmelo Anthony had been cited for marijuana possession at the Denver airport and told officials the pot had been left in his backpack by a friend. A friend who surfaced the next day and corroborated the account. The friend's street name was "Slim." No further questions, Mr. Zig Zag Man.

*(**Cavaliers give tryout to Jayson Williams...**)* A long-distance fall-away jumper at the buzzer by Ed Markey.

THE **CUTS**

6–0 Eagles, T.O., OT Browns 34–31. What a break. If Philly had lost to Cleveland, Terrell Owens would have had to start making disparaging remarks about Dick Cheney's daughter. This was a reference to a reference I had referred to before, concerning Owens's cracks about former teammate Garcia's sexuality. Good callback, unfortunately too far away from the original to get people not to assume it was a cheap shot at John Kerry's alleged "outing" at the last debate. Yeesh....

NBC is getting way too cautious with NASCAR. First, they impose a five-second delay, now they're insisting Mark Martin's Viagra car stay at least three rows off the pole. This was a reference to impotence, and despite being three rows back, not far enough away for people to assume it was anything but a dick joke. Which it, uh, is not.

I don't get this. If the Braves had reached the World Series, Rafael Furcal would only have been allowed to use a designated driver to get to the American League park. Furcal had violated his DUI probation and had to serve 21 days in jail after the Braves finished their season. Maybe if I had made his designated driver Mark Martin...nah.

THE **HIT(S)**

"Billy, Don't Be a Hero"

Good to be here. Just got back from the parade. I can't tell you what a thrill it was to be with three million Red Sox fans listening attentively for the other shoe to drop.

NOMAR GARCIAPARRA VOTED A FULL SERIES SHARE Don't get excited, the Red Sox also voted one to the 28-inch actor Pedro Martinez keeps by his locker.

Curt Schilling's contract called for a $2 million bonus if the Sox won the World Series. That works out to $667,000 a suture.

Free-agent-to-be Derek Lowe became the first pitcher to win three series-clinching games in a single postseason. The only way Lowe could have made more money on Fox would have been by winning *Rebel Billionaire*.

The Cardinals hit .190 for the Series. Let's be honest. That little AOL guy got better hacks.

The Series was over so quickly, Tony La Russa didn't even get to double-switch his hotel room.

STEELERS END PATS' WINNING STREAK 34–20 O.K., so the other shoe was a cleat....

FedEx Field has expanded to 91,665 seats. The Redskins had to handle all the overflow NASCAR fans who come out hoping to see a crash involving Joe Gibbs and Dan Snyder.

And a new Hooters restaurant was added to the club level at FedEx Field. It's a real Redskins Hooters: All the waitresses are well over the cup limit.

Dolphins receiver David Boston, who's out for the season, was arrested last week at a Vermont airport after he allegedly assaulted a 59year-old gate agent. I have a question: Can you get andro at a duty-free shop?

The NFL may not renew its contract with Madison Square Garden to host the draft. It's looking for a bigger venue, like Mel Kiper Jr.'s mousse warehouse.

NBA UNLOCKS-OUT REGULAR SEASON The Heat will play on national TV 24 times this season. (That sound you hear is the *Queer Eye* guys rushing to Stan Van Gundy's house.)

Shaquille O'Neal plans to join the Miami Beach police department as a $1 a year volunteer. Shaq will head up his own crack investigative division, Thong Patrol.

OHIO STATE–MICHIGAN BACKS OUT OF NAMING-RIGHTS DEAL WITH SBC FOR ANNUAL FOOTBALL CLASSIC SBC was going to pay $1 million for the Ohio State–Michigan game for the next two years. Damn. Art Schlichter had the over at 2½.

NCAA president Myles Brand applauded the decision to back out. Too bad. I was hoping that for the right price, he'd be Myles (Your) Brand (Here).

Elsewhere, Georgia beat Florida 31–24. I had to turn this in before Election Day. Just wondering: Were Florida voters able to get the "Deport Ron Zook" referendum on the ballot in time?

North Carolina shocked unbeaten Miami. Before this season the only experience most Miami football players had with the ACC was with the word *accessory*.

PARIS HILTON SEEN WITH MARK PHILIP-POUSSIS, THEN ANDY RODDICK Makes sense. She dumped Philippoussis for a guy who could perform well on all surfaces.

METS PITCHER JOHN FRANCO QUES-TIONED OVER TICKETS HE PROVIDED TO THE BONANNO CRIME FAMILY IN EARLY '90s That's more than 10 years ago. I guess the feds can talk to him under the Rico Brogna statutes.

My time is up. You've been great. Enjoy the Electras.

THE **NOTES**

(Just came back from the parade...) Like most Red Sox fans, I was just glad it was finally over and I could get on with my life at 47. Here's an example of my sober restraint in victory: During the parade, Pedro Martinez was hit in the forehead with a ball thrown by a fan. I *did not* write the joke *Sure he got hit. Grady Little decided to leave him out there.* Okay, I thought about it. Hell, I'm still thinking about it.

(The series was over so quickly, Tony La Russa...) The Cardinals manager had been whining during the first two games that the Red Sox had purposely put his team in a hotel in Quincy, 45 minutes from the ballpark and with no room service after 10:00. Grady Little, him I'll let slide, but not this guy. What a baby. No room service after 10:00? Hey Tony, Mr. Genius, next time call your butt boy George Will. I'm sure he would have waited on you....Sorry. I don't know if I'm cranky, or emotional because we've come to the end of the collection.

(Mets pitcher John Franco questioned over tickets he provided...) Rico Brogna was a great fielding first basemen with the Mets who went on to become an All-Star RBI machine with the Phillies. He deserves better than to be the butt of some inspired wordplay. Wait. Just let me look at this again....*Rico Brogna Statutes.* Nah. This is quite a tribute.

THE **CUTS**

Good to be here. Have you seen the latest tape of Osama? You know it's recent, because in the middle, "Scooter" comes on to demonstrate a screwball. I loved this opener, but even with a magazine that turns over as fast as *SI*, you have to worry about the dangers of things happening during lead time. And by "you," I mean people other than me who aren't trying to be funny.

Elsewhere, Green Bay beat Washington, 28–14. In every presidential race since 1936, when the Redskins lose the Sunday before Election Day, the incumbent is defeated. Hmm. Does Dan Snyder have enough room under the cap to sign five Supreme Court judges? Same reasoning as above, given this column closed the day before the election. And we already had the much more accessible Hooters "cup room" groin-slapper. Speaking of groin-slappers, how *did* the election turn out?

THE **HIT(S)**

None. (I had to put Kerry's band in here. You know, the one whose album is only worth $2,500....)

Acknowledgments

In the fall of 1999, a year before he became the Industry Known as Tony Kornheiser, the *Washington Post* columnist/talking head/radio host decided he was already too busy to do all he was doing and continue his column at two-year-old *ESPN Magazine*. Steve Wulf, the executive editor, had read a humor piece I had written about Bill Parcells for the Sunday *Times* and called to ask if I was interested in maybe doing something in the page Kornheiser had occupied. This is a little like Theo Epstein throwing you a glove and asking if you'd be interested in maybe wandering out to centerfield.

So, here's my point: Blame Tony Kornheiser for all this.

O.K. now that we've handed out blame, let's be grateful. Rick Wolff at Warner Books took about 10 minutes before deciding to publish this collection and another minute and a half before making an offer to my gleefully tenacious agent, Jennifer Rudolph Walsh. In addition to being a fellow member of the ever-growing secret society, Tragically Underutilized Ivy League Infielders, Rick always understood that we needed to do more than just reprint columns readers had already seen. His suggestion: Write another 600 jokes, not including 25 personalized cracks about the University of Michigan for his boss, Larry Kirshbaum. Did I tell you he was underutilized?

Twenty-four years ago, I had a chance to become a writer at *Sports Illustrated*. It didn't happen then. It wasn't supposed to happen then. So, you can imagine my eternal karmic shock when, at a

lunch arranged by my fiction rabbi, David Hirshey of HarperCollins, *SI* executive editor Rob Fleder offered me the chance to bring my column from *ESPN Magazine* over to his little book in July 2002. The chance to produce every week and work at the same place where my uncle, the golf laureate Herbert Warren Wind, had worked almost a half-century before, was cup runneth overwhelming.

Unaccustomed as I am to shamelessly sucking up to editors, I have received nothing but encouragement and enthusiasm for my column from the crow's nest of the masthead on down: Terry McDonnell, David Bauer, Rob Fleder, Charlie Leershen, Bob Roe, Jim Herre, Marc Bechtel and Paul Fichtenbaum.

My editor for 90% of these columns, Kostya Kennedy, received more than a few shout-outs during my annotations. If you haven't figured out that he's invaluable, well, call me and I'll give you another couple hundred examples.

As you can tell from his introduction, Rick Reilly has always been way, way too supportive for someone so successful.

Every week, whether the jokes are lame or not, you get to see inspired comic artwork in my column from Jeff Wong. We couldn't afford to reproduce all of it here, so you just got the dynamite cover.

Then there are the *SI* people I've annoyed over the years: Barbara Fox, Brian Clavell, Lena Elguindi, Caryn Prine, Aimee Crawford. Yeah, I know. The list should be much longer.

There's no "The Show" without "The Monologue," the *ESPN Magazine* column that preceded it for two and a half years. You're already met Steve Wulf. You never forget your first great editor. Ridiculously belated thanks to John Walsh, Dan Patrick, Lynn Crimando, John Papanek, Gary Hoenig and anyone who ever laughed at anything I said during the Tuesday morning editorial meeting.

Somebody once told me the acknowledgments should not be longer than the book. (Kostya, probably). So, in no specific order other than alphabetical . . . Jonathan Alter, Larry Amoros, Dave Anderson, Danny Arndt, Tom Aronson, Sam Beer, Peter Beilin, Kevin Benchley, Bill Carter, Celia Converse, Bob Costas, Curt Chaplin, Larry David, Hugh Fink, Tom Fitzgerald, Barbara Gaines, Fred Gaudelli, Jimmy Golen, Tom Griswold, Peter Grunwald, Don Harrell, Bob Kevoian, Kristi Lee, Jill Leiderman, Dave Letterman, Mike Lupica, Ed Markey, Tim McCarver, Chick McGee, Pat McGrath, Mike McIntee, Phil Mushnick, Mike Muth, Chris Nolan, John O'Leary, J.P. Patterson, Mark Patrick, Jason Pinter, Dean Reilly, Gerry Rioux, Francis Santos, my brothers John and Tom Scheft, my parents Bill and Gitty Scheft, my sisters Andrea, Sally, and Harriet, Greg Simetz, Cara Stein, Kevin Talty, Jeff Toobin and Ben Walker.

And finally, to my wife, Adrianne Tolsch, the nth power of example. When I want to really laugh, really experience art or really know courage, I never have to look farther than right next to me.

My time is more than up. You've been great. Enjoy the Truants.

Bill Scheft
November 2004

About the Author

BILL SCHEFT...

... waits 20 minutes after eating before entering his NCAA office pool.

... was the brains behind the rejected Portland Trail Blazers ad campaign, "I Courtney Love this game!"

... is developing a show for MTV Sports about the University of Colorado, *Pimp My Free Ride.*

... is the creator if the Rotisserie League of Women Voters.

... is working on a book with Steven King, *The Girl Who Loved Ramiro Mendoza on the Disabled List.*

... has written 32 first-round jokes for his annual Mock NFL Draft.

... is working on a four-part investigative series, "Is the Powerball Juiced?"

... has pitched a book idea to Mitch Albom, *The Five People You Meet at the Will Call Window.*

... grabbed a chunk of sod from the finale of Survivor All-Stars.

... is almost finished writing a television pilot for David E. Kelley, *The Practice...Tee.*

... is creating a midseason reality show for Fox, *My Big, Obnoxious, Steroid-Ingesting Fiancée*

.... is the former head monologue writer for Rahal-Letterman racing. He was the 11th guy to come up with the phrase Stupid Pit Tricks.

... is in court over his latest book, *Harry Potter and the Magic Salary Cap Room.*

... is celebrating the 25th anniversary of his brain-child, the College World Series of Poker.

... is an uncredited screenwriter on the upcoming Ben Stiller project, *TV Tag!*

... is awaiting word from the Elias Sports Bureau on if it will recognize his proposed new statistic, Quality Blown Saves.

... has been the editor of *The Lance Armstrong Chafer's Guide to France* since 1996.

... once spent 10 minutes trying to find Kathmandu on Teddy Atlas.

... is still looking for a corporate sponsor for Oscillating Fan Appreciation Day.

... is trying to get Street Cred Luge added to the X Games as a demonstration sport.

... was a semifinalist in *Sports Illustrated*'s "Fresh Mouths" competition.

... is the creator of the new Golf Channel reality series, *Last Comic Slicing*.

... will be at the Hall of Fame celebration of Jewish baseball players next week, running the Richie Scheinblum memorabilia booth.

... plans to promote five jokes from the PCL after Sept. 1.

... once ruptured a vocal cord auditioning for ESPN's *Around the Horn*.

... had his Aug. 16 column used as anesthesia during President Clinton's bypass surgery.

... may have given a forged Mickey Mantle autographed baseball to Dan Rather.

... purchased the Riddick Bowe comeback fight on Pay-Per-Cruel.

... has been volunteering at an NFL suicide pool hotline.

... recently completed his first *Who's the Boss?* Marathon.

... sent Tiger and his new wife a set of fondue irons.

... prevented a last-minute pro-choice demonstration at the Breeders' Cup.